Business and Democracy in Latin America

Ernest Bartell, C.S.C. and Leigh A. Payne, Editors

D1521919

University of Pittsburgh Press ● Pittsburgh and London

Published by the University of Pittsburgh Press, Pittsburgh, Pa., 15260
Copyright © 1995, University of Pittsburgh Press
All rights reserved
Manufactured in the United States of America
Printed on acid-free paper

LIBRARY OF CONGRESS CATALOGING-IN-PUBLICATION DATA
Business and democracy in Latin America / Ernest Bartell and
   Leigh A. Payne, editors.
      p. cm.—(Pitt Latin America series)
   Includes bibliographical references.
   ISBN 0-8229-3853-7. —ISBN 0-8229-5537-7 (pbk.)
    1. Business and politics—Latin America. 2. Latin America—
Politics and government—1980– 3. Democracy—Latin America.
  I. Bartell, Ernest, J., 1932– . II. Payne, Leigh A. III. Series.
HC125.B77 1995
322'.3'098—dc20   94-39787
                                      CIP

A CIP catalogue record for this book is available from the British Library.
Eurospan, London

Contents

Acknowledgments

This volume grew out of a workshop on Business Elites and Democracy in Latin America sponsored by the Helen Kellogg Institute for International Studies of the University of Notre Dame, held on May 3–5, 1991. The organization of the workshop and the preparation of the volume relied on the efforts of a number of individuals.

It brought together a number of scholars involved in recent research on business elites, many of whom had been Residential Fellows of the Kellogg Institute at different times. These individuals have authored the excellent case studies included in this volume.

In addition to presenting the case studies on business elites, the conference was designed to initiate a comparative framework for analyzing business elites and democracy in Latin America. To assist in the development of a comparative framework, several scholars were invited to share insights into the case studies based on their own areas of expertise. These individuals included: Lovell Jarvis, Robert Kaufman, Jaime Ros, Philippe Schmitter, Lee Tavis, Samuel Valenzuela, Raymond Vernon, Francisco Weffort, and Lynne Wozniak. We have used their insights in revising the papers and in preparing the conclusion to the volume. An interpretive report of the conference, prepared by Juan López, helped us think through the excellent contributions made at the conference.

We wish also to thank Erika Valenzuela, Nancy Hall, Caroline Domingo, Albert LeMay, Jeffery Cason, Judith Lawton, and Darren Hawkins for their generous efforts at various stages of the project, from the organization of the conference to preparation of this manuscript. We are fully aware that this volume would not have emerged without the contributions of all those mentioned here, but we also acknowledge the shortcomings that are our responsibility.

ERNEST BARTELL, C.S.C.,
AND LEIGH PAYNE
Editors

Introduction

There is little doubt that business leaders are important political actors in Latin America. In some countries they helped to undermine the democratic regimes of the 1960s and 1970s and provided one of the few bases of civilian support for the authoritarian regimes that replaced those democracies. In other countries, they endorsed or contributed to the return of democracy. In less dramatic but equally important ways, they have influenced political outcomes, using their extensive financial, organizational, and social resources. They have helped elect individuals to public office, lobbied the executive and legislature, and shaped public opinion. They have also undermined or bolstered the stability and legitimacy of specific governments by reducing or increasing their investments, production of consumer goods, and employment opportunities.

Despite their obvious political importance, business leaders are often reduced to stereotypes in discussions of Latin America by social scientists. Scholarship has been largely devoted to labor, political parties, the military, and social movements in Latin America. In the absence of empirical research, explanations of business leaders' political activities or behavior are generally derived from the dominant theoretical literature, which analyses business leaders in the context of larger political questions. These studies are not based on empirical research nor do they seek to explain the political attitudes and behavior of business leaders. Two examples are the theory of the bureaucratic-authoritarian state and discussions of transitions from authoritarian rule.

With his theory of the bureaucratic-authoritarian state, Guillermo O'Donnell sought to explain the breakdown of democracy in a number of Latin American countries in the 1960s and 1970s.[1] In the theory, domestic business played a peripheral role. Business people are subordinate actors in a triumvirate comprised of business (mainly transnational), technocrats, and military officers who aimed to replace democratic rule with a political system more capable of ensuring political and social order and economic growth. According to the theory, domestic business people join the triumvirate because they believe that an authoritarian regime is essential to eliminate threats from labor and the left and to stimulate and subsidize investment opportunities. In time, domestic entrepreneurs come to believe that the authoritarian regime is not acting in their interests, but rather in the interest of international capital. As business withdraws its support from the regime, thereby removing one of its national bases of legitimacy, the military rulers attempt to win back support by adopting economic policies more favorable to business.[2] Several assumptions have been derived from this theory: (1) business leaders are generally weak; (2) their political and economic weakness leads them to seek protection from an authoritarian state; (3) they have enough political power to ally themselves with other social forces to install such a regime; and (4) they can also influence political outcomes under an authoritarian regime.

The transitions from authoritarian rule under way during the 1970s and 1980s called into question some of these assumptions. In most cases, Latin American authoritarian regimes had proved incapable of protecting the interests of business. Instead, they created disastrous economic conditions, used arbitrary and uncontrolled violence against their own citizens, and failed to prevent the emergence of social movements opposing the regime. The failure of authoritarianism led many business leaders to endorse a transition to democracy. In some cases they joined other political actors to push for change. In others they were themselves the engine of political change. And as the democracies evolved, business leaders proved increasingly able to assert their demands in a democratic context.

Despite an apparent departure by the business elite from past authoritarian attitudes, scholars studying transitions from authoritarian rule have viewed this change with great skepticism. They distrust business leaders' commitment to democracy. They assume that if they prove unable to control the democratization process—which, given their limited political power, is a plausible assumption—and if liberalization goes "too far," business leaders will again unite with other social sectors and reverse the process. In other words, according to skeptics, the only variant of democracy business leaders will accept is a highly restricted one.[3] Once again, then, business leaders are perceived as too weak to assert their demands in a democratic context, although powerful enough to replace democracy with authoritarian rule, and generally preferring authoritarianism or highly restricted democracy to democratic rule.

How accurate are these characterizations of Latin American business leaders' political attitudes and behavior? This volume approaches that question by analyzing the role of business in the democratization process in three subregions of Latin America: the Andean region (Bolivia and Peru), Brazil and the Southern Cone (Chile and Argentina), and Mexico. Each of the six country studies is based on several years of empirical research conducted in the field. The authors analyze reasons underlying business support for democracy, the likelihood that business leaders will achieve their demands in a democratic system, and the limits of their tolerance for democracy.

While each chapter focuses on the particulars of a case study, there is a set of common themes. Therefore, in addition to a set of empirically based country studies on business leaders and democracy, the volume includes a comparative conclusion with implications and suggestions for analyzing differences and similarities among these actors.

In chapter 1, Carlos H. Acuña suggests that the Argentine transition to democracy begun in 1983 marks a departure from the traditional pattern of political mobilization followed by business leaders since the 1930s. Acuña argues that although business leaders strongly supported the 1976 military coup and have faced a serious economic crisis during the transition to democracy, they are unlikely to turn back now. He argues that business leaders perceived that the cost of democracy, primarily the expansion of trade-union power and state control over the economy, were not as great as the costs incurred under the military's politically and economically inept leadership. These views were confirmed during the first few years under democratic rule. Business learned that democratic governments could control labor and might even improve the business climate.

In chapter 2, Ernest Bartell explains and challenges the prevailing view that other Latin American nations should attempt to replicate Chile's success in incorporating business leaders into the democratic political process and a competitive international economy. In contrast to their counterparts in the rest of Latin America, Chilean business leaders have successfully competed with foreign and domestic competitors without special privilege and dependence on the government. He also uses extensive interview material to illustrate how democratic rule has allowed Chilean business leaders to overcome certain traditional traits that formerly prevented them from participating in democratic government, particularly their defensiveness about their social legitimacy and skepticism regarding prospects for economic expansion under democratic rule. However, he notes that Chilean business leaders are likely to thwart any attempts to redistribute wealth that are not market-motivated, thereby limiting one of democracy's most substantive goals. He further surmises that Chile's pattern of incorporation into the international economy is not readily replicated elsewhere in Latin America.

In chapter 3, Catherine M. Conaghan examines the development of business interest group activism in Bolivia. She argues that during the 1980s, business interest groups became high-profile political actors that worked openly to reshape the country's policy-making and ideological landscape. The thrust of the campaign was to promote neoliberal economic ideas and to create a more positive public image of the private sector. While these efforts met with some success, challenges by popular-class organizations and criticisms by politicians tempered the effects of the business campaign to remake public opinion. Moreover, the continued reluctance of domestic capitalists to undertake substantial new investments further undercut attempts by business to project itself as progressive and productive. Nonetheless, the mobilization was effective in heightening class consciousness and solidarity. Conaghan shows that the mixed political and economic record of the Bolivian private sector underscores the continuing problems involved in constructing bourgeois hegemony in Latin America.

In chapter 4, Francisco Durand examines the successful struggle of Peruvian business leaders to develop a strong national business association (CONFIEP) during the 1980s. Peruvian entrepreneurs recognized that they had to organize in order to overcome their vulnerability to economic policies. Yet they faced serious obstacles in forming an organization. Some are inherent to all business communities—that is, the diversity of interests, needs, and viewpoints of the members of that community that leads to individual rather than collective action. The business community must overcome attempts by the state to weaken the collective power of business and society's indifference or hostility to business leaders' demands. CONFIEP was able to overcome those obstacles because of a number of propitious factors: state policies that created a universal threat to business and mobilized it against the government; early victories by the association in fights with the government which increased its appeal to the business community; and effective and creative leadership that persevered when the chips were down. In discussing the creation of business associations, Durand illustrates how the transition to democracy creates new challenges to and opportunities for business leaders to assert their political demands and argues that they are not doomed to play a weak role subordinate to the state.

In chapter 5, Blanca Heredia uses the Mexican case to analyze what general conditions might encourage rational profit-maximizers (that is, Mexican business leaders) to favor—or at least not hinder—a transition to democracy. The conflict between the state and the private sector in Mexico during the 1980s stopped just short of rupture, and business's political activism can hardly have contributed to a democratic transition. By focusing on the strategic interaction between Mexico's economic and political leaders, Heredia shows how the relatively strong economic and political assets of the Mexican government enabled its political leaders first to withstand and then to respond effectively to business demands.

In chapter 6, Leigh A. Payne argues that Brazilian business leaders were the key civilian supporters of the 1964 military coup. During the transition to democracy begun in 1974, they faced the same threats that had prompted their support for the coup: economic crisis, capital-labor conflict, and threats to private property. Yet in recent years they have not endorsed an authoritarian solution to their problems. This chapter provides new insights into business leaders' political attitudes and behavior based on an analysis of these two democratic periods. It argues that the lack of political options, rather than the severity of the social crisis, determines business leaders' involvement in antiregime activities.

In the concluding chapter, Ernest Bartell and Leigh A. Payne move beyond the conventional view of business leaders in the theoretical literature as politically and economically weak and dependent upon a strong authoritarian state to defend their interests. As Latin American democracies adopt neoliberal economic policies in response to the failures of state-led development and international pressure, the private sector has emerged as potentially the primary engine for economic growth. Success in this central economic role has enhanced the social status of business and its ability to demand appropriate economic institutions—for example, property rights—as well as consistent economic policies efficiently administered. Business interests are neither homogeneous nor uniform, but the leaders' ability to adapt actively to political opportunities offered in democratic societies, including engaging in collective action, has resulted in political power that goes well beyond a mere tolerance for democracy. Since democracy is potentially vulnerable to attacks from both a strong business sector as well as a weak one, Bartell and Payne suggest strategic guidelines for government efforts to moderate and channel the new economic and political power of business toward democratic stabilization.

Notes

1. Guillermo O'Donnell, *Modernization and Bureaucratic-Authoritarianism* (Berkeley and Los Angeles: University of California Press, 1973). See also *The New Authoritarianism in Latin America*, ed. David Collier (Princeton: Princeton University Press, 1979).

2. Guillermo O'Donnell, "Reflections on the Patterns of Change in the Bureaucratic-Authoritarian Regimes in Latin America," *Latin American Research Review* 13 (1978): 3–38.

3. Guillermo O'Donnell and Philippe C. Schmitter, *Transitions from Authoritarian Rule: Tentative Conclusions about Uncertain Democracies* (Baltimore: Johns Hopkins University Press, 1986).

Business and Democracy
in Latin America

Carlos H. Acuña

1. Business Interests, Dictatorship, and Democracy in Argentina

This chapter examines the organization and political behavior of the Argentine bourgeoisie, with special emphasis on the implications of this activity for the emergence and breakdown of democratic regimes. The central hypothesis is that the transition to democracy in Argentina that began in 1983 represented a substantial break with the bourgeoisie's past political behavior. Specifically, I argue that because of the wide variety of changes that took place in the Argentine economy beginning in the mid-1970s, business redefined its understanding of both authoritarianism and democracy. This political redefinition has led to a long-term "bet" on the part of bourgeoisie in favor of democratic stability.

The Bourgeoisie as a Collective Actor in Argentina

By the 1930s, business associations in Argentina were quite active. Business sought to influence economic policy and to change political regimes. For example, both the Argentine Rural Society (SRA) and the Argentine Industrial Union

(UIA) supported the overthrow of Yrigoyen in 1930. In the 1930–1945 period, most of the world witnessed a revolution in the interests and cost-benefit analyses of capitalists and their collective representatives because of the Great Depression and its political and economic consequences. In Argentina this upheaval resulted from several factors, including profound changes in the nation's socioeconomic structure, the redefined role of the state, and the rise of Peronism. Because of these changes, business saw the political environment as increasingly threatening.[1]

The new social and political arrangements threatened the traditional leadership of the large industrial bourgeoisie and the exporting landowners. Peronism threatened these traditional interests when democratic rules were in place, since the Peronist movement dominated electoral politics. This was true not only because of Peronism's support for strengthening the unions, but also because of the emergence of new capitalists. These new business interests had taken advantage of import substitution opportunities and were willing to challenge the business sector's traditional political leadership. The threat of Peronism became clear when Perón dissolved the UIA shortly after assuming office. The UIA had incurred Perón's wrath by its active support for the coalition of parties opposed to Perón in the 1946 election. Thus, democracy meant not only greater rights and political influence for the working class; in addition, it threatened the very existence of the associations that represented key sectors of business.

The struggle over the form of political regime had clear consequences for how business would be politically organized and represented. This is apparent in the reestablishment of peak business organizations under a Peronist regime and their subsequent fate. The General Economic Confederation (CGE) was founded in 1952 as part of the Peronist project to base economic policies on neocorporatist agreements between the state and representatives of labor and capital. The CGE represented the newer local capitalists, and its history is tied closely to changes in political regime. The military government that overthrew Perón in 1955 banned it, alleging that it was a totalitarian organization. The CGE was then reestablished by the Frondizi government elected in 1958. This reestablishment was part of the Perón-Frondizi accord that also returned the General Workers Confederation (CGT) to a leadership elected by the workers. The CGE was again banned in 1976 in the wake of that year's military coup and was finally reinstated by the National Congress in 1984 after the return to democratic government.

At the same time, those sectors of business tied to large local and foreign capital interests (the UIA, the SRA, and the Argentine Chamber of Commerce [CAC]) formed their own organizations during two periods: the Coordinated Action of Free Business Institutions (ACIEL) from 1958 to 1973 and the Permanent Assembly of Entrepreneurial Entities (APEGE) from 1975 to 1976. These entities established relationships with authoritarian governments and provided political and ideological support. In many cases, key state bureaucrats during the authoritarian periods were members of these business organizations.[2]

The 1955–1976 period was characterized by widespread social and political conflict in Argentina. Struggles between labor and capital were resolved in a number of ways, with business either calling for or supporting repression of workers, or granting wage increases to workers and then increasing prices to compensate for higher costs. However, intercapitalist conflicts could not be resolved through such simple means. Issues such as exchange rate policy, export taxes, and tariff barriers were much more contentious and had clear winners and losers. Clashes over these economic policies pitted different sectors of industrial capital against one another, and industrial capital against agro-exporters.

Authoritarian governments that defended the interests of entrepreneurs as "employers," repressing workers and their organizations, also forced important transfers of resources between these entrepreneurs as "producers" through changes in export taxes, tariff barriers, or price controls. In the industrial sector, for example, because industry provides its own inputs, business organizations have pressured the state for reducing tariffs on members' inputs, while pressing for maintaining or increasing tariffs on their own products. The desire to buy cheap and sell dear has created a permanent struggle between industrialists with "backward" and "forward" linkages. Those who have been inefficient in gaining access to government decision makers have often lost out. And contradictions between capital- and labor-intensive groups, and between those more or less dependent on the internal market, state credit, or regional economies, are at the center of conflicts such as that between the UIA and the General Industrial Confederation (CGI), an industrial confederation affiliated with the CGE. Thus the state was inevitably an arena of conflict.

The fact that no decision was ever considered *final* intensified this conflict. Successful political pressure by a specific sector of business in favor of particular policies could later be neutralized by pressure from either labor or another faction of capital. There was thus permanent struggle between different social sectors. In a context of great instability—both in economic policy and political regime—the bourgeoisie pursued short-term political strategies, including support for military coups. Because they always stood a reasonable chance of success, they preferred these short-term political strategies to other business strategies such as increasing investment in more sophisticated technologies or pursuing risky export markets. As a result, political conflict among capitalists in Argentina was much more intense than in other Latin American countries with relatively closed economies.

Until 1976, the conflicts among different sectors of capital led to both authoritarian regimes and inflation. With the exception of the CGE, authoritarianism was frequently encouraged by business. However, the military coup of 1976 that overthrew Peronism marked the beginning of a reevaluation of politics by the Argentine bourgeoisie. This was due primarily to the radically different diagnosis of Argentina's economic ills by the new military government. The new government and the technocrats who staffed it argued that the crisis was due not only to guerrilla activity, "excessive" union power, or Peronism; they argued that fundamental problems included a semi-closed economy in which resources were not well allocated. Subsidized industrialization shielded inefficient producers from healthy competition. Most relevant for this discussion, technocrats condemned the politicization of economic policy that erupted in violent struggles over the distribution of resources and the crisis of accumulation in Argentina.

This new interpretation of Argentina's political economy after 1976 led the military government to discipline not only the working class, but important groups of capitalists as well. Its economic policies included both opening up the economy and substantial deregulation, which implied less political influence for business. The opening as a way of controlling inflation placed a ceiling (defined by international prices) on domestic price increases and pressured the productive sectors to become more competitive. Deregulation was a way of reducing the capacity of sectoral interests to force inefficient transfers of resources in their favor through pressure on the state.

The technocratic diagnosis of Argentina's economic crisis called for neutralizing the traditional pressures that business had exerted on the state through corporatist channels or other lobbying activities. (In interviews, several entrepreneurs affirmed that it was easier to gain access to top-level government military authorities than to second-level functionaries in the economics ministry; in fact, sometimes the way to reach a subsecretary of economy with a demand might be through the interior minister.) Thus, even though capitalists were in a privileged position as *employers* (because of the high priority that the dictatorship placed on repressing the popular sector and unions), they were unable to influence policies that affected them as *producers*. Conflicts between capitalists were not resolved because one sector had the state's ear, as had happened in previous military governments. In general, all capitalists saw their capacity to influence policy greatly reduced.

This is not to say there were no winners and losers as a result of the changes in economic policy. In fact, the financial sector, industrial groups with state contracts, and horizontally diversified businesses did quite well. In contrast, nondiversified and vertically integrated industrial sectors incurred substantial losses as a result of changes in economic policy.[3] Associations linked to the APEGE unconditionally supported the military regime and its "philosophy," even when there were complaints about the military government's handling of the economy in areas such as interest rates, the speed of economic adjustment, and the exchange rate. Such policy areas had clear distributional implications in the struggle between various capitalist groups.

The military dealt with the business organizations aggressively. In 1976 the government of General Videla took control of the CGE and abolished it and its member confederations in 1977, expropriating their assets. In addition, the Videla government nullified the merger within the Argentine Industrial Confederation (CINA) of the UIA and the General Confederation of Industry (CGI) that had occurred under Peronist government pressure in 1973–1974. The UIA had its legal recognition and status restored, but it was placed under the control of an army officer. The effect of these actions was to nearly paralyze the activities of the association until the end of 1980, when a new "General Regulation" of the UIA was approved.

The bleak circumstances facing industry during this period eventually led the UIA to emerge as an independent actor in a context of increasing tension between the military regime and business.

The increase in political and economic pressures after the military disaster in the Malvinas/Falkland Islands led to a breakdown in internal military cohesion and left the government impotent in the face of advancing social and political forces. The economic crisis of the post-Malvinas period also increased tensions between the government and industrialists. The heavy foreign debt and the inevitable limitations that IMF-sponsored stabilization programs placed on the government intensified this conflict, especially between the government and the UIA. Even the "statization" of the private external debt—which amounted to half of total foreign debt, which had grown from under $7 billion in 1975 to $47 billion by 1984—did not mitigate the conflict. Thus, given the increasingly uncertain consequences of continued social protest, business organizations recognized that opting for a democratic opening would be the least risky strategy. As at other historical conjunctures, these organizations dusted off the principles of liberal ideology and expressed their support for a democratic regime.

Socioeconomic Strategies of the Radical Government and the Capitalist Class

The surprising victory of the Radicals in the 1983 election marked the beginning of a change in the meaning of democracy for entrepreneurs.[4] The first redefinition concerned the relationship between democratic elections and Peronism. The "iron law" that Peronists were the natural electoral majority was no longer valid, and thus democracy was not automatically associated with Peronism. In addition, the anticorporatist discourse of the Radical party during the campaign seemed aimed at restraining the demands of unions that were expected to increase under the new democratic government.

The government of Raúl Alfonsín concentrated decision making at the executive level, justifying such concentration by arguing that the socioeconomic crisis allowed little room for maneuver. The most salient features of the crisis were massive fiscal and foreign debt, a falling investment rate and real wages, and stagflation. The gross investment rate as a proportion of GDP fell from around 20 percent between 1970 and 1981 to 15.0, 13.5, and 11.6 percent in the next three years.[5] Real wages suffered a sharp drop in the adjustment period in 1981 and 1982 and then rebounded in the last semester of 1983 when the military government was especially weak and acceded to labor demands to control social tensions. GDP increased by only 1.6 percent in 1980, and declined in the next two years by 6.7 and 4.5 percent, recovering somewhat with a growth rate of 2.8 in 1983. Finally, annual inflation continued to accelerate in the same period from around 70 percent to around 200 percent. Dealing with this crisis involved three simultaneous objectives: increasing real wages, achieving a modest level of growth, and paying less to foreign creditors than the IMF or creditor banks demanded. Despite the adverse situation, Economics Minister Bernardo Grinspun sought simultaneously to increase both investment and wages.

After centralizing decision making, the Alfonsín government undertook to reformulate the structure of union representation. It attempted to carry out a profound transformation of the workers' movement and tried to extend the government's reach into the labor movement. Nevertheless, this attempt at union reorganization and the meager economic results achieved by the economic team provoked sharp reactions from different socioeconomic sectors. Entrepreneurs, for example, objected to not having access to decision making and objected to some key policies of the new economic team, such as price controls, increased export taxes, and expanded public spending.

In addition, the Alfonsín government was unable to get congressional approval for its union legislation, which had serious consequences for the Radical government. To begin with, the failure to pass the new legislation resulted in increased tensions between union leaders and the minister of labor, Antonio Mucci, which led to the minister's resignation. Second, the government maintained its decision to control the economic variables even in the face of its inability to change union structures. This led the government to "delay" legislation that dealt with changes in the labor market, and the government resorted to using the legal mechanisms of the military government to control wages and prices. Finally, union leaders began to develop new alliances with capitalists. This strategy was pursued both because of the threat that the unions felt came from the government as well as the demonstrated weakness of the labor movement after the electoral defeat of Peronism.

Remarkably, the central business actors in these meetings were organizations that had traditionally confronted the CGT, such as the UIA, the SRA, and the CAC. Meetings initiated by labor primarily ended in demands for collaboration in formulating socioeconomic policy. As a result of these negotiations, the business-labor "Group of 11" was formed. In the group, the UIA and the CGT deepened joint activities and elaborated a series of declarations and documents with common demands and interpretations of the economic situation and the government's economic policies. The Group of 11 also included the CAC, SRA, CRA, the Argentine Chamber of Construction, the Coordinator of Business and Merchant Activities (CAME), the Intercooperative Agricultural Confederation (CONINAGRO), the Chamber of Commerce, Industry and Production, the Argentine Bank Association (ADEBA), and the Union of Argentine Commercial Associations (UDECA).

In sum, during 1984 real wages and production increased

somewhat, but by the end of the year inflation was accelerating, reaching a monthly rate in excess of 20 percent. By late 1984 there were also clear signs of a recession in production: in spite of a 2.5 percent growth in GDP in 1984, industrial production began to decline, and between the third trimesters of 1984 and 1985, industrial production declined by 19 percent. The exclusion of both business and labor representatives from decision making, and their decreasing control over the main macroeconomic variables, led to a climate of uncertainty that had two consequences: an unprecedented alliance between union leaders and liberal-leaning business associations, and the increasing isolation of the Economics Ministry and its confrontation with the most powerful social actors. In this context, the government sought to counter the setbacks of the Grinspun administration by naming a new economic team in January 1985, headed by a new economics minister, Juan V. Sourrouille. The new team launched the Austral Plan in June of that year.

Reaction to the Austral Plan

The fundamental objective of the Austral Plan was to contain price increases by way of an anti-inflationary shock aimed at generating credibility for the government in both internal and international capital markets. The latter were particularly important, given the need to refinance the foreign debt on more favorable terms. The plan was designed to provide more effective state control over the principal macroeconomic variables such as prices, wages, interest rates, and exchange rates.

Among the most important measures taken were the monetary reform and the reduction of the fiscal deficit, targeted to fall from 12.5 percent of GDP in the first semester of 1985 to 2.5 percent in the second semester. This reduction would be achieved through measures such as increased public utility charges as well as taxes on foreign trade. Changes in tax laws would tax the more prosperous sectors of society. The government would refrain from printing money to finance any eventual fiscal deficits. The monetary reform also included reduced regulated interest rates, changing the currency from the peso to the austral, and a conversion table that applied to contracts that were in effect at the time of the plan. This table was meant to gradually decrease tendencies toward indexation in the economy.

This table, however, did not apply to labor contracts. Instead, salaries were increased 22.6 percent, which amounted to 90 percent of the May inflation rate. The plan also included measures to avoid medium-term problems that would result from the reactivation of the economy, including bottlenecks and balance-of-payments pressures. These included stimulating industrial exports through subsidies as well as reducing export taxes.

The freezing of prices and wages found the business sector with prices high enough to avoid any threat to profits. On the other hand, labor entered the new world of the Austral Plan having suffered a loss in real wages. Despite these relative differences, the plan achieved nearly unanimous support by a society threatened with the specter of hyperinflation. Business leaders accepted the price controls as necessary, even though they insisted that such regulation should be only temporary. In short, business confidence in government policies increased significantly as a result of the Austral Plan.

Indeed, the initial results of the anti-inflationary measures were impressive: consumer prices fell from 30.5 percent in June to 6.2, 3.1, 2.0, and 1.9 percent in subsequent months. The Austral Plan was also accompanied by a change in government strategy regarding the nation's social actors. The old (and useless) state-sponsored negotiations between business and labor (*mesa de concertación*), which had been put on the back burner shortly before the Austral Plan was unveiled, were replaced at the end of July by the Economic-Social Conference (CES) at the government's initiative. The government's strategy did not include negotiating its economic policy; instead, it was reduced to dividing business from the labor movement, as well as dividing industrialists from the rest of business. As a result, business did not frame its demands on the government in the "twenty points" document that was agreed upon by the Group of 11, and the group itself dissolved shortly thereafter. Unions, increasingly isolated from the busines sector, developed several strategies for changing government policy. These included a series of contacts with different political parties, as well as applying direct pressure on the government through strikes and periodic withdrawals from and adherence to the CES.

Until the second stage of the Austral Plan (initiated in March 1986), business organizations such as the UIA and the CAC reaffirmed their support for the plan. At the same time, they supported a gradual freeing of prices, as well as lower interest rates and a reduced tax burden. In addition, this business support did not imply endorsement of the medium-term measures such as increasing industrial exports, which would imply achieving greater efficiency and international competitiveness on the part of Argentine industry. At any rate, 1985 ended with indications of political stability and social support for the government's efforts; in spite of the costs associated with the adjustment policies, the Radical Civic Union (UCR) won the November parliamentary elections. It increased its representation in the Chamber of Deputies by one seat, while the Peronists lost eight, the Intransigent party (PI) went from three to six seats, and the liberal Central Democratic Union (Ucedé) gained one seat.

The Second Stage of the Austral Plan

The next stage of the Austral Plan, to relax wage and price controls, began in February and March 1986. The new stage included policies related to the revision of the incomes policy, privatization of state-owned industries, and promotion of industrial exports. Such policies were pursued with a reactivation of the CES and support for collective bargaining, with salary increases limited to the official estimates of inflation for 1986. In this context, the government announced the privatization of several key state industries in February 1986, including petrochemical and steel firms. At the same time, a number of measures promoting industrial exports were announced.

Business reaction to these new measures was mixed. While industrial associations continued to support the government, agricultural interests pressed for changes in policy. The alarm of agricultural interests was understandable: while industrial production increased 12.8 percent during 1986, agricultural production declined 2.8 percent, and international grain prices declined 30 percent between 1984 and 1986. Thus, in addition to calls from the agricultural sector to further reduce export taxes came other demands to decrease taxes unrelated to exports and interest rates. Growers also brought pressure against the proposed tax on unimproved land, which had been advanced by the agriculture secretary to force an increase in investments on the part of the agricultural sector. In general, these objections reinforced the notion that the struggle between the agricultural and industrial sectors was a zero-sum game.

One of the aims of the process of unfreezing price and wage controls was to minimize the uncertainty commonly associated with such deregulation. As a result, it attempted to break inertial inflationary expectations by setting minimum and maximum wage increases on the basis of projected future inflation instead of past inflation. However, since the CGT did not accept these targets for wage increases, the Alfonsín government set minimums and maximums as of April 4. In addition, by the end of April, meetings of the CES resumed, with the objective of discussing labor reforms and salary guidelines.

Although industrialists supported these attempts to unfreeze the economy, their analysis coincided with that of the agricultural interests represented by the SRA. Both sectors saw a zero-sum game, and the UIA and its leaders declared on several occasions that "distributive possibilities were exhausted." They asserted that real wages could be increased only if productivity gained as well.[6]

In confronting this situation, however, the strategies of industrial and agricultural interests were quite different. Whereas industrialists were willing to participate in the tripartite dialogue within the CES framework, agricultural producer groups initiated a confrontational strategy beginning in April. This strategy consisted of owner lockouts, mobilization, and denunciations of the government's economic policies. Such confrontation had four main consequences. First, ideologically opposed associations, including the SRA, the Argentine Agrarian Federation (FAA), the Argentine Rural Confederations (CRA), and the Intercooperative Agricultural Confederation (CONINAGRO) carried out joint activities. Second, bilateral negotiations between the state and agricultural interests were institutionalized in the Agricultural Council on Economic Emergency. Third, export taxes on agricultural products were reduced. Finally, Agriculture Minister Lucio Reca was replaced by Ernesto Figueras. Because he was tied to the SRA, Figueras was understood to represent the sector.

This influence from agricultural producers was only part of the pressure that the economic team faced during 1986. Inflation began to accelerate in August. Moreover, besides the direct pressure of the agricultural producers, the Radical party began to point out that agricultural interests would have to be accommodated for electoral reasons. Given the importance of agriculture in provinces such as Buenos Aires, their support would be needed in the 1987 gubernatorial and congressional elections. As a result, the SRA succeeded in having its own representative on the economic team in the person of Figueras. Because of the economic team's new sensitivity to agricultural producers, further reductions in export taxes were forthcoming. In addition, the team abandoned the project to tax unimproved land and made more "flexible" price controls on agricultural products. As a result of these changes, the joint activities of the agricultural associations came to a halt, and the SRA pursued greater collaboration with the most important business associations such as the UIA and the CAC.

The government also faced difficulties on the labor front. The most important conflict took place in the metalworking industry between the Association of the Metallurgical Industry of the Argentine Republic (ADIMRA) and the Metallurgical Workers' Union (UOM). Although the economic team wanted wage adjustments to reflect anticipated inflation, the UOM insisted on recouping past losses. After a thirty-three-day strike, however, the government pressured ADIMRA to accede to labor demands. Thus, from the business point of view, the negotiations had been a disaster. Not only had they lost thirty-three days' worth of production and been forced to grant wage increases, but also business had lost confidence in the government's resolve as well as its political capacity. The Alfonsín government never fully recaptured the confidence of business.

This settlement with the metallurgical workers set a pattern for other industrial sectors. Because of wage increases, business increased prices, which contributed to the jump in inflation in August 1986. In fact, the government had apparently underestimated the impact of the settlement of the metalworkers' strike: consumer prices rose from 4.5 percent in June to 6.8 percent in July and 8.8 percent in August; wholesale prices increased in these months by 4.6 percent, 5.1 percent, and 9.4 percent.

Despite rising inflation, the government continued to insist on lowering price increases and putting a ceiling on wage increases. In fact, inflation fell during the last months of 1986, from 7.2 percent in September to 4.7 percent in December. The overall economic results were encouraging: GDP grew by 5.3 percent, the fiscal deficit fell from a high of 8.3 percent in 1984 to 4.1 percent in 1985, and then 2.7 percent in 1986. Gross domestic investment increased by 18.2 percent over the 1985 level, and fixed gross domestic investment grew 7.8 percent in the same period. Annual inflation fell to 81.9 percent for retail prices and 57.8 percent for wholesale prices, while real wages increased by 2 percent.[7]

At the same time, the Austral Plan faced serious obstacles. The events of August demonstrated that inflation remained a latent threat. In addition, wages and investment were at much lower levels than during the previous decade. The deterioration in the terms-of-trade, combined with the burden of foreign debt, hampered development prospects. Furthermore, the government could no longer count on the business support it had enjoyed earlier. Business was increasingly critical of government policies for several reasons: continued high interest rates, continued price controls, and the uncertainty generated by the resurgence in inflation. Although the economic team had planned to continue administering wage and price levels in 1987, the January inflation rate jumped to 7.6 percent, primarily as a result of the increase in food—especially meat—prices. The strategy of controlling inflation through price controls and guided salary negotiations had evidently not checked inflation.

The Third Stage of the Austral Plan

Despite its initial success, the Austral Plan had not been able to unfreeze the economy without reproducing the conditions that might lead to another inflationary spiral. Once again, the economic team concluded that the accumulation model that had been in place for five decades was exhausted, with little chance for growth and redistribution without inflationary consequences. From their point of view, the only way to decrease the inflationary potential was to make it more difficult for various social actors to influence the struggle over how resources were distributed. The team proposed to open up the economy.

This opening would have several consequences, which included lowering the costs for inputs of manufactured exports and increased export levels, expanded reserves, and altering the behavior of both capitalists and workers in the distributive struggle.

Once again, the economic crisis was diagnosed as follows: because of Argentina's relatively closed economy, distorted prices permit increases in nominal wages that are quickly reflected in prices. The economic team's argument was that while international conditions might allow for the transfer of resources from the agro-exporting sector during certain periods, conditions in the 1970s made it much more difficult to capture foreign resources. In addition, the military regime's policy of increasing the foreign debt had only worsened the distributive conflict. Following this logic, opening the economy had made it harder for business to transfer wage increases to consumer prices. Union demands were also limited by business's resistance to raising wages as well as by fear of unemployment in a recessionary economy.

While this general diagnosis may have been appropriate, the Alfonsín government faced more immediate problems: the need for short-term responses to the increase in inflation and the loss of control over labor policy. The jump in inflation in January 1987 led the economic team by the end of February to abandon the policy of setting general price and wage guidelines. Instead, wages and prices were again frozen, at least through the first six months of the year.

At the same time, the government began to adopt policies that threatened business. Facing new elections, the Radical party and the president himself pursued initiatives to increase their chances of success. Thus, conflicts emerged between the "economists" and "politicians" in the government itself. The new "political" initiatives included not only naming Figueras agriculture secretary, but also involved policies meant to satisfy labor. For example, shortly after introducing the new freeze in

February, the government began negotiations with the secretary-general of the UOM, Lorenzo Miguel, and a group of labor leaders known as "the Fifteen." This alliance brought together powerful unions from key economic sectors whose leaders were ideologically identified with "orthodox" Peronism. Most of these unions had once been quite militant, yet open to negotiation, regardless of the character of the government.

The fact that government strategy had changed became clear on 25 March, when Labor Minister Hugo Barrionuevo resigned and was replaced by Carlos Alderete, a leader of the light and power union and one of the Fifteen. The executive strategy was to defuse the confrontation by including some of the more powerful unions in economic decision making. But business viewed this strategy as contradicting the government's main policy thrust since the beginning of its term. In addition, even though business remained silent, the naming of Alderete confirmed one of business's main fears: in a democratic context, the labor ministry would fall under union control.

The new labor minister focused on reopening discussions on a social pact. In April the UIA and CGT began to discuss issues such as labor legislation, social programs, economic policy, and salaries. Although both sides made some concessions, in the end business associations were reluctant to accept most of the proposals presented by labor.

Thus, the Alderete administration was unable to conclude a social pact. In fact, the most significant outcome of the labor minister's tenure was an agreement between the Labor Ministry and the Economics Ministry at the end of May that again unfroze prices and wages. The policy of controlled increases was reintroduced. However, given the previous failure of the attempt to control wage and price increases, as well as the fact that the Labor Ministry was in the hands of a union representative, the new attempt lacked credibility, especially for business. Success seemed even more unlikely, given the upcoming elections in September. In fact, inflation accelerated gradually from a May level of 4.2 percent to an October level of 19.5 percent.

The government did not give up the hope of stopping inflation, however. In an attempt to attack the structural causes of inflation, on 20 July 1987 the economic team introduced the July Plan. This plan focused both on an opening of the economy and reforming the public sector. The minister, in presenting the program, made its objectives clear: "What Argentines experience . . . is the crisis of a populist and easy model, of a closed model, that is, of a centralized and statist model" tied to a semiclosed economy.[8] The July program inaugurated state deregulation in transportation and communication, privatization in the chemical and petrochemical sectors, restructuring of the state oil company YPF, and opening the oil industry to private activity. At the same time, the new plan set internal energy prices at international levels and restructured the state banking sector. Measures also included reactivating housing plans with the participation of private capital, promoting industrial exports, and lowering taxes on agricultural exports. At the same time, the foreign accounts complicated these measures, since by midyear it became clear that the trade surplus would not reach even 50 percent of the expected surplus for 1987.

As expected, business leaders immediately endorsed the plan and criticized the government for not adopting it sooner. Pleased with the new plan, business now focused its political energies on delaying the adoption of new labor legislation supported by the CGT. The Group of 8, made up of the most important business associations, began a series of meetings with government officials and legislators. These efforts bore fruit when in August the Senate decided to postpone consideration of the labor laws until after the September elections.

The results of the elections were surprising. Unexpectedly the Peronists won the gubernatorial elections in fourteen provinces—garnering 41.5 percent of the vote—while the governing Radicals won in only two provinces and received only

37.4 percent. The Peronists also won the key province of Buenos Aires and achieved a majority in the Chamber of Deputies. It appeared that the political strategy of incorporating a member of the Fifteen as labor minister had not succeeded, and Alderete resigned in September. Some sectors of the governing party blamed the defeat on economic policy. At the same time, President Alfonsín reiterated his support for the plan and pledged to continue opening markets, deregulating the economy, and pursuing privatization of state-owned companies.

The economic situation continued to deteriorate, as did the power of the government to implement its economic policies. On 14 October 1987, the economic team once again froze the main economic indicators in order to control rising inflation. It also announced an acceleration of the structural reforms that were designed to make many industrial sectors more competitive. Nevertheless, the Radicals' electoral defeat had significantly limited the government's room for maneuver. In addition, the increase in the government deficit in 1987 made necessary a tax reform that would probably include increases in real estate and other taxes. (The deficit in nonfinancial bank operations of the public sector jumped from 2.7 percent in 1986 to 4.4 percent of GDP in 1987.)[9]

At the same time, the government was attacked by business associations and saw itself forced to negotiate with Peronists, who now controlled the lower house of Congress. Thus, in exchange for a tax reform package, the government was forced to accept a new law governing workers' professional associations and free collective bargaining between employers and workers.

This agreement represented a significant loss of power on the part of the Economics Ministry. Granting workers and capitalists the freedom to negotiate wages left the government without one of its principal tools for controlling aggregate demand and inflation. Once again, the principal economic indicators showed signs of stagflation. As noted, the budget deficit had increased and the trade surplus was much lower than expected; annual inflation had been 175 percent for consumer prices and 182 percent for wholesale prices. Economic activity declined in the third trimester of 1987 and average wages and number of hours worked fell 9.7 percent and 6.9 percent, respectively.[10] The year ended with increasing uncertainty, as business waited to confront demands from labor, which would attempt to recover some of the losses in wages that had occurred during the year. This time, the government would not supervise these negotiations.

Economic Chaos and the Peronist Electoral Victory

The year 1988 began with the Radical government facing familiar pressures. On the one hand, it confronted short-term political and electoral competition. On the other hand, it had medium- and long-term goals for economic restructuring. However, the government now faced a situation that can more appropriately be termed "post-austral." Since the agreement with the Peronists that provided for tax reform and removed state controls over collective bargaining, the principal government mechanism that might have slowed inflation was removed. Business faced increasing uncertainty as well, since the proximity of national elections invoked the fear of Peronist victory, especially given an accentuated the economic crisis. Since the Peronists had won the 1987 elections, it became apparent that they could capture the presidency again. Such an out-come was quite troubling to business, since a Peronist president could easily strengthen union power and the state's role in the economy.

Indeed, in early 1988 the economic crisis intensified. Business, labor, and the state expected an increased competition for economic resources given the rise in the government deficit, the lower trade surplus, the increase in the foreign debt, and the fall in real wages and employment. The distributive struggle was not long in coming and had an immediate effect on inflation. Between January and August 1988, the monthly inflation rate increased consistently, from 9.1 percent to a dangerous level of 27.6 percent. According to the National Statistical and Census Institute (INDEC), annual inflation between September 1987 and August 1988 had reached 440 percent, while wholesale prices increased 606.5 percent. By April, the government had suspended payments on the foreign debt.

Given these deteriorating circumstances, the government, under pressure from both the IMF and the Radical party presidential candidate, took further steps to control inflation. At the beginning of August, they announced the Spring Plan. The plan included an alliance with the UIA and the CAC, two associations that were particularly concerned about the possible electoral triumph of the Peronist presidential candidate Carlos Menem. The measures included a price control agreement for 180 days with the UIA, formation of a group to follow up on the accord—the secretary of internal commerce, the UIA, and the CAC—a 11.4 percent devaluation of the austral, a 30 percent increase in public utility rates, and establishment of different exchange rates for imports and exports. In addition, the government agreed to gradually reduce the budget deficit to 4 percent of GDP, reduction of the value-added tax by 3 percent, and several other measures.

The plan had almost immediate results: inflation declined to 11.7 percent in September and 5.7 percent in November. Foreign creditors also approved of the new plan, with the U.S. Treasury Department, the IMF, and the World Bank approving a set of loans that would be disbursed in a scaled fashion. These new loans were crucial, since the plan's success depended on controlling the exchange rate, which the new foreign credits would facilitate.

At the same time, a struggle emerged among capitalist factions. Whereas the UIA supported the new plan, the agricultural associations—including the SRA, CRA, CONINAGRO, and FAA—presented a document denouncing the Spring Plan. The agricultural associations were especially incensed at the differential exchange rates for imports and exports, which they argued "plundered" the countryside and consumers. Although some associations such as the Argentine Construction Union (UCA) and the Argentine Confederation of Industry (CAI) "moderated" their opposition to the new plan, it became clear by 10 August 1988 that the plan's only supporters were the UIA and the CAC.[11]

Conflict between business factions and the government continued in a meeting at the presidential estate, where 500 entrepreneurs tied to the UIA, CAC, CAI, and CGI, representing the most important economic groups in the country, expressed support for the plan. President Alfonsín called this an "alliance between production and democracy."[12] However, at the inauguration of the exhibition of agriculture and cattle of the SRA, the president was massively jeered.[13] The new plan was threatened on other fronts as well. Not only had the intercapitalist struggle intensified, but also salary negotiations increased inflationary pressures. On 21 August 1988, the UOM negotiated a 47.4 percent wage increase with the metallurgical business associations, with further agreements to reconsider wage levels less than a month later. This settlement foretold greater union pressure. In addition, the intensified presidential election campaign and the Peronist candidate's threat to declare a moratorium on foreign debt payments and to decree a *salariazo* (a large salary increase) were reflected in the December inflation rate of 6.8 percent.

At the same time, the government attempted ever more desperately to keep a lid on inflation. One tactic was maintaining a "cheap" dollar. The overvaluation of the austral was buttressed by Central Bank sales of the dollar as well as high interest rates on bank deposits to decrease the overall demand for dollars. Expectations, however, made this foreign exchange policy untenable. Since capitalists did not believe the government would be able to maintain the overvaluation for very long, they used the surpluses obtained from high interest rates to buy dollars, thus increasing pressure on the dollar and reducing Central Bank reserves. By the end of 1988, both internal and external confidence in the plan had disappeared, what with increasing inflation, high interest rates, declining investment, recession, devaluation, and a growing foreign debt. The crisis was extremely severe, even by Argentine standards. When the Central Bank declared a bank holiday on 6 February 1989 and decided to suspend its sale of dollars, the effects on the exchange rate and inflation were devastating.

The business associations that had supported the new plan abandoned the government at the end of February and declared that they were no longer bound by price agreements. Exporters also began to refuse to exchange their dollars at the official exchange rate. On 3 March, the government announced that the World Bank had suspended a $350 million loan, and on the last day of March, Radical presidential candidate Eduardo Angeloz demanded the resignation of the economic team. The two Radical ministers who succeeded Sourrouille were helpless in the face of the intensifying crisis, which lurched toward hyperinflation. Retail prices increased 33.4 percent in April and nearly 80 percent in May, while wholesale prices increased over 100 percent in May.

Given this wretched performance of the economy, Radical party arguments that a Peronist victory would only make matters worse had little resonance. In the election held on 15 May, Peronist candidate Carlos Menem achieved a majority in the electoral college on the strength of his garnering of 47 percent of the popular vote. The Radical candidate, Eduardo Angeloz, received just 32 percent of the electorate's support. Peronism also obtained a majority in the Senate, achieving 56.5 percent of the seats. In the Chamber of Deputies, Peronism maintained its position as the largest bloc, with 44.1 percent of the deputies. For the first time in Argentine history, a democratic government had lost a presidential election to an opposition party.

Menemism as the Missing Piece for the Bourgeoisie's Democratic Bet

At the moment of the Peronist electoral victory in May 1989, Peronism itself was still an unpredictable movement. The campaign proposals of the president-elect, Carlos Menem, had been unclear, as had been his ideas on dealing with the foreign debt and the relationship between wages and profits. His proposal for a *salariazo* as well as the contemplated "productive revolution" were not clear either, until the economic team was named. Those in business were especially concerned because many in the candidate's entourage pushed for a moratorium on debt payments and traditional demand-stimulus economic policies.

Peronism Begins to Surprise Even the Peronists

Business, however, need not have worried. The unexpected nomination of Miguel Roig to head the Economics Ministry left no doubt about the direction of economic policy. Roig represented the Bunge and Born group, one of the most powerful Argentine multinational oligopolies associated with food production and commerce. (Oddly enough, this group, presented by the government as a model of success and efficiency, had historically been seen by Peronism as a capitalist enterprise whose profits did not serve the "national interests.")

Other appointments to the new government included advisors of associations like the UIA and the CAC, as well as leaders of the principal part of the liberal right, the Ucedé, which accepted the unusual invitation to collaborate with the Peronists in supporting the new economic policy. For example, the incoming secretary of internal commerce, who would be negotiating price agreements with leading firms and their associations, had advised the UIA and COPAL before his appointment and was a militant of the Ucedé. In general, the new policies deepened the neoliberal reforms that the Radicals had already haltingly attempted to implement.

The Menem government adopted several emergency measures to confront the hyperinflationary situation. The first measures, announced on 9 July 1989, included a 300 percent devaluation of the austral, increases in energy and public utility rates of between 200 and 600 percent, suspension of export subsidies, and the continuation of export taxes of 30 percent for agricultural products and 20 percent for manufactured products. Other emergency measures included the cessation of printing money to finance the budget deficit, increases and subsequent freezes (until October) of wages and pensions, a ninety-day price freeze retroactive to 3 July, elimination of restrictions on foreign investments, reduced public spending, and privatization of public services. A tax reform was also announced, which extended the value-added tax to most economic activities.

Business associations generally supported the new direction of the government's economic policy, even though they criticized the temporary price freeze. In addition, following Minister Roig's death only six days into the Menem government, the president made a point of publicizing his consultation over the minister's replacement with Jorge Born, head of the Bunge and Born group. The legitimacy of the new economics minister, Néstor Rapanelli, was based on his representing this key economic group. Only two days after assuming office (17 July), the new minister reached an agreement with 350 business leaders to stabilize prices in exchange for maintaining stability in interest rates, the exchange rate, and public utility charges. These measures achieved short-term success, with a decline in the inflation rate from 197 percent in July to 38 percent in August, 9.4 percent in September, and 5.6 percent in October. The numbers from September and October were especially impressive, considering that they were achieved after a round of new wage negotiations without a "ceiling" on increases imposed by the government.

At the same time, the government realized that its room for maneuver was quite limited. Real wages had declined substantially in the face of hyperinflation, and exporters faced losses because of the frozen exchange rate. Thus, the government decided to try to broaden its margin for action. The new government took advantage of the crisis (and the Radical party's promise not to oppose economic measures) and its ability to manipulate pro-government congressmen to pursue new initiatives. These included the approval of the State Reform Law on 17 August and the Economic Emergency Law on 1 September. These laws authorized the state to partially or totally privatize all state firms (service, productive, or extractive) and to suspend promotional subsidies to industry and mining. It also suspended the policy of giving preference to local producers in state purchases. State hiring was also frozen, and job security for state employees was temporarily discontinued. These measures fundamentally threatened regional economic interests, firms that supplied the state, and public employees.

As a result, capitalists' initial surprise was transformed into active support for the Peronist government. For example, while Menem was well received and applauded at the inauguration of the SRA exposition on 12 August, the support at "Industry Day" ceremonies on 2 September was much more specific and enthusiastic. Business backed the economic plan in general, as well as the measures that were meant to decrease the budget deficit and to reform the state apparatus. Business also expressed support for the government's intention to eliminate export taxes in twelve months, reform the tariff system, establish incentives for industrial reactivation, and provide more financing for exporters.[14] At the same time, support from industry was more qualified than that of agricultural interests. Industrialists were especially concerned about the internal recession and their exclusion from decision making.[15]

While this set of policies might appear to be quite anti-Peronist, President Menem considered his introduction of a "popular market economy" an "updating" of Peronism. In fact, at this point, Menem enjoyed more support from business and the right-wing parties than he did from the unions and the governing party. Sensing this resistance from the unions, the government took steps to neutralize the most combative ones. The government named representatives of the Fifteen to key posts in the Labor Ministry, who were well disposed to negotiate with the executive (given their experience during the Alfonsín government in 1987) and had better relationships with business leaders. With the pro-Menemist union leaders controlling the Labor Ministry and the CGT (led by Saúl Ubaldini) remaining intransigent toward the government, the Menem administration succeeded in achieving a split in the CGT on 10 October 1989. Both factions of the CGT insisted on being the sole representative of workers, but the Menemist "San Martín" faction enjoyed official state recognition, while the more confrontational "Azopardo" wing was isolated. The government's policy vis-à-vis unions was clearly meant to signal its determination to carry out its economic reforms.

Although the passage of the state reform and economic emergency laws, as well as divisions within the CGT, created conditions that were conducive to medium- and long-term reforms, immediate economic policy remained a contentious issue. Beginning in November 1989, exporters responded to the still frozen exchange rate by refusing to exchange their dollars for australs; the total withheld during 1989 was estimated at around $2 billion. Inflation also began to increase in November, to 6.5 percent. Conflict over the direction of economic policy, and especially over policy relating to the undervalued exchange rate and low interest rates, led to several resignations from the economic team, including the president of the Central Bank. Finally, on 11 and 12 December, several new economic measures were announced, which included a 54 percent devaluation of the austral, a dual exchange rate (one official and one free), and a lowering of import tariffs. To decrease the budget deficit, the economic team declared a new round of price increases in the energy sector and public utilities and increased export taxes.

These new measures led to only greater instability and were criticized roundly. One liberal leader noted, "What has been done should not be confused with a realistic liberal program."[16] After only a few days, policy direction changed again. On 15 December, Economics Minister Néstor Rapanelli was replaced by Antonio Ermán González, a Christian Democrat economist who had served as economics minister under Menem when the latter was governor of La Rioja Province.

González's set of economic reform measures included freeing prices, unifying exchange rates and liberalizing the exchange rate market, eliminating all regulations on the sale or purchase of foreign currency, repealing the increase in export taxes, and, given the likely increase in inflation, a substantial wage increase. Business associations, as expected, supported the new plan because of the liberalized exchange rate market or newly freed prices. Also as expected, businesses raised their prices: consumer prices increased 40 percent in December, and the value of the dollar increased from 960 to 2,000 australs. Hyperinflation returned in 1990, with consumer prices increasing nearly 500 percent in the first three months of year. During the year that saw the first democratic transfer of government to an opposition party in the nation's history, Argentina reached a record of dubious merit: from April 1989 to March 1990, consumer prices increased 20,594 percent.

The economic policy initiatives taken in December 1989 marked the beginning of a pattern that the Menem government has continued: in the face of economic crisis, the government response has been to intensify the reform process by speeding up initiatives already adopted or by proposing new reforms. Thus, faced with a deepening crisis, the economic team launched new measures on 1 January 1990. These included converting the majority of bank deposits (some $1.5 billion with short-term maturities) to long-term debt tied to the dollar. It suspended the prefinancing of exports and postponed bidding on government contracts for four months. Dollar bank accounts were also legalized.

In general, the government strategy was to stop the rise in the dollar to control inflation, using a combination of several measures. Since the government had decided to stop printing money to finance the budget deficit and payments on bank deposits had been suspended, the monetary base shrunk dramatically in a context of hyperinflation. The coefficient of liquidity (M2/GDP) fell from 12 percent in the last trimester of 1989 to 6 percent in the first trimester of 1990. This decline in the monetary base induced a sharp rise in interest rates (from 38.5 percent a month in December to 74 percent in January) and deepened the recession. The shrunken monetary base also affected the exchange rate: since australs were hard to come by, firms had to sell their reserves of dollars to obtain needed cash. The value of the dollar fell from 2,500 australs at the end of December to 1,300 in the first week of January.[17]

At the same time, the high rate of inflation led to an undervaluation of public utility rates. The recession and the consequent decline in economic activity also reduced tax revenues. Both factors led to a larger budget deficit, and the government responded on 1 February 1990 by increasing utility rates by 90 percent and by extending the value-added tax to activities previously exempted from the tax. Business remained silent, since their agreement to support the general thrust of economic policy did not imply their endorsement of specific policy measures.

This lukewarm support echoed business's response to the reforms adopted in December. The government responded in December by trying to drum up support for its policies from "authorities" whose backing for Peronist economic policies was still novel. For example, presidential advisor Alvaro Alsogaray, president of Ucedé, supported the government in a speech on national radio and television by declaring that "December 18 will mark the boundary between two different eras."[18] A letter from President Bush noted that the United States would "continue encouraging" the reforms and offered support "for the success of the program."[19]

Economic reforms continued unabated, however. On 4 March 1990, Economics Minister González announced a new "package" of policies designed to reduce the budget deficit. The Housing (Hipotecario) Bank was closed, and 136 secretariats and subsecretariats were abolished within the executive branch. These measures tended to reduce the state's operational expenses. Taxes on agricultural exports were also increased by 5 percent, payments to state contractors were suspended for sixty days, and public firms were forced to save an equivalent of 5 percent of total income. Finally, the Central Bank was prohibited from printing money to cover the budget deficit.[20]

As a result of these measures, inflation fell substantially after March, stabilizing at a rate of 11–16 percent per month from April to September. Nevertheless, inflation appeared to be rising by August, which gave the economic team another opportunity to deepen the reforms. On 31 August, the economics minister announced an acceleration of the adjustment process. The new measures included spending cuts for central government administration and public enterprises, forced retirements and layoffs in the public sector, the elimination of tax exemptions, tax indexation, and accelerated privatization of state-owned enterprises.[21]

The plan succeeded from the government's point of view: inflation dropped to a 4.7 monthly rate by December 1990, and privatizations were indeed speeded up. Both the national telecommunications firm, ENTEL, and the national airline, Aerolineas Argentinas, were privatized in November. Although these moves were plagued by inefficiency and accusations of corruption, for capitalists they were a new sign of the government's determination to achieve structural reform.

The bidding process was accelerated for other public enterprises, including railroads and 40 percent of the road network, as well as firms in sectors such as petroleum, chemicals, and metallurgy. The government began to make interest payments on its foreign debt; since payments had been suspended since April 1988, Argentina was $5.8 billion in arrears in interest. In July the government had also signed integration agreements with Brazil that laid the basis for the Southern Cone Common Market (MERCOSUR).

Finally, the government concentrated more political power in the executive to neutralize any potential opposition to its economic reforms. Among the salient measures was limitation of the right to strike, instituted by decree without congressional approval. In addition, the government sought to assure that none of its measures would be declared unconstitutional by getting parliamentary approval to enlarge the Supreme Court from five to nine members, and it named judges that would approve the new policies. This blurring the line between the executive and the judiciary as an attempt to concentrate power in the executive obviously calls into question the democratic legitimacy of the regime.

This dizzying pace of change marked 1990 as a year of rupture with the past. To begin with, the implementation of neoliberal policies led to intra- and interparty redefinitions. Not only was there significant collaboration between the Peronist executive branch and the right-wing parties, there were tensions between the Peronist government and the Peronist party itself, especially in the passage of the state reform and economic emergency laws. In addition, there was a growing rapprochement between the Peronist government and the United States. This improvement in relations concerned both the substance of economic policy as well as important aspects of foreign policy.

At the beginning of 1990, diplomatic relations were reopened with Great Britain, Argentina did not condemn the U.S. invasion of Panama, and during the conflict with Iraq Argentina sent ships as part of the allied forces led by the United States. The executive carried out the last action without consulting Congress, and Argentina was the only Latin American country that actively participated in the anti-Iraq coalition. Finally, on 19 September 1991, Argentina withdrew from the nonaligned movement, which it had joined under the Peronists in 1973.

Nevertheless, 1990 presented mixed economic results. While inflation had declined from 1989 levels, Argentina was certainly still experiencing stagflation; consumer prices increased 1,344 percent during the year, while GDP fell 3.5 percent, industrial production declined 4 percent, and real wages dropped 3.5 percent. The recession did improve the balance of payments, with exports increasing 21 percent and imports declining 4.5 percent, leading to a balance-of-payments surplus of $8.22 billion.[22] Reserves reached $3 billion by the end of the year. Nevertheless, the dollar was undervalued by 54 percent, compared to its level at the beginning of the year.

Given these economic results, business was not enthusiastic about the direction of economic policy. Industrialists and the construction sector were affected adversely by the recession and the elevation of the tax burden. Agricultural producers were also hurt by the increased tax burden as well as the growing undervaluation of the dollar. The equilibrium was clearly unstable, and business was not confident in the state's ability to control the budget deficit. This uncertainty, borne out by a budget deficit of $50 million in January, combined with the usual year-end increase in demand for dollars to rapidly increase the value of the dollar by over 60 percent between the end of December and the end of January. Although inflation grew only 7.7 percent during January, the projection of a budget deficit of $200 million for February led to the resignation of Economics Minister González and his replacement by Domingo Cavallo.

"El Cavallazo"

The economic situation that Cavallo faced was certainly more manageable than that of many of his predecessors. Although there was a short-term threat from inflation, reserves were at a high level. To confront the imminent inflation danger, Cavallo introduced yet another adjustment plan that was notably severe. Tensions increased between Peronists and the executive over this plan, and the most severe congressional resistance to the new measures came from the Peronist bloc of deputies. The plan called for increasing the value-added tax and doubling the tax on assets, and other tax increases. The new plan also raised public utility rates 25–50 percent and proposed small increases in public-sector salaries and pensions to counteract the expected increase in inflation.[23]

When Cavallo met with the Peronist bloc, he faced intense criticism and demands to know why such austerity was needed, a plan that did not take into account the circumstances and crises in the provinces. Cavallo responded, "If you don't like the economic plan, tell Carlos [Menem] to name another economics minister." The minister left the meeting in the midst of threats that the bloc would reject the plan.[24] Nevertheless, after heavy pressure from the president, the new tax structure was approved both by the Chamber of Deputies and the Senate.

Another immediate problem facing the new economics minister was a railroad workers' strike called on 5 February 1991. The government followed the same policy it had adopted since coming to power in 1989: it used the law that limited strikes and took immediate action. The government declared the strike illegal because it affected public services, undertook mass firings, intervened in the railroad workers' union, and began the closing of shops as well as four of the railroad lines. Cavallo also accelerated the privatization of the national railroads. The strike finally ended after fifty-four days. By the end of the strike on 29 March, the only union demand was for the reinstatement of workers who had been fired, but even this was not a condition for ending the strike.

The government faced conflicts on other fronts as well. Agricultural associations proposed a "fiscal pact" that would lower their tax burden. The government did not respond. When the growers threatened to stop paying taxes, Cavallo announced that he would confront the agricultural sector "with the same firmness with which he had faced the railroad strike." Three of the principal agricultural associations (CONINAGRO, CRA, and FAA; the SRA did not participate) responded by calling for a two-day production stoppage. The conflict was finally resolved when the government announced a series of concessions, which included eliminating export taxes and new lines of credit for agricultural producers.[25] This new flexibility on the part of the government convinced the agricultural producers to call off their plans to stop production.

Once these problems had been overcome, the Economics Ministry announced a new scheme on 20 March 1991. Even in the context of greater political stability, the plan was presented as an all-or-nothing gamble. It was to take effect on 1 April and would peg the dollar at an exchange rate of 10,000 australs. To assure a fixed exchange rate, the Central Bank was required by law to maintain the current relationship between the monetary base and the level of reserves. The government also vowed that the budget deficit would disappear as of April, and if one were incurred in the future, it would be covered by domestic borrowing and not by printing money.[26] On 27 March 1991, the so-called Convertibility Plan was approved by Congress, with the support of the right-wing parties and a majority of the Peronist deputies.

The effects on financial markets were immediate. The level of reserves made the fixed exchange rate credible, and the dollar exchange rate stabilized. On 1 April, annual interest rates dropped from 44 percent to 22 percent. Inflation also declined from 27 percent in February and 11 percent in March to 5.5 percent in April. The May and June increases were in the 3 percent range.

Other indicators were positive as well. Import tariffs for industrial inputs had already been reduced to an average of 11 percent in February. This reduction in costs, combined with increased economic stability, the decline in interest rates, and negotiations with different industrial sectors (such as automobiles, steel, and foodstuffs) to exchange tax reductions for price reductions, led to an impressive recovery in the second trimester of 1991. The stock market showed an upward trend, overall demand increased, and most industrial sectors experienced striking growth. The following figures show the increase in output in the second trimester compared to the first: electronics, 221 percent; autos, 108 percent; metallurgy, 97 percent; chemicals, 45 percent; glass, 40 percent; tractors, 28 percent; and auto parts, 23 percent.[27]

The new plan has ten general goals. The first five are connected to overhauling both the public accounts and the role of the state in the economy. First, the plan to extend privatization has the aim of reducing the budget deficit, since the state can free itself from money-losing enterprises that are a drain on state resources. It will also be able to increase the inflow of foreign exchange through privatizations; $2 billion had already come in by the end of August 1991. Finally, the foreign debt will be reduced by the use of debt bonds that can be exchanged for equity in the privatized firms; the total reduction had reached $7 billion by the end of August 1991.

Second, Decree 2284/91 stated the government's intention to deregulate the economy and revoked state authority in several of its previous functions. It has also removed the state from a number of markets, abolishing regulatory commissions that oversaw production, the National Sugar Directorate, the Meat Council, and the National Council of Grains, among others.

Third, the administrative reform has continued, which reduces the size of the state apparatus. From 1989 to the end of 1991, the number of employees of the central government administration had been reduced by 147,000, for a total of 200,000.

Fourth, the state has obtained more financial resources through negotiations with international creditors. The government signed a stand-by agreement with the IMF in mid-1991 and lived up to the agreed targets. This permitted the inflow of loans from the IMF itself, and also freed up loans from the IDB and the World Bank. The government also renegotiated its foreign debt with creditor banks and entered the Brady Plan, which allowed the government to achieve a 35 percent reduction in state-controlled debt after an accord was reached in April 1992. These agreements increase state resources by lowering the required payments of principal and interest to foreign creditors and make it possible to obtain resources at market interest rates, which until this point had been impossible for the Argentine state.

The fifth goal is to increase the collection of taxes. This has been done by raising the value-added tax and the income tax, as well as prohibiting the deduction of past losses from one's income tax. Taxes now have to be paid on the current year's income, and past losses are converted into long-term bonds tied to the dollar. These changes, effected in February and March 1992, are particularly relevant in Argentina, where large economic groups have used past losses to reduce their tax burden, with a consequent income tax–GDP ratio in Argentina similar to that in Haiti.

There have also been efforts to reduce tax evasion by simplifying the tax structure and establishing a single billing procedure for the service sector, industry, and commerce as of January 1992. Labor costs were also reduced (to be discussed shortly), and a series of publicly administered punishments of tax evaders made it seem more risky to keep operations informal and undeclared.

The sixth goal relates to prices and production costs, and the continued opening of the economy to international competition. The opening serves two functions: it acts as a ceiling on domestic price increases of tradable goods and it reduces the cost of inputs for domestic industry. The mean tariff had been 37 percent in 1982–1988, 17 percent in 1989–1990, and was 10 percent in 1991. When Cavallo assumed office, 80 percent of products were tariffed at the maximum of 22 percent, while the rest had no tariff. Cavallo reduced the mean tariff to 10 percent on the basis of a three-tiered tariff structure: tariffs on 5,000 products were lowered to zero, those on 2,700 were lowered to 11 percent, and those on 3,800 remained at 22 percent.[28]

The final four goals concern labor costs and the relationship between capital and labor. The seventh goal is to make labor costs more "flexible," which has been translated into new laws covering work accidents and employment (both approved in November 1991). These laws have lowered labor costs by limiting settlements relating to work accidents, making hiring temporary workers more feasible, and reducing settlement limits for unjustified dismissals.

Eighth, Decree 1334 (issued in July 1991) makes salary increases contingent on increased productivity. The objective is to keep wage increases from being transferred to prices.

Ninth, the government has attempted to weaken the political and economic power of unions by redefining the laws governing professional workers' associations and collective bargaining agreements. It has removed prohibitions against the existence of more than one CGT and to the formation of unions based on either trade or firm. The government has also reduced the role of peak negotiations on the basis of economic sector, and has instead encouraged negotiations over wages and working conditions at the level of the firm.

Tenth, and finally, the new social security law as proposed would attack a traditional union power base. It would annul the requirement that workers must contribute to the social security fund of the union that represents them. The state would also unify the system and would replace the unions as receiver and controller of social security contributions.

As is evident from the description of the measures implemented and/or in progress, Argentina has experienced a true neoliberal revolution in its accumulation model and the structure of its social relations. As Minister Cavallo himself said— with the naiveté of a child who declares that the emperor has no clothes on in the face of hypocrites who praise an invisible robe—"Menem is changing everything that Perón did after the Second World War."[29] With further declines in the inflation rate in July, August, and September 1991 (to 2.7, 1.3, and 1.8 percent, respectively), and cheered by signs of economic recovery, the electorate ignored the imputations of corruption attached to Menem's government and gave the Peronists an important victory in the elections for governors and deputies in September and October 1991. Peronists won in ten provinces, while Radicals won in only two and in the federal capital. Peronism gained seven seats in Chamber of Deputies, while the Radicals lost five and Ucedé lost one.

Business support for the Peronist government was also apparent. The political context presented an image of stability that was reinforced by the aforementioned signs of economic recovery and the continued decline in inflation after the elections to rates extremely low by Argentine standards. Inflation amounted to only 1.4 percent in October, 0.4 in November, and 0.6 percent in December. At the end of 1991, consumer prices had risen 84 percent, and wholesale prices had increased only 57 percent. GDP also rebounded, posting a 5.1 percent gain. Given this political and economic stability and a transfer of resources from the working class and public sector to business, a majority of entrepreneurs both at the firm and association level supported the Peronist government.[30]

Even though all business leaders support measures to weaken unions and reduce the budget deficit, however, some in sectors like textiles, electronics, and auto parts are not necessarily happy with the direction of economic policy in Argentina. Because of the drop in state spending, the reduction in subsidies, and the economic opening with an undervalued exchange rate (by historic standards), they have been unable to take advantage of the new structure of lower costs. Yet despite the democratic character of the regime, these groups are unable to contest economic policy. With the CGE quite weak, they depend on the willingness and capacity of the UIA to articulate their demands before a government that is quite inflexible in economic policy. Israel Mahler (elected president of the UIA in May 1991) described his reduced margin of action: "The level of deterioration of the productive sector, reflected in the fact that industrial production per capita is today almost 40 percent less than in 1970, had a decisive influence on the avoidance of combative attitudes that led nowhere." Consequently, the strategy of industrial representatives in crisis was to look for channels of dialogue with the government.[31]

The plan succeeded in convincing business that even if they were affected adversely by the new economic plan (and whatever the eventual results of the plan), the result, as in any revolution, would be a social order far different from the one prior to the Menem government and the Cavallazo.

Conclusions

Business associations were commonplace in Argentina by the 1940s. Even earlier, they had been active in the configuration and the policy making of governments and had also played a role in breaking down and replacing political regimes, as had happened in the coup that overthrew Yrigoyen. The rise of Peronism as an electoral majority made democracy seem especially risky for the bourgeoisie. Thus, beginning in the 1950s, the organization and political strategies of capitalists followed their interpretation of the meaning of democracy and authoritarianism in light of their interests. Business developed defensive and/or conspiratorial activities during periods of democratization or democracy and was usually behind the installation of military regimes. Until recently, only the latter were regarded as favoring the vital interests of capital. After 1976, however, military authoritarianism changed its meaning for the bourgeoisie, and after 1983, the meaning of democracy began to change as well.

Regarding authoritarian regimes, the experience of a military dictatorship between 1976 and 1983 modified the perception of important capitalist groups about the costs and benefits of such regimes. In many ways, the economic policies of the military regime were more devastating than any applied during democratic periods. In addition, policy had been designed and implemented with no business input. The effects of government economic strategies were no longer predictable and threatened to lead to technocratic policies that would have a strongly negative impact on important business groups. They could also lead to such adventures as the takeover and war in the Malvinas, followed by the uncontrolled disintegration of the regime.

Even more risky for business are other military groups who oppose the above-mentioned "liberal" policies. These elements, who emerged after Holy Week 1987, present mostly populist themes and denounce U.S. and British "imperialism." Fearing these more radical alternatives within the military, the main business associations such as the SRA, UIA, and the CAC opposed the military uprisings and supported democracy during the crises of Holy Week, Monte Caseros, and Villa Martelli. This was in clear contrast to their previous support for military demands, or at least their "neutrality" when military groups opposed democratic governments.

At the same time, between the 1940s and 1983, democratic rule has usually had negative consequences for business. Democratic governments have usually meant Peronist control, which led to the political advance of unions and of business groups and associations (such as the CGE) linked to regional and small to medium-sized firms that depended on the domestic market. Peronism also usually involved a stronger state and less trust in the market to allocate resources. In addition, some business organizations such as the UIA or the ACIEL were sometimes dissolved. Finally, democratic governments often clashed with the bourgeoisie over issues such as nationalization of industries or higher taxes on foreign capital.

When the Radical party won the 1983 elections, these patterns were broken, and thus the meaning of democracy was redefined for business groups and organizations. The "iron law" that Peronism would triumph in any open election no longer held. Furthermore, the Radicals' anticorporatist discourse during the campaign seemed aimed at thwarting the expected increase in union demands. From the elections of 1983 until June 1985 when the Austral Plan was inaugurated, the democratic alternative offered business several advantages. These included the electoral defeat of Peronism, less risk that some business organizations would be excluded from politics, the government's recognition of the political hegemony of the UIA instead of the CGE/CGI, and a confrontational stance toward unions, especially with respect to collective bargaining or control over social security programs.

After the introduction of the Austral Plan (and the later Spring Plan), the Radical government also became more receptive to the participation of capitalists and their organizations in decision making. There were modifications in economic policy and in the model of accumulation that business preferred. These included opening up the economy, privatization of state-owned enterprises, confrontation with unions, and a reduced role for the state in the economy. It became apparent that such policies were supported by interests other than the political right or the armed forces.

At the same time, the Peronist victory has deepened this neoliberal direction in economic policy and in the reorganization of society. Not only that, but the Peronists' pursuit of neoliberalism is proving to be much more successful than either the Radical or military variants. The Peronists have done a better job of stabilizing the economy and confronting the potential opposition of unions. The policy changes undertaken by the Menem government are revolutionary in their swiftness and scope. Yet the direction of policy is fundamentally different from that expected by the political movement that brought Menem to power. In effect, the present model entails more oligopolic control of the economy and less distributive justice.

Nevertheless, it is not difficult to understand why Menem is achieving his objectives more effectively than either the Radicals or the military were able to do. He has the support of business as well as the electoral majority, in spite of the costs of his government's policies to the popular sectors. The two great conflicts that have characterized the political and economic struggle since the rise of Peronism until the military coup of 1976 have been resolved in favor of powerful capitalist interests. The local bourgeoisie tied to the CGE has disappeared as a threat to organizations such as the UIA, the SRA, and the

CAC. At the same time, the cycle initiated by Menem's government presents a weakened working class that today places a higher value on stability in poverty than on risking social change. Recent Argentine history has associated such risks with state terrorism and the uncertainty of recession and hyperinflation.

Given these circumstances and the longer-range effects of the measures already adopted, the bourgeoisie has accepted the possible political variants associated with democracy in Argentina. For business, democracy has become much more functional and less risky than authoritarianism. Furthermore, since installing an authoritarian regime is impossible without the support of the large economic groups and the most important business associations, even a worsening economic situation is unlikely to result in a breakdown of democracy. The bourgeoisie clearly has bet on the long-term stability of the democratic regime.

Notes

This chapter was translated by Judith Lawton, with substantial revisions by Jeffrey Cason.

1. See also Carlos H. Acuña, "La relativa ausencia de exportaciones industriales en la Argentina. Determinantes políticos y sus consecuencias sobre la estabilidad y tipo de democracia esperables," *Realidad Económica,* 1991: 100; Acuña, "Políticas públicas, estructura económica y lucha política en la Argentina: Su relación con la organización y el comportamiento de los empresarios," in *Organizaciones Empresariales y Políticas Públicas,* ed. CIESU/FESUR/ICP (Montevideo: FESUR/Trilce, 1992); Acuña, "Empresarios y politica (Parte I). La relación de las organizaciones capitalistas con partidos y regímenes políticos en América Latina: Los casos argentino y brasileño," *Boletín Techint,* 1988: 255; Carlos Acuña et al., "La relación estado-empresarios con referencia a políticas concertadas de ingresos. El caso argentino" in *Politica económica y actores sociales,* ed. (Santiago do Chile: PREALC-OIT, 1988); and G. Alberti, L. Golbert, and Acuña, "Intereses industriales y gobernabilidad democrática," *Boletín Techint,* 1984: 235.

2. See John W. Freels, *El sector industrial en la política nacional* (Buenos Aires: EUDEBA, 1970); Jorge Niosi, *Los empresarios y el estado argentino (1955–1969)* (Buenos Aires: Siglo XXI, 1974); Guillermo O'Donnell, "Estado y alianzas en la Argentina, 1956–1976," in *CEDES/CLACSO, 1976,* 5; and Guillermo O'Don-

nell, "Notas para el estudio de la burguesía local, con especial referencia a sus vinculaciones con el capital transnacional y el aparato estatal," *Estudios Sociales* (CEDES, 1978): 12.

3. Moreover, works along the lines of D. Azpiazu, E. Basualdo and M. Khavisse, *El nuevo poder económico* (Buenos Aires: Legasa, 1986) demonstrate that in the process of nationalization/statization of the private external debt in 1982 and 1983, 85 percent of the nationalized debt belonged to only 5 percent of the total of debtors, and it was only this small group of debtors that benefited from the transfer. Furthermore, this is a group of firms that was commonly identified as the "captains of industry" because of their leadership in different industrial sectors and the preferential political treatment that they received during the Radical government.

4. A more detailed analysis of the political processes from the democratic opening through 1987 is contained in Acuña and Laura Golbert, "Los empresarios y sus organizaciones. Actitudes y reacciones en relación con el Plan Austral y su interacción con el mercado de trabajo," in *Estabilización y respuesta social,* ed. PREALC-OIT (Santiago de Chile: PREALC-OIT). This work, with some revisions, was published in Argentina under the title "Empresarios y Politica (Parte II). Los empresarios y sus organizaciones: ¿Qué pasó con el Plan Austral?" *Boletín Techint* (1990): 263.

5. BCRA, "Trimestral Estimates of Global Supply and Demand."

6. UIA document; *La Nación,* 26 March 1986.

7. Data from the Economics Ministry and the Foundation for Latin American Economic Investigation (FIEL).

8. *La Nación,* 21 July 1987.

9. Accord reached with the IMF in November 1987.

10. INDEC, on the basis of a survey of 1,300 industrial establishments.

11. *La Nación,* 11 August 1988, 1.

12. *La Nación* and *Clarín,* 13 August 1988, 1.

13. *La Nación,* 14 August 1988, 1.

14. See *La Nación,* 2 September 1989, 1, 14, 16, 17.

15. *Clarín,* 3 October 1989, special supplement for the Metallurgical exhibition '89, 3.

16. *La Nación,* 14 December 1989, 1, 26.

17. Data based on reports of CEPAL cited by Aldo Vacs, in "Argentina," in *Latin American and Caribbean Contemporary Record,* ed. James Malloy and Eduardo Gamarra (New York and London: Holmes and Meier, 1991), 9:3.

18. *La Nación,* 10 January 1990, 1.

19. *La Nación,* 11 January 1990, 1.

20. *La Nación,* 5 March 1990, 1.

21. *La Nación,* 1 September 1990, 1; Vacs, "Argentina," 4.

22. Figures cited by Vacs, "Argentina," 5.

23. *La Nación,* 4 February 1991, 1.

24. *La Nación,* 7 February 1991.

25. *La Nación,* 17 March 1991.

26. *La Nación,* 21 March 1991.

27. *La Nación,* 15 August 1991, 1.

28. *La Nación,* 9 November 1991, 6.

29. *La Nación,* 11 February 1992, 13.

30. A survey by Price Waterhouse of representatives of the 500 firms with the highest sales in Argentina showed that, for 1992, 56.3 percent expected a growth in GDP greater than 3 percent, a budget surplus, and inflation around 21 percent. Of the same group, 58.2 percent foresaw growing profitability, and 85.1 percent expected the general economic situation in the next two years to be either good or very good (*Página* 12, 10 November 1991, 8–9).

31. *La Nación,* 1 September 1991, sec. 3a, 1.

Ernest Bartell, c.s.c.

2. Perceptions by Business Leaders and the Transition to Democracy in Chile

The transitions to democracy in Latin America in the 1980s and 1990s have been accompanied by economic policies and social expectations that do not always coincide. The conversions to neoliberal economic policies over the past quarter century by many authoritarian regimes give fresh significance, both political and economic, to the behavior of the private sector within the national economy, and especially to entrepreneurship in those sectors on which the performance of neoliberal policies depends. The state was said to be justified in taking a leading role in economic development because the private sector was inadequate as the primary engine of development: Latin American markets were unable to effectively provide goods and services to meet basic needs and control the undesirable and costly external effects of market-led development—for example, the inadequate provision of public and social services. It was held that private enterprise could make only a limited contribution to sustained and equitable economic development because of a lack of entrepreneurial spirit in Latin American economies and because income distribution associated with market-led development had become badly skewed.[1] There was also concern about inefficient monopolies that dominated small markets as a result of minimum firm size needed for efficient production and about the barriers to entering the market created by limited access to capital and technology. Private-sector markets were also deemed inherently inefficient because of market uncertainty, limits on the ability to acquire and analyze information, including the "imperfect perception of information,"[2] as well as social stratification and cultural and political traditions that frowned on the pursuit of private profit.[3]

The result was that Latin American governments, both capitalist and socialist, adopted a wide variety of interventionist policies toward the ownership and regulation of productive property and control of prices, wages, and flows of resources, domestic and international, under various ideological banners: socialism, state capitalism, and mixed enterprise. These policies were typically justified by arguments identified with the Economic Commission for Latin America and the Caribbean (ECLAC) that advocated protecting domestic markets and subsidizing domestic production of import substitutes to expand national markets and stimulate domestic savings and investment. The results—rates of economic growth, patterns of income distribution, and provision of public and social goods and services—varied nationally and cyclically and were perceived differently by different sectors. Government institutions that were seen by some as necessary to redress the deficiencies of private-sector markets were for others economically inefficient bureaucracies that fueled inflation and stifled entrepreneurship and efficiency. Despite robust economic growth in many Latin American countries during the early years of import substitution in the 1950s and 1960s, these results and the perceptions of them were so mixed and so unstable that coherent models of sovereign national development could not be worked out.

Meanwhile, the neoliberal economic claim that free markets

can elicit the entrepreneurship needed for sustained development—though sometimes only with direct and indirect government support—were buttressed by high and relatively stable market-led economic growth in some OECD countries and in Asian NICs. Many Latin American authoritarian regimes adopted varying mixes of neoliberal policies and programs in search of new economic strategies in the 1960s and 1970s.

However, Chile's experiment came to be seen as a paradigm for comprehensive restructuring because of the high economic growth rates, moderate inflation, and relatively stable capital markets and exchange rates achieved in the last three years of Pinochet's seventeen-year regime. However, the strong and repressive role of government in that restructuring, especially during its earlier years, is not to be forgotten.[4] Intervention was marked not only by human rights abuses, but by unprecedented numbers of bankruptcies, high unemployment, and increasing inequalities in wealth and income. Nevertheless, the continued reliance on many features of the successful neoliberal model by the subsequent democratically elected government has strengthened Chile's image as a paradigm for concurrent economic liberalization and political democratization.

Whether Chile can be a model for other countries depends on many variables, not least of which is the political and economic behavior of the business sector, where decisions affecting macroeconomic performance and market development are often made on the basis of subjective perceptions. In a market economy, decisions made in the private sector about investment, production levels, and marketing targets obviously affect macroeconomic policy objectives regarding employment and wages, capital formation, growth rates, prices and interest rates, allocative efficiency, and market integration, domestic and international. They help to determine the composition of output, rates of technological change, distribution of income and wealth, the burden of foreign debt, and balance of payments constraints, and thus can influence the political determination of national economic policies and social realignments.

Business decisions are made under constraints of time and resources. Rational market behavior in the real world is based not on perfect information shared by all—according to neoliberal microeconomic theory, a necessary condition for efficiency—but on subjective perceptions. Because of these limitations, macroeconomic and microeconomic business decisions, by both individuals and groups, are made under uncertainty. And even when greater certainty might be achieved in principle, limited time and resources make it economically infeasible. These realities undermine the simplistic assumption that a centrally planned economy, whether socialist or state-capitalist, is a more rational way to achieve social objectives than a market-driven economy. However, they also undermine the argument for the inherent efficiency of a market model with economic actors whose perceptions are neither equally valid nor mutually consistent.

Therefore, the success of the neoliberal economic model that has accompanied the transition to democracy in Chile does not automatically translate into a paradigm that can be replicated in other economies, societies, and cultures. Replicating the model elsewhere requires conditions that elicit a dynamically motivated, entrepreneurial private sector that can survive outside the chauvinist interventionist state and compete effectively in the international marketplace. These conditions include how business people perceive economic parameters and variables and how they interpret social and political institutions, policies, and programs influencing their economic opportunities and risks. Chile is unique in Latin America for its long, relatively uninterrupted tradition of democracy and for having elected a socialist government whose economic failures helped to mobilize unusual support for the military coup by General Pinochet, who repressively imposed a neoliberal economic regime. Therefore, responses by Chilean business to the transition to democracy are not necessarily like those of other Latin American private sectors facing transitions to democracy and a market-driven economy. Nor can we assume that effects on entrepreneurial behavior will be the same or that Chile's success with an open, free-market economy can be reproduced elsewhere.

It is beyond my scope to analyze how Chile's historical experience conditioned the nation to endure seventeen years of authoritarian repression, two waves of business bankruptcies, persistently high unemployment, and a greatly worsened distribution of income before the transition to an open, free-market economy began to demonstrate sustained growth. This chapter examines, through interview data, the perceptions of members of Chile's private business sector regarding the economic and political influences on their entrepreneurial behavior.[5] In addition, it will draw some inferences about the compatibility of the economic expectations and political attitudes of business leaders with the social goals and participatory processes of democratic society. This inquiry may shed light on the likelihood of replicating Chile's success with an open economy in a newly democratic society. To sharpen the issue, I will make some comparative observations based on similar interview data with private-sector decision makers in Brazil.

Comparing these perceptions may also reveal the conditions and variables that encourage the sort of dynamic business behavior that is essential for the liberal, open economy to succeed, and will suggest possible limitations on the trajectory and replicability of Chile's success. Perceptions about current economic conditions and future expectations are obviously important; private-sector decision makers must subjectively assess the impact of macro- and microeconomic changes on a complex mix of objectives and opportunities—for instance, operating profits, portfolio returns, stability and growth of sales, domestic market share, international market penetration, maintaining and strengthening their sociopolitical status.

Macroeconomic perceptions include judgments and expectations about inflation, credit conditions, stability of currencies, growth rates, and capital movements. Microeconomic perceptions include opportunities for individual saving and investment behavior, including credit availability and costs, interest rates, subjective risk assessments and evaluations of individual market opportunities in light of competitive market conditions that help determine costs, markups, prices, and profitability of investments.

Equally important to private sector–led economic growth are business leaders' perceptions of their own competence, especially their competitiveness, in domestic and international markets. The typical neoliberal development strategy stresses production for export, partly to test competitive efficiency and partly because of the constraints of relatively small domestic markets. However, relatively large minimum firm sizes for efficient production and the possibilities for economies of scale in some industries suggest that entrepreneurs' views on their ability to compete will be influenced by both domestic and international market opportunities.

It is commonplace to emphasize that political stability is essential to economic risk taking and to confidence in democratic institutions. Much of the short-term, speculative, and nonproductive behavior typically attributed to Latin American investors—for example, capital flight—may be based on a rational assessment of the economic effects of political instability, of which the region has a long history. The confidence engendered by perceived political stability is obviously basic to maintaining the long-term savings and investment, domestic and foreign, needed for substantial economic growth.

However, perceptions of stability are influenced by unique characteristics in each setting. Observable consistency and continuity in economic policies and strategies is an important component of business confidence. So too are attitudes toward institutions considered fundamental to market-led development—for example, private property and the free movement of market prices. Social and political attitudes and norms of social equity—regarding poverty, distribution of income and wealth, and access to social services—obviously contribute to perceptions of political stability. However, their impact on business confidence will depend upon culturally defined attitudes about social responsibility. Perceptions among Latin American elites about the most effective way to protect against social unrest have ranged from support for armed repression to participating in democratic determination of equitable social policies.

Closely related to perceptions of political stability and of business competence are views about the appropriate role of the state in the economy. Although the neoliberal ideology typically articulated by business leaders may give the state a minimal role in the economy—for instance, a role limited to protecting property rights—in practice, business people expect varying degrees of intervention based on their experience with government and, at least implicitly, on confidence in their ability to function effectively in the existing economic environment. Expectations about possible economic growth also affect perceptions about the appropriate role of government— for example, in providing physical and technical infrastructure, granting access to credit and to external markets, and maintaining acceptable levels of inflation and variations in the exchange rate.

Business tolerance for government intervention in the economy is also affected by perceptions of the competence of those who design and administer economic policies and strategies. Here too experience with government personnel at all levels is likely to shape attitudes more than abstract ideology. Respect for the professional and ethical competence of public servants breeds respect for government and the political system. At the same time, the magnitude and complexity of public servants' responsibilities can raise doubts about their competence. Public administrators are more apt to be seen as capable in a relatively simple, integrated economy with easily identified technological and economic opportunities than in a poorly integrated, multisectored economy dependent upon vertically complex, capital-intensive, and technologically demanding industrial output.

Business leaders are also more likely to accept a government role in the economy when they feel they can influence the exercise of that role. Influence can be applied at the political level—for example, in choosing public officials and determining policy. Or it can be at the level of public administration—for example, in getting fair or preferential treatment from public servants. Those who are successful in securing favorable legislation or in manipulating bureaucratic regulation are likely to be more satisfied with current levels of government intervention than those who are not.

Methodological Note

The interviews for the following case studies, typically lasting an hour or more, were conducted with a sample of business people in Santiago, Chile, in the fall of 1987 and the spring of 1988, just prior to the plebiscite that set the stage for the democratic election in 1989. I again interviewed a cross section of the same respondents in early 1991, approximately a year after the installation of the newly elected coalition government. As a comparison, to shed light on the feasibility of replicating the Chilean model elsewhere, in 1989 I carried out similar interviews in São Paulo, Brazil, before the election that installed Brazil's first democratically elected government since the exit of the authoritarian regime, and held follow-up meetings in early 1991.[6]

The interviews were intended to elicit how business people perceived a range of macro- and microeconomic variables, government policies, and social indicators that might affect their decisions, especially about investment. Held shortly before elections and again after the new governments' policies had been announced and were being implemented, the interviews also sought to learn how perceptions were affected by expected changes in government policy. In turn, interview responses can suggest how perceptions by business can facilitate or thwart the effectiveness of economic liberalization policies and can suggest some practical limits to the pace and extent of liberalization.

The forty-one respondents in Santiago and the thirty-six in São Paulo interviewed in 1987–1988, as well as in follow-up meetings in 1991, were decision makers identified by their peers and academic observers as either successful and representative of significant sectors of the economy or as positive examples of modernizing behavior—that is, as members of a new entrepreneurial generation, especially in nontraditional and export sectors. All Brazilian respondents and all but two in Chile were male. The firms they represented were either medium-sized or large, relative to the national mix. Traditional small businesses, microenterprises, and the nontradeable sectors—for example, transportation and real estate—were not included. About 10 percent of those interviewed were executives of foreign multinational firms, so that I could benefit from "external" opinions of national entrepreneurship and learn something about national private-sector attitudes toward foreign participation and competition in national economies.

Attitudes of Business Before the Transition in Chile

By the time of the 1987–1988 interviews, the business community in Chile was an elite group who had survived the market liberalization policies of the 1970s and the economic crises of the mid-seventies and the early eighties. The annual number of bankruptcies had risen from 25 in 1973, the year of the

Pinochet coup, to 810 in the 1982 recession. Even during the "boom" years of 1978–1981, the annual bankruptcy rate in the liberalized Chilean economy was double that of the economically unspectacular years of the Frei administration in the late 1960s.[7] The industrial sector was especially hard hit by the liberalization policies of the Pinochet regime, the international oil shocks, and the international economic slump of the early 1980s. By 1983, Chile's industrial productive capacity had declined by over 9 percent from 1969 levels (over 19 percent, if the nonferrous metal basic industry sector is excluded). Out of twenty-nine identifiable industrial-sector classifications, twenty-three had experienced stagnation or retrenchment during that period.[8]

Agriculture experienced some of the same direct pressures of liberalization of markets as industry, including changed relations between prices of products and of inputs. As markets were liberalized, agricultural producers complained that market prices of their products dropped, while costs of inputs such as fertilizers and pesticides rose.[9] The effects of macroeconomic restructuring on Chile's agricultural producers, however, may have been more benign than those on the industrial elite. The import substitution industrialization policies pursued in Latin America (as in other developing countries) in the two decades after World War II typically favored industrial growth at the expense of agriculture. Some of the discrimination was the result of direct measures—for example, price controls on agricultural products—and some came from indirect policies. The latter included macroeconomic measures such as exchange rates that raised the cost of agricultural inputs and overvalued agricultural exports in international markets. Similarly, tax and subsidy schemes for industrial import substitutes had the effect of lowering costs to industrial producers. These indirect measures, which in effect taxed agricultural producers more than their industrial counterparts, often overwhelmed the benefits of direct supports or subsidies for domestic agricultural production.[10] In sixteen agricultural-exporting nations in Latin America, Africa, and Asia, the combined effects of direct and indirect economic policies favoring domestic industrial import substitutes amounted to an average tax of 36–40 percent on agricultural exports during 1975–1984.

Chile, however, was an exception. Because it abandoned import substitution policies in the 1970s, fruit exports during the last five years of the decade, according to the above calculation, received almost no direct subsidy because of market liberalization but were effectively subsidized by 22 percent as a result of indirect effects of macroeconomic policies. (In the first half of the 1980s, the direct subsidy was zero, but there was a relatively small indirect tax effect of 7 percent as a result of macroeconomic policies, which included substantial overvaluation of the Chilean currency during the first two years of the period.)[11] These atypical macroeconomic effects, along with the effective dismantling of agrarian reform during the 1970s, contributed to the boom in export agriculture and to a reallocation of industrial priorities that has continued through the transition to democracy. The effect was to redirect private investment from traditional import substitute industrial production to agricultural development for export, in conformity with Chile's comparative advantage in natural resources.

Growth in Agriculture and Industry

In the process, private investment in agriculture began to rise alongside those in traditional industrial, financial, and nontradeable sectors. With macroeconomic policies less biased toward urban industrialization and with restrictions on large landholdings eased with the dismantling of the agrarian reform programs of the Frei and Allende regimes, large corporate firms and groups, domestic and foreign, reemerged in a wave of speculative accumulation. By 1978 the forty-six largest agroenterprises held assets valued at over $1 billion, with the largest enterprise accounting for almost half the total.[12] The dominant economic conglomerates of the 1970s, whose growth was largely characterized by financial transactions and investment in nontradeables—for example, urban and rural real estate—were replaced by conglomerates, like the Angelini and Matte groups, that invested heavily, often through joint ventures with foreign firms, in agricultural and wood products for export—as well as in other natural resource ventures like commercial fishing and methanol, also for export.[13]

In some respects, there has been a reemergence of the traditional Chilean class system in which large landowners and corporate executives and bankers were found within the same families.[14] Now, however, it is conglomerate corporations, often in joint ventures with foreign capital, that take the place of families (though sometimes with a significant family presence). And now agricultural investments are determined on the same criteria of productivity for profit maximization as other ventures in the conglomerates, often as part of a vertically integrated production process. Agricultural production for export has grown even more rapidly than total exports, from 8 percent of the total in 1970 to 28 percent of the total in 1990, and growth in commercial agriculture has substantially exceeded that of peasant agriculture.[15]

The end of land reform and the liberalization of agriculture have, not surprisingly, been accompanied by changes in the land markets. Land prices, which remained relatively stable between 1917 and 1970, took off with the restructuring of landownership after the 1973 coup and increased at an average annual rate of over 12 percent during the first five years of the Pinochet regime.[16]

At the same time, the relative absence of economies of scale in the cultivation of fruit for export, along with the availability in the public domain of nonproprietary modern agricultural technology, made it possible for those with medium-sized properties to benefit along with large landholders. As a result, by 1988 there were approximately 11,000 producers of export fruit and about 100 export firms, the four largest of which exported over 40 percent of total fruit exports.[17] This shift also meant increased agricultural employment, at least seasonally;[18] however, without effective labor organization and given persistent rural unemployment and underemployment, wages remained low.[19]

By 1987 aggregate growth in gross domestic product (GDP) was over 5 percent, and growth rates in industry had recovered from their lows of the early 1980s. There were about 270,000 private business firms of all sizes operating in six major sectors: manufacturing, mining, construction, agriculture, transport, and commerce.[20] The firms represented in the 1987–1988 interviews were primarily involved in tradeables, that is, commercial agriculture and fishing, forestry and wood products, copper, finance, and nontraditional activities such as computer software.

Self-Evaluation by Business Leaders

Interviews held in 1987–1988 discredited the stereotype of the Chilean businessman as a patrimonial, risk-avoiding, rent-seeking, nonmaximizing property owner, fearful of modern competition, with a short time horizon and a low propensity to save and invest; this image is certainly not typical of entrepreneurial activity in the economy's dynamic sectors.[21] Clearly, a new generation of Chilean entrepreneurs was emerging, competitively professional and self-confident and committed ideologically or pragmatically to a liberal economic model.[22] In 1987–1988 the new generation saw themselves as liberated from what one called the "paternalistic, *rentista* mentality" of the past and quite capable of competing successfully with foreign as well as domestic competitors, without special privileges and dependence on the government.

Many of the new breed have earned graduate or professional degrees abroad and continue to read the same professional literature as their foreign peers. They also identify successful foreign counterparts as their models, use international sources of professional advice, and reflect an awareness and acceptance of international business standards, methods, and practices. Although the Chilean economy in 1987 was only beginning to emerge from the recession of the early 1980s, my interlocutors were generally optimistic about the state of the economy and virtually unanimous in their support for an internationally open economy, expressing little or no fear of foreign competition in domestic markets while at the same time manifesting confidence about their ability to compete with foreign businesses and investors in domestic and international markets.

The Competitive Market Model and Social Legitimacy of Business

Chilean respondents were almost unanimous in supporting foreign investment in Chile and expressed little fear of debt equity swaps, which foreign investors were beginning to use to buy Chilean assets under the relatively liberal terms offered by the government.[23] Chilean entrepreneurs did not complain about the windfalls realized by foreign investors, who could exchange at near par value Chilean government bonds that could then be purchased at 55–60 percent of face value on international secondary markets. Rather, they complained of government restrictions that prevented them from engaging in debt-equity swaps on the same terms. A few also objected to capital restrictions that blocked them from expanding their businesses abroad through direct foreign investment of their own—that is, that prevented them from becoming multinationals in their own right.

Respondents virtually unanimously supported the competitive market model as the sine qua non for economic development in Chile, and all believed that Chile had made a transition to a liberal economy from the protectionism of the ECLAC model of the 1950s and 1960s, although several acknowledged that some sectors were still dominated by oligopoly and monopoly—for example, banking—and still benefited from government privilege and patronage. Several respondents identified competitive success in export markets as the single most important determinant of Chile's successful transition to a competitive market-oriented economy. Many saw an open economy as the most important market force to maintain productive efficiency in monopolistic or oligopolistic domestic firms. Many were proudly convinced that they owed their success not to privilege and patronage, but to their own efforts and initiative, given the political freedom to pursue it.

Paradoxically, however, Chilean entrepreneurs in 1987–1988 expressed a decidedly traditional insecurity and defensiveness about the social legitimacy of what they represent: the pursuit of material gain through business. Despite modernization and its economic opening to the external world, Chilean society was described as in the Hispanic tradition, valuing intellectual effort, political activity, and public-sector administration more highly than the pursuit of profit, and assigning a higher ethical value to labor than to management.[24] Self-confident before the international economy, Chilean respondents were defensive and unsure of their place in their own culture.

Business and the Democratic Transition

The paradoxical self-evaluation of Chilean business people in 1987–1988 was reflected in ambivalence toward the transition to democracy. Whereas almost all respondents supported a return to democracy and several were embarrassed over Chile's international reputation for human rights violations, they almost unanimously backed the neoliberal economic policies of the Pinochet regime, the political stability (however repressive) it had achieved, and the competence of the regime's economic policy makers and administrators.

Virtually all were quick to distinguish between political regime and economic model, and most were at least somewhat

confident that features of a liberal economic model were sufficiently embedded and accepted in Chilean society to make a
radical economic change unlikely after the transition to
democracy. When asked to identify the most important characteristics of the liberal capitalist model that should be preserved,
almost all cited the preservation of property rights as most crucial to maintaining business confidence and stimulating private
investment. So much concern during a period of market-led
economic improvement about something as fundamental as
property rights, in retrospect, indicates the degree of uncertainty with which even relative optimists faced the transition to
democracy. So strong was this concern that there was virtually
unanimous opposition to any policy of redistributive agrarian
reform, even among those who acknowledged the need for
more equity in the distribution of wealth and income.

Tolerance for government regulation of markets varied
somewhat among my respondents, but the free movement of
prices without direct price controls (described by one as "indirect expropriation") was most often cited as essential to a
healthy private sector. Opposition to price controls was typically more pragmatic than ideological. Price controls during
the Allende regime were vividly remembered as inconsistent,
unworkable, and destructive to normal business operations
that depend upon the relationship between prices of inputs and
of final products. Price controls were also criticized as socially
burdensome, because of administrative costs—for instance, the
cost of assigning hundreds of prices to all the labels and vin-
tages of domestic wines—and because they encouraged corruption and evasion.

Despite some affirmations of confidence that the basic elements of the market model would be preserved, most respondents were uneasy about the social acceptance and political
treatment that private enterprise would receive in a democratic
society. In spite of a rising tide of reassuring statements by political leaders in the center-left coalition pressing for a

plebiscite and a return to democracy, there was widespread suspicion regarding the attitudes toward business by political parties and their leaders in the democratic coalition. Collective memories of agrarian reform policies and price controls during the last Christian Democratic regime, and especially during the economically "chaotic" years of the Allende regime, were much more vivid than those of the economic crises of 1976 and 1982, and were cited frequently. A significant number, while affirming democratic values, worried openly about political leaders' ability to resist sectarian pressures for forms of government intervention in the economy that would be inimical to a strong private sector. The most optimistic respondents, who hopefully assumed that fundamental principles of property rights and market signals were firmly enough established to preclude any assault by a new government, tended to be executives and owners of the largest firms and business associations rather than representatives of smaller enterprises.

Expressed in various ways, there was widespread suspicion of political coalitions as the vehicles for coherent and stable economic policy. The fear was frequently mentioned that a democratic coalition, which might hold together long enough to defeat General Pinochet and regain political power, would later disintegrate over economic policies and strategies. This fear was buttressed by self-appraisals of the Chilean character as ideologically intransigent. There was little confidence that Chile's political parties would be willing to compromise, not only because of party rivalries, presumed to be strong after the return to democracy, but also because of the Chilean propensity to attach fundamental ideological significance to even the most trivial political positions. Some respondents worried that even the dominant party in the democratic coalition opposing the Pinochet regime, the Christian Democrats, would not be able to develop coherent economic policies because of the broad spectrum of passionately held ideological positions within the party itself.

It should be noted that spokesmen for the opposing democratic coalition assumed that business leaders were as ideologically intransigent as well. Interviews with active members of the coalition during this period revealed a stereotype of the business elite as homogeneous and tradition-bound. At the same time, there were indications that significant political differences were emerging within the private sector, with a movement of the "new generation" toward a progressive side of the center-right Renovación Nacional party. Nevertheless, few felt a need for dialogue on either side before the plebiscite of 1989. A prominent opposition leader responded to an outsider's suggestion of dialogue with the comment, "Why bother? [Businessmen] will never vote for us anyway."[25]

A few respondents had already concluded that if the Pinochet regime lost both the plebiscite and the election that would follow such a loss, economists with a Christian Democratic orientation from the Corporación de Investigaciones Económicas Para Latinoamérica (CIEPLAN), an opposition economics research institute well known in the private sector, and especially its president, Alejandro Foxley, would be influential in determining and administering economic policy. (Foxley was, in fact, named finance minister in the new government.) Some had already read Foxley's 1987 book, *Chile y su futuro: Un país posible*,[26] looking for clues about economic policy in a government led by Christian Democrats. While they found the book's content and author tolerable, some respondents criticized some of the author's associates at CIEPLAN who were judged "leftist" and threatening to the fundamental principles of property rights and market-determined prices—considered to be essential rules of the game for preserving the liberal economic model.[27]

In light of collective memories and the absence of widespread communication between business leaders and members of the opposition, it is not surprising that only a slight majority of business respondents believed that, in the current political climate, property rights would not be jeopardized by a transition to democracy and that price regulation for ideological or social objectives would not be a political issue that could threaten efficient business operations in most economic sectors. Respondents familiar with investment plans across several areas of the private sector gave different assessments of how far such plans were currently affected by the political uncertainties surrounding the transition to democracy. Executives of foreign firms producing for both export and domestic markets, however, expressed more confidence in the future of the Chilean economy and acknowledged continuing commitments to long-term investment strategies.

Business and Social Responsibility

At the same time, many respondents clearly recognized that the private sector should address the social issues raised by increased concentration in the distribution of income, wealth, and influence after the imposition of the liberal economic model. This awareness contradicted the conventional judgment that the Chilean businessman "has no social conscience."[28] Sensitivity to social issues and policies, however, is understandable in a defensive business community in a political and cultural climate perceived to be hostile to the materialist values of the economic model, and does not necessarily reflect a moral conversion. Concern for social issues and policies was most often articulated in comments about wages and employment. Virtually all who mentioned wages affirmed the necessity of maintaining competitive levels consistent with productivity. In addition, a substantial minority acknowledged a need to raise wages, mostly as a means to ensure the political and social stability essential for uninterrupted economic progress. Similar exhortations came from some business associations such as the Sociedad Nacional de Agricultura. A few, especially those affiliated with the Unión Social de Empresarios Cristianos (USEC), a business group identified with principles of Christian Democracy, cited moral or ethical foundations for social policy based on Chilean cultural antecedents or drawn from philosophic and religious sources, especially Catholic social teaching. However, only a few respondents, all younger than average, favored direct government intervention in setting wages.

Consistent with reliance on market mechanisms, most favored wage increases only when based on increased productivity. There was widespread uneasiness about the effects of allowing union bargaining beyond the individual plant and of restoring centralized union activity at national, regional, or industrywide levels. Many candidly expressed their fear that large union organizations could become politicized in ways that would undo growing public acceptance of market criteria in all phases of economic activity. Some respondents were more nuanced in supporting existing union restrictions; they argued that industrywide or regional and national bargaining would penalize workers in the most productive firms by forcing them to accept an average wage kept down by lower productivity in firms restrained by more political influence over bargaining outcomes—for instance, state-owned enterprises. Some believed or hoped that workers were currently more interested in steady work and financial security than in politically motivated union movements.

Most who addressed social questions affirmed a legitimate role for government in providing social services, but invariably emphasized services that represent an investment in human capital, such as health care and education, that would increase workers' productivity. Some explicitly acknowledged the inadequacy of social services in the Pinochet regime. There were varied responses to the question of public financing for social services. A few complained that taxes were already too high, using as a comparison the lower marginal income tax rates of the United States. Many felt that more efficient tax administration, that is, reducing tax evasion, would significantly increase revenues. Some, however, expressed the belief that marginal tax rates in the higher brackets could be raised without unfavorable effects on savings and investment. Some of the younger respondents also suggested reducing defense expenditures as a source of revenue for social spending, seeing most defense spending as unnecessary.

One respondent criticized what he considered the ambiguity and equivocation of his cohorts in their attitudes toward social expenditures—wanting the government to assume responsibility but seeking to avoid the cost. In his opinion, to be consistent with the principles of the neoliberal model, the private sector itself should voluntarily provide social services. So lofty a sentiment might be easily dismissed as interview rhetoric, but it is worth noting that this respondent, without mentioning the fact, had personally financed a church-sponsored housing development program in a working-class *población*.

Capitalism and Democracy

In light of the mixed ambivalence and concerned tolerance expressed by respondents about likely relationships between political democracy and economic liberalism, it is not surprising that the more progressive political right wing of Chile's business community, as represented in the Renovación Nacional party, was willing to join coalition parties in support of democratic constitutional reform but unwilling to back the Christian Democratic presidential candidate supported by the center-left coalition. Instead, the party was joined by other right-wing parties in supporting Hernan Büchi, the last minister of finance in the Pinochet regime. Although some prominent USEC members publicly supported the democratic coalition, several respondents agreed that USEC did not represent more than about 10 percent of the business community.

The perceptible but ambivalent acquiescence by business leaders on the prospects for joining liberal economic policies to a democratic transition was mirrored in the public statements of leaders in the democratic coalition who began to affirm the "compatibility" of capitalism and democracy and who, in their published economic program, accepted "the idea of an economy open to the outside, with low tariffs, oriented to exports . . . with stability in the rules of the game, without recourse to political expropriation."[29] Moreover, regular, informal conversations were begun during the election campaign between Alejandro Foxley with others in the democratic coalition and business leaders in the private sector.

Despite the uncertainties and misgivings associated with the plebiscite and the subsequent electoral campaign leading to the transition to democracy, business confidence in the relatively open Chilean economy remained high before the installation of the new government. The annual growth rate in GDP that had hovered near 5 percent through 1986 and 1987 rose to 7.6 percent in 1988 and then rose again during 1989, the year of the election campaign, to 9.3 percent, by far the highest growth rate of any Latin American country in that year.[30] This growth was marked by an exceptionally high domestic savings rate of over 17 percent of GDP, a gross investment rate of 20 percent of GDP, and exports that accounted for about one-third of GDP in 1989, compared with a level of approximately 25 percent during the last boom at the beginning of the decade.[31]

The 1989 miniboom, however, contributed to rising inflation which, after declining to an annual rate of 12.7 percent for consumer prices in 1988, rose to 21.7 percent the following year. Although urban unemployment continued to fall in 1987–1989, growth in real wages slowed to 1.9 percent in 1989 after a record growth of 6.6 percent in 1988, and real wages at the end of the decade were still below 1981 levels.[32] Moreover, social spending, which had been as high as 22.5 percent of GDP early in the decade, had fallen to 17.6 percent by 1988.[33] Thus, the new government faced the challenge of controlling inflation without inducing a recession, all the while trying to respond to the social expectations of an electorate that had experienced high unemployment, falling real wages, and diminished social spending for most of the past decade.

Attitudes of Chilean Business Leaders After the Transition

By the time the new government was installed and proceeding with legislative initiatives, there was some evidence that the communications gap between Chile's democratic coalition and the private sector had been bridged and that there was less ambivalence about the prospects for linking the liberal features of the existing economic system with the move to democracy. An early policy measure of the new government following its installation in March 1990 was tax legislation that raised both the marginal income tax rate as well as the tax rate on value added. The rise in taxes was justified as necessary for a financially responsible, noninflationary expansion of social services.

One of the first collective public expressions of support for this legislation came from the Renovación Nacional party, while the Confederación Unitaria de Trabajadores (CUT), Chile's major trade union association, found fault with it, criticizing the increase in the value-added tax. Moreover, the Centro de Estudios Públicos, a conservative research and policy center supported by the business community, published a favorable commentary on the tax legislation that defended both the levels and progressivity of the tax increases as well as the social expenditures to which they would be applied.[34]

Nevertheless, during its first year in office the new government's allegiance to liberal economic policies was severely tested. The inflation rate in an already overheated economy was further fueled by the rise in oil prices following Iraq's invasion of Kuwait in August, with the result that inflation reached 29.4 percent for the year. Meanwhile, the price of copper, Chile's principal traditional export, which had almost doubled during the final three years of the previous regime, producing a windfall of foreign exchange, suddenly dropped by 5.9 percent in 1990. As a result, despite an increase in export volume of 12.4 percent (the highest in recent years), the value of Chilean exports increased only 4.5 percent during 1990. Restrictive monetary policies[35] and careful management of exchange rates, along with some restrictions in the use of petroleum products, in the context of noninflationary fiscal policies reduced the growth of imports from 27.1 percent in 1989 to 1.3 percent in 1990. Another result, however, was a drop in the GDP growth rate to 0.2 percent, its lowest level since 1985. In addition, urban real wages rose by only 1.6 percent, the smallest increase in four years, although urban unemployment continued to fall, averaging 6.6 percent for the year.[36]

New labor legislation also tested support for the new government's economic policies by the business community, including employers like many of those interviewed in 1987–1988, who favored the restrictions on bargaining and strikes and who feared the political behavior of centralized unions. To respond to such concerns, before introducing new labor legislation the new administration secured a business-labor accord in which each side pledged to respect certain essential principles. Labor thus agreed to the importance of property rights, free markets with flexible prices, and an open economy. In turn, business acknowledged both that the income generated by a free-market economy should be fairly distributed and that labor's rights to organize effectively to create conditions for equitable negotiations should be recognized.

The law proposed by the new government permits labor organization at the national level and bargaining above the plant level—for example, at sectorial or regional levels. Moreover, the proposed law removes the sixty-day limit on strikes which had been allegedly abused by some employers who dragged out strikes beyond the limit to avoid paying retroactive workers' benefits. (Under the law, these benefits must be paid only if the strike is settled within sixty days.) The proposed law also allows the negotiated extension of severance pay beyond the limit of one month's pay per year of service, up to a maximum of five months' pay. This provision has the effect of restricting the market mobility of workers by penalizing moves made by those with more than five years of service, as well as penalizing early retirees covered by the same restriction.

Although this last provision is consistent with the principles of liberal market economics, along with the other provisions mentioned it was formally opposed by the business community and its employer associations in testimony before the government. According to those close to the legislative process, the strongest organized opposition was against abolishing limits on the length and cost of strikes. Along with this organized opposition, however, many were pleased with the accord reached by the Ministry of Labor in negotiations with the stevedores' union and relevant parties. Labor minister René Cortazar was praised inside and outside government for forging a consensus out of complex discussions involving all parties—employers, exporters, brokers, and workers—with the result that a comprehensive voluntary accord was achieved without need for legislative or judicial determination, except for legal ratification.

By March 1991, when I conducted follow-up interviews, Chile's economic indicators were buoyant. Accumulated inflation for the previous four months was estimated at 1 percent, and for the month of February had reached a low of 0.1 percent.[37] The exchange rate in the parallel market was virtually identical to the official rate.[38] Unemployment had dropped to 5.6 percent in February, its lowest level in almost two decades. Real wages had, for the first time since the 1973 coup, equaled their 1970 peak,[39] partly because of low unemployment and because of the lagged response of wage adjustments to the fall in inflation. Real interest rates had been falling and total investment was running over 20 percent of GDP, with foreign di-

rect investment having set a record of $1.5 billion, excluding
bank credits and debt equity swaps, which was equal to about
5 percent of GDP. Chile was no longer on creditor banks' lists
of countries in need of restructuring, and Chile's external debt
instruments had risen in value on international secondary markets to 80 percent of par value, the highest of any South American country.[40] A survey of 442 investment projects planned by
the private sector for 1990–1995 (which does not claim to be
exhaustive) reveals a total value of planned projects equal to
over 80 percent of the 1989 value of GDP in Chile. Almost 60
percent of the projects represent production for export, concentrated in mining and industrial production of exportable
products and services based on Chilean natural resources—for
example, wood, processed agricultural products, and tourism.
Reflecting the same openness to foreign investment revealed in
the 1987–1988 interviews, a majority of the export projects
were joint ventures with foreign firms, and 35 percent were totally foreign-owned.[41]

Follow-up interviews with business leaders in March 1991
reflect both the buoyancy of the economy and better communication with the new government. I chose to reinterview primarily those who had expressed the sharpest doubts about the
prospects for a liberal economic policy following the transition
to democracy. However, none of my interlocutors expressed
disapproval of the new government's economic performance.
The statement, "It has been a surprise that has exceeded all my
expectations and couldn't be better," was typical. Concerns
about the continuity of basic principles of the liberal economic
model, especially property rights and free markets with market-determined prices, had simply evaporated. Indeed, one respondent, when asked about changes in economic policy introduced by the new government, quipped, "What changes?"
There was little worry about long-term inflation, even though
inflation rates had begun to rise late in the first quarter of
1991.

Some of the praise for the new government was slightly backhanded. Conservative respondents who, three years earlier, had thanked General Pinochet for saving the country from socialism were quick to credit the previous regime for having laid the foundation for current economic success. They praised the leadership of the present government for honestly admitting the wisdom of the policies it inherited and for having the courage and flexibility to abandon interventionist and protectionist economic thinking in favor of the liberal model introduced by the Pinochet regime.

Still, even this limited praise reflected confidence in the present government and avoided the negativism of public comments made by several of the previous government's economic leaders, who had been quick to pass judgments like the following: "For Aylwin, the economy is a world completely alien, where he is weakest and most insecure," and who criticized the new government's proposed social expenditures, new tax legislation, and slower-paced privatization policies.[42] Some respondents explicitly criticized the negativism of Chile's leading newspaper, the conservative *El Mercurio*, toward the new government, mentioning that more reliable business and economic commentary could be found in an increasingly widely read business trade paper. As respondents discussed prospects for long-term investment opportunities in Chile, enthusiastically projecting as far as twenty years ahead, one could detect a sense of national identification and pride that contrasted sharply with the alienation, expressed three years earlier, from what seemed to be the traditional mores of Chilean culture. Despite the public negativism of some political leaders on the right, my interview respondents readily agreed that the center-left democratic coalition of the transition period had in practice been extended to the center-right.[43] The fact that basic elements of a liberal economic model had been validated by a popularly elected government, apparently with the help of constructive dialogue with the business community, seems to have encouraged a sense of social acceptance and legitimacy that was lacking under the authoritarian government, even one that overtly supported the liberal economic paradigm.

In the 1988 interviews, business people had pointed out that economic policy and administration under the Pinochet regime, while favoring the private sector, were technocratic and objective, not patrimonial and clientelistic in the familiar Latin American tradition. Consequently, although the new government was not perceived as probusiness, its continuation of consistent market-oriented policies and technically competent administration provided the necessary continuity for business support.

The result is a growing sense of national pride and loyalty that elicited generous responses to queries about social issues. When asked about the new tax laws, not one respondent objected to them. Most described them as "reasonable" or at least politically necessary, and one simply dismissed them (in English) as "window dressing." These responses are consistent with comments made three years earlier by some who believed—as noted—that taxes on higher incomes could be raised without unfavorable effects on savings and investment. One respondent then said confidentially that the Pinochet tax reform had been an unnecessary windfall for the wealthy, and that the only effect of a rise in marginal income tax rates would be a socially desirable reduction in imports of Mercedes-Benzes.

Opinion was more divided about the proposed new labor legislation, though the fear expressed three years earlier that centralized, politically powerful labor unions might upset the apple cart of free enterprise was not mentioned as often or as vehemently as before. Rather, concerns about the pending labor legislation were directed more to bread-and-butter issues than to political concerns. There was some anxiety, for example, that negotiated wage increases should not exceed gains in productivity to the extent that they weakened international competitiveness. There was uncertainty about the treatment of special situations—for instance, of part-time agricultural labor, and about prudent administration of the new provisions. In fact, real wage rates leveled off in the first quarter of 1991 and remained stable into the last quarter.[44]

At the same time, some respondents worried that wages and salaries in some sectors had not kept up with the recent inflation. There was widespread support for the kind of social programs proposed by the new government, stressing education, nutrition, health care, and other investments in human capital. Moreover, despite the prevailing climate of social peace, a few respondents volunteered the opinion, widely held among lower-income groups, that implementation of social programs for the poor was too slow. "This government seems to be fascinated with capital," was the comment of one investor. Again, the fact that such candor could be expressed outside the context of a narrow, self-interested preoccupation with the necessity of social stability reflected confidence in the new government's economic leadership and policies.

In fact, after a "honeymoon" year of labor peace and labor-management consensus, labor conflict began to sharpen in Chile. One of the first major strikes occurred in the state-owned copper industry at CODELCO's Chuquicamata mine, which was closed for fourteen days by the work stoppage. Nevertheless, the subsequent labor agreement is viewed as a precedent-setting accomplishment for labor-management relations because the union accepted wage increases tied to increases in productivity.[45] The principle of linking wages to productivity is obviously important to preserving international competitiveness in a small open economy whose development strategy is based so heavily on exports.

Strong business confidence in 1991 was further reflected in responses to direct questions concerning worries or preoccupations about the future. None of the concerns reflected doubts about the economic policies or integrity of the present government. Most had to do with the future—namely, whether the present positive trajectory of economic policy and administration could be sustained, especially through another election. More than one respondent asked in some form, "What will happen when Aylwin and Foxley are no longer in charge?" At this point, fears expressed three years earlier about the heterogeneous cast of characters in the democratic coalition surfaced again: populist demagogues might gain ascendancy once the present administration left the scene.[46] This time, however, there was a new variation—namely, fear of right-wing populism of the sort expressed by Francisco Errázuriz, a minority presidential candidate who fared better than expected in the presidential election and who is apparently intensely disliked by much of the business sector. Some of these fears were supported by polls later in the year that indicated a decline in popular approval of the incumbent administration and growing political apathy.[47] Some political analysts, however, suggest that the triumph of the liberal economic model is delinking an increasingly "technocratic" government from political parties, while they interpret settlements with the copper miners' union as indications of the unions' loss of influence in both the government and the political parties.[48]

Equally significant were fears that foreign exports, on which the economy of Chile increasingly depends, will be threatened by protectionism in foreign markets in response to fears about the effect of foreign competition on incomes and employment. Since the time of the 1991 inverviews, the Chilean business community has supported efforts of the Aylwin government to secure entry into the North American Free Trade Association (between the United States, Canada, and Mexico) as soon as possible after the treaty is signed.

Meanwhile, international confidence in the Chilean economy and low interest rates due to countercyclical monetary policies in the United States and other OECD countries resulted in a substantial flow of capital into Chile, which, along with an increasingly favorable trade balance, put pressure on the exchange rate of the Chilean peso throughout 1991 and into 1992. As a result, minimizing the rise in value of the peso has been an issue for those in the business community concerned about foreign competition and for the authorities alike.[49] The central bank continued to increase its reserves of foreign exchange, and in January 1992 the peso was revalued by 5 percent against the dollar and was allowed to float in a wider band than previously. Nevertheless, despite upward pressure on the peso and the tax increases begun in 1990, domestic savings and investment continued to grow. As an indication of continued business confidence in Chile, private savings alone in 1991 reached over 14 percent of gross domestic product, a rate almost 50 percent higher than the rate of total savings, public and private, throughout the eighties.[50]

Brazil: A Contrasting Case

The evolving self-confidence of Chilean business and its confidence in the democratic regime contrasts sharply with the perceptions of Brazil's business leaders interviewed in 1988 and again in 1991. In relatively industrialized Brazil, I concentrated my attention on leaders of industry, including producers of capital goods, as well as producers of minerals, chemicals, and other primary products, finance, textiles, commerce, and commercial services. Although Brazilian business people, like their counterparts in Chile, were looking forward to democratic elections in 1988, the political and economic climate differed greatly between the two countries.

In Brazil a formal transition to democracy had already occurred in 1984. However, the president-elect died before being inaugurated, and the vice president–designate (though not popularly elected), José Sarney, was inaugurated in early 1985. Although democratic institutions were in place, President Sarney's electoral mandate was less than clear. This ambiguity, coupled with the perceived failure of his economic policies, re-sulted in unanimous disapproval by the business leaders I interviewed in March and April 1988. Nevertheless, there was universal approval of the transition to democracy itself and frequent expressions of optimism for the future, along with a sense of expectation (and uncertainty) in the face of a new constitution just then being developed and Sarney's political maneuvers to extend his term, despite a remarkable lack of popularity.

The economic policies of the Sarney government in its first year were not marked by significant liberalization of the traditionally chauvinist, interventionist, and highly protected economy, despite pressures in that direction by the IMF and by the creditor banks during debt negotiations. The economic issue most commented on by business respondents in 1988 was Brazil's persistent high inflation, and the government policies most noted were the succession of anti-inflationary programs that began with the Cruzado Plan at the end of February 1986.

At the heart of the Cruzado Plan was an attempt to halt the inertial component of total inflation through a concerted deindexing of the entire economy by freezing wages and prices and eliminating the inflationary correction of all major monetary assets except passbook savings accounts. As a result, increases in the consumer price index, which had been rising at an accelerating rate for four months, averaging 10–15 percent per month, dropped dramatically in the first month of the freeze and remained below 2 percent per month for ten months.[51] At the time, some hailed this accomplishment as a victory for the political strategy of concertation among various social segments. However, as the price freeze was phased out and prices of public-sector goods and services were readjusted, price levels and real interest rates escalated; the economy once again adjusted to inflation by returning to the fully indexed status that existed before the Cruzado Plan.[52] By January 1987, consumer prices were rising by more than 16 percent a month and the rate exceeded 23 percent by June. A second stabilization program, the New Cruzado Plan or Bresser Plan, reimposed wage and price controls, but less severe than the first, and attempted to deal with the fiscal deficit—seen by many to be as virulent an inflationary force as indexation—through tax reform, reduced subsidies, and controls on government spending. The monthly rise in the consumer price index slowed to less than 7 percent under this plan for three months, but was again over 15 percent by early 1988.[53]

Why these measures failed is much debated; explanations range from microeconomic to macroeconomic, from political to social to psychological.[54] For the businessmen I interviewed in 1988, the price and wage freezes were extremely distasteful experiences, even though some admitted to having profited in the short run from the consumer buying boom that accompanied the first Cruzado Plan, when wages were raised while consumer prices were frozen. Like their Chilean counterparts, Brazilian business leaders were quick to point out the microeconomic inconsistencies in a blanket freeze that trapped some businesses just before scheduled price increases, while others had raised prices just before the freeze. Some complained that input prices, especially of public-sector goods and services, had been allowed to rise more than output prices. Evasion by those not bound in practice to public accounting of all transactions—for example, small businesses and providers of professional services—was cited as another inconsistency. The lessons from these experiences were clear: the prudent business person must be prepared in advance to minimize the costs of unannounced freezes—for instance, by always maintaining official price lists that secured margins larger than needed as a hedge against a price freeze.

More broadly, the freezes, the regulations that accompanied them, and measures to evade them were perceived as inducements by the private sector to divert activity from the formal economy into an unregulated underground economy, which differed from a typical informal sector by implicating not only microenterprises, the marginal self-employed, and the under-employed but also large mainstream enterprises. An example of such an inducement was high real interest rates for regulated bank loans, which resulted from the failure of nominal bank rates to fall as price levels dropped during the freezes, thus encouraging unregulated loans between nonfinancial firms—that is, from firms with available retained earnings to those without liquidity.

The failure to control inflation meant that business people were not only preoccupied by compliance with (or evasion of) anti-inflationary programs but also compelled by inflation to devote considerable resources, including their own time, to protecting their liquid assets. Several executives of industrial firms indicated that their principal operating responsibilities had moved from their enterprise's primary mission to the financial arena. Some complained about the amount of time they had to spend with financial officers planning short-term financial strategies to hedge against inflation—for example, to identify and place in "overnight" investments all cash balances at the end of each working day. The head of a branch of a large foreign bank indicated that his computer accounting programs for daily detailed management of liquid assets were more sophisticated and detailed than those used by the home office in the United States.

The result was a relatively short time horizon and crowding out private borrowers from capital markets, as the government kept short-term interest rates high to finance its own deficits through short-term borrowing in, for example, the overnight market. The combined effect on the private sector was to divert effort and resources from productive activities like investment for expansion and technological improvement. However, domestic business leaders responded to this issue very differently from executives of multinational firms. On the one hand, domestic leaders complained much less than foreign business people about the diversion of their efforts and the cost of coping with accelerated inflation and the bureaucracy to comply with new provisions and regulations. "We are accustomed to these realities and know how to deal with them," was a typical response from the latter. Paradoxically, managers of foreign firms, while conscious of and frustrated by the diversions, expressed the most optimism about Brazil's economic future and could point to more concrete plans for relatively long-term productive investment. More than one indicated that the current stabilization difficulties were not a deterrent to scheduled investment plans.

Unlike their Chilean counterparts, Brazilian business people lacked confidence not only in the new political regime but also in the productive efficiency of the national economy and in their ability to compete. According to one prominent business leader, "Brazil will always produce goods of mediocre quality at above average costs." Except for export-oriented sectors, Brazilian business leaders expressed much less confidence than Chileans in their ability to compete in open markets, domestic and international, and supported import barriers. Among domestic firms there was less than universal enthusiasm for promoting exports and opening the economy to imports. Several respondents described export promotion as a secondary, backup activity for many exporting firms; export markets were pursued only when necessary to even out fluctuations in domestic markets and to minimize the costs of cyclical retrenchment and expansion. Regarding Chile's successful promotion of trade, more than one respondent noted that Chile's entry into competitive world markets was an unpleasant necessity because of the inefficiently small size of its domestic markets, in contrast to Brazil's large, protected domestic markets. Since many multinational firms were in Brazil primarily to gain access to these protected markets, their presence was not uniformly appreciated by domestic entrepreneurs.

Some Brazilian industries—for instance, production of auto

parts and specialty clothing—are internationally competitive. Explaining this internal discrepancy in a protected domestic economy was beyond the scope of interviews with managers of such firms. An explanation would have to take into account various historical factors, links with other domestic industries (for example, in the production of autos, direct and indirect state subsidies), peculiarities of specific international markets, possible domestic comparative advantages, and the personal characteristics of successful entrepreneurs in those industries.[55] However, respondents associated with successful export firms exhibited more competitive self-confidence and less interest in the traditionally chauvinist, intervenionist reputation of the Brazilian economy. One did complain that the cavalier attitude of many Brazilian firms toward export markets as secondary backup opportunities meant that Brazilian industry had a poor external competitive image because exporters failed to meet export delivery schedules and were not reliable suppliers of foreign clients.

Although state enterprises were perceived to be frequently inefficient, few complained about them. Indeed, respondents in sectors where the presence of state enterprise dictated market share and prices were generally content with the arrangement. Business associations like the Federação das Indústrias do Estado de São Paulo (FIESP) were seen as useful for lobbying and negotiating with government agencies. Smaller associations, especially those limited to specific industries or groups of firms, were also seen as helpful for regulating behavior within particular economic sectors. While such regulation might refer to business standards, it apparently also served to limit competition among members. At the same time, Brazilian respondents, unlike their Chilean counterparts, were socially and politically self-confident, affirming the identification of their own materialist values with the dominant cultural values of Brazilian society.

Perhaps because of this self-confidence, Brazilian business

people were much less concerned than Chileans with social questions, including potentially destabilizing issues like poverty, high concentrations of wealth and income for the elite, wage levels, working conditions, and labor unrest. Although respondents recognized that these issues affected political stability, few saw them as the private sector's responsibility. "The unions work out all that with the government, and we abide by the results" was a typical answer to a question about labor relations. More than one expatriate head of a foreign firm, while praising the abilities of Brazilian executives, mentioned their typically obsolete personnel management styles and lack of consideration for labor as significant management problems.

Despite complaints about the results of the Sarney government's stabilization policies and universal disapproval of the president, there was general optimism about the future, even among those who acknowledged the stagnation of productive investment plans in the current uncertain climate. There was a widely shared belief that, if a reasonable candidate were elected to succeed Sarney, economic stability would return and Brazilian growth would resume. Although there was some fear of a leftist demagogue, and Lionel Brizola was the principal named threat, no one was interested in returning to an authoritarian government. Instead, they discussed how to institutionalize democracy in Brazil—whether in a parliamentary or a presidential system. While some thought a parliamentary system was superior in principle, most felt that political parties in Brazil were too weak, opportunistic, and unfocused to maintain it. A minority, however, believed that a parliamentary system could help compensate for the weakness of the party system. By 1991 this sentiment had become more widespread, with the failure of stabilization programs under a new constitution and a new president.[56]

Between early 1988 and early 1991, a new president, Fernando Collor de Mello, had been elected in Brazil and three more economic stabilization programs had been attempted, one by the Sarney government and two by the Collor government. Growth in gross domestic product was zero in 1988, but rebounded to 3.6 percent in 1989.[57] However, despite a short-lived stabilization plan, the Summer Plan, that reduced the monthly increase in the consumer price index to less than 10 percent for three months, consumer prices for 1989 rose by 1,764.9 percent and were rising at a monthly rate of 84.3 percent by the time of Collor's inauguration in March 1990.[58]

Collor's economic team immediately implemented a new stabilization program designed to attack sources of inertial inflation, this time relying in part on a controversial freeze of liquid assets, including overnight investments and bank balances above a fixed level, estimated to equal $27 billion or 6 percent of GDP.[59] This plan succeeded in keeping the monthly rise in the consumer price index below 10 percent for two months, but by the end of 1990 consumer prices had risen at an estimated 2,359.9 percent for the year as a whole. Meanwhile, economic growth was sharply negative, with gross domestic product shrinking by 4 percent during 1990.[60] At the time of my 1991 interviews, a second Collor Plan had just been introduced that froze prices and wages (after a 25 percent upward readjustment), controlled interest rates (which had failed to fall as rapidly as prices during previous stabilization plans), forbade any further indexing, and abolished the indices (BTN) previously used for indexing. The new plan also abolished the existing overnight short-term investment market, proposing to substitute the Fundo de Aplicações Financeiras (FAF or "Fundão"), a government-regulated short-term investment fund designed to channel domestic savings into socially desirable investments such as economic infrastructure and education.

Although I specifically included in the 1991 follow-up interviews those who had been most optimistic three years earlier about the prospects for business in Brazil, there was no discernible difference among respondents, regardless of sector, in their unrelenting pessimism. Even raising the question of long-term investment in Brazil was perceived by most as irrelevant, if not foolish, when short-term financial survival was the dominant preoccupation. Bankruptcies were increasingly common, and survivors worried about their ability to continue for more than a very short time.

Confidence in the government, especially in the economic team, had simply vanished and was generally replaced by exasperation and overt antagonism. There was frustration over unproductive communications with government and business's lack of influence over economic decisions. While the government charged that firms were going bankrupt because they were unwilling to lower prices to increase sales, respondents argued that profit margins were too low.[61] Only some non-Brazilian managers of foreign firms were somewhat sympathetic with the new government, considering the massive structural changes it was trying to effect. Managers of multinational firms criticized the obstructionist or reactionary behavior of Brazilian industrial associations in the face of change. One foreign executive, a member of the board of FIESP, mentioned that he had simply stopped attending its meetings out of frustration. Managers of some medium-sized businesses complained that accords negotiated by trade associations with the government often served the interests of the largest firms in the association, which were not necessarily those of smaller ones.

However, even managers of multinational firms were almost universally pessimistic about the prospects for successfully transforming a highly protected economy dominated by oligopolistic markets, with heavy government participation and intervention, into an open, liberal, capitalist system. Moreover, contrary to their relatively bullish behavior in 1988, foreign firms were now reducing or shelving investment plans for expansion in Brazil, and financial losses by subsidiaries of foreign firms in many sectors of the economy were common.[62] One respondent noted that a scheduled multimillion dollar investment project described in an interview three years ago had since been canceled and transferred to the United States. Domestic entrepreneurs tended to ridicule the government's neoliberal economic rhetoric, arguing that government intervention in the Brazilian economy had never been higher, and complained about the impact of the perceived populist politics of a maverick presidential regime that lacked a clear base in the political party system. They attacked the confiscation of their wealth after the freeze of liquid assets in the first Collor Plan, were highly critical of the price freeze in the second Collor Plan, and repeatedly complained that the present government did not consult or negotiate with them before announcing new economic measures. Several were exasperated by the confusion generated by successive, often inconsistent, revisions of regulations—for instance, of import quotas and duties—following complaints about earlier versions by affected sectors. There was wide agreement that stabilization plans with wage and price freezes were decreasingly effective, as the useful life of each plan proved to be shorter than the last.[63] Business's general disapproval of the second Collor Plan contrasts with the plan's high ratings in an early public opinion poll, reflecting widespread popular agreement with the government's accusations that business was abusing its power to raise prices.[64] Such sentiments call into question the self-confidence articulated by interview respondents about their social image only a few years before.

In my 1991 interviews, there was much less concern about the effect on profits of the current price freeze than I heard in 1988 about similar policies of the Sarney regime. "Rational expectations" had obviously influenced the development of protective, anticipatory pricing policies of some firms who had been burnt in the first price freezes. However, independent analysis suggests that, despite anticipatory price increases, industrial profit margins were indeed squeezed during the first year of the Collor regime because of wage adjustments and changes in relative prices of other inputs, especially goods and services purchased from state-owned enterprises.[65] It was also clear from respondents' comments that no one expected the freezes to last, so there was also visible impunity in their refusal to comply. Expectations of ineffectiveness were becoming self-fulfilling prophecies.

Yet there was none of the self-confidence in the viability of the Brazilian economic model manifested three years earlier. One respondent described the protectionist, noncompetitive ECLAC model as a "leftist" model that had the perverse effect of favoring the industrial elite. In the 1991 interviews there were more declarations about the need to become more efficient for international competitiveness and a wide acknowledgment of, if not enthusiasm for, the necessity of opening the Brazilian economy. One of the successful exporters interviewed in 1988 was still thriving and his business was growing. However, he was pessimistic about Brazil's prospects and acknowledged that all his major current investment plans for expansion were outside Brazil—for instance, in the European common market. Control of another successful industrial firm had passed from a father to a U.S.-educated son since the last interview, and the son had begun to implement a comprehensive and sophisticated restructuring of the firm, using European and American management consultants. The objective in this case was not so much to enter export markets as to prepare to compete effectively in traditional domestic markets against the foreign competition that he believed would accompany the eventual liberalization of the economy. Other respondents spoke simply about the continuing apparent rise in capital flight—something that, three years ago, was seen as atypical of Brazilian investment behavior. Part of the blame for increased capital flight, however, was placed on the new government's abolition of anonymous bearer accounts, which had provided safe havens in the Brazilian banking system for revenues from underground economic activities.

Weakening self-confidence on the part of Brazilian respondents did not, however, translate into a heightened concern for resolving problems of poverty, unemployment, and unequal income distribution, despite their potentially destabilizing social and political effects and despite a rise in unemployment by almost 1 million during the previous month. Instead, the government was faulted for inconsistency in criticizing private-sector layoffs while urging enterprises to become more cost-conscious and efficient.

Lack of confidence in the Brazilian model was also evident in changed attitudes toward the liberalization of the economy of Chile. Whereas in 1988 attitudes had been complacent and patronizing toward Chilean business, now there was admiration. One respondent saw Chile as having moved beyond the orbit of Brazil and other Southern Cone countries, preferring to pursue free trade with North America while eschewing participation in a regional common market.[66] In more than one instance, admiration was qualified by the suggestion that the Chilean economy, being smaller and less complex, was more adaptable to change.

Others, however, blamed differences in government policy but did not move to the easy conclusion that the nation's economic prospects would have benefited if there had been no democratic transition in Brazil. Rather, ineffective policies were blamed equally on democratic governments and on the previous military ones, which were criticized for failing to pursue a coherent economic restructuring like that maintained through much of the Pinochet regime in Chile. Brazil's military regime was accused of having begun properly, but of selling out to economic interests. There was no hint of support for a return to authoritarian government, but neither was there optimism about an emergence of economic leadership and economic viability in the current political climate. There were relatively few proposals for institutional reforms to improve the economy, and these sometimes conflicted, with some favoring greater liberalization and others strong government intervention, but of a different sort. Instead, there was fear that essential social values needed to drive the economy were disintegrating. For one respondent, the present system was running on corruption at all levels of government and in all sectors. For most, this was at best a risky moment and at worst a dark one.

By late 1991, Collor's original economic team had been replaced, but many economic indicators continued to worsen, as though confirming a self-fulfilling prophecy proclaimed earlier in the regime. Despite a contraction in federal expenditures of 25 percent (in real terms) during the first half of 1991 (due to the lower cost of debt servicing and lower government salaries), the federal deficit continued to grow: there had been a 30 percent decline in the real value of revenues, as well as expanding deficits in state and municipal budgets and in off-budget programs like social security.[67] The new constitution exacerbates the public deficit problem by increasing the share of tax revenues transferred to states and cities and by mandating a number of specific social benefits such as paid maternity leaves, indexing of pensions, and pension entitlements unrelated to age.

As a result, the government proposed a number of structural alterations. These included constitutional changes limiting retirement benefits, creating mechanisms for financing state and municipality deficits, and permitting the dismissal of public officials. Plans for privatization of state enterprises, including telecommunications and the USIMINAS steel company, were announced.[68] However, the pace of privatization in Brazil has been slower than in Mexico and Argentina. By November 1991, only four state companies had been sold, and many of their shares were sold to other state companies and to state pension funds.[69] However, political and economic time lags in realizing any tangible effects of these measures left the economy subject to continuing inflationary pressures, and by July the annual rate of inflation for consumer prices was once again in triple digits and indexing mechanisms were again introduced.[70] On the other hand, the gradual return to circulation of the liquid balances frozen under the first Collor Plan, beginning with a $2 billion release in August, was apparently not being channelled to circulation but being used largely to finance the public sector under new instrumentalities created to replace the earlier "overnights."[71] There is survey evidence that the vast majority of previously blocked balances will likely be maintained in financial instruments following release.[72]

At the same time, there was some recovery in economic growth and capital formation following large declines in the first quarter of 1991. Nevertheless, with the gradual release of a total of $24 billion of blocked balances, Brazil could hardly continue to finance its deficits at the relatively low real interest rates paid on the blocked balances (6 percent) or on the new short-term instruments (8.5 percent) without severe anti-inflationary measures.[73] In fact, the restrictive monetary and fiscal policies of the new economics minister, known as the "liberal shock," which began in August 1991, was moderately successful in reducing inflation, but at the cost of a 6.5 percent drop in per capita income for the year.[74] Meanwhile, highly publicized charges of government corruption and widespread disapproval of the president persisted into 1992, when on March 30 about half the cabinet resigned following accusations of corruption.

The familiar recurring pattern of countervailing financial maneuvers by government and by the private sector in a climate of mutual mistrust hastens the disintegration of the sort of financial mediation that is normally assumed to stimulate private investment. Instead, entrepreneurs and administrators focus on short-term protective reactions against inflation. Moreover, prolonged and repeated inflationary cycles dominated by government borrowing gives rise to private-sector defensive strategems to protect against threatened "surprises," conventional or heterodox, in macroeconomic stabilization policy.

Conclusion: Some Comparative Reflections

The contrast between the self-perceptions of business people in Chile and Brazil against the background of two transitions to democracy, already evident in interviews conducted in 1988, had reached almost the sharpness of caricature by 1991. If perceptions have self-fulfilling power, one can argue that the personal self-confidence of Chilean business leaders interviewed in 1988 contributed to the subsequent economic growth, which in turn has reinforced the sense of stability and continuity that justifies further optimism. And one can argue that anxiety about Brazil's lack of competitiveness has contributed to declining entrepreneurship, investment, and growth since 1988. However, it is also true that the uncertainty generated by the new government's poorly understood and fluctuating actions contributes to the pessimism and stagnation that characterize Brazil's private sector. There is an axiom in economics, usually attributed to Keynes, that in circumstances of complete uncertainty, the typical response is to expect the present situation to continue. In crisis conditions, the result is expected to be more of the same, at best. Thus it would be inaccurate to conclude that Brazil lacks the entrepreneurial capability of Chile.

The reality, of course, is a complex interaction of individual and social behavior with institutional and structural characteristics that makes facile comparisons precarious. Complaints about the government's behavior in Brazil could be in part personal expressions of pain accompanying a competitive shakeout in a liberalizing economy. Interview respondents in Chile, on the other hand, were survivors or were successors to a generation of private-sector entrepreneurs who had been exposed to relatively unrestricted foreign competition and then devastated by the economic crises of 1976 and 1982, which wiped out a manufacturing sector and bankrupted many firms. The fact that the survivors are performing successfully in the neoliberal model that was maintained throughout both crises may be a tribute not so much to ideological or structural transformation as to a Darwinian principle of survival of the fittest. The losers, if they had been interviewed again, may well have sounded as pessimistic as those currently threatened by market changes in Brazil.

The business community as a whole in Chile had been a dominant force in the civil resistance to the Allende regime.[75] So it is understandable that the survivors of the economic shakeouts that followed should be loyal supporters of the neoliberal economic model that they had mastered and of the political regime that had imposed and sustained it.

At the same time, respondents' comments in both countries affirm the importance of consistent and enduring economic policies in creating a perception of stability that is essential to encouraging risk-oriented business behavior—for example, in productive investment. The rapid acceptance by Chile's business leaders of new economic policies, and Brazilians' criticisms of the economic policies of their nation's recent military regimes, show that perceived stability does not inherently depend on whether a regime is authoritarian or democratic but on the judgment that the rules of the game are clear, consistent, and enduring.

Similarly, the persistent complaints by Brazilian respondents that the new government failed to consult or negotiate with the affected parties before imposing new policies and regulations, in stark contrast to the new Chilean government's excellent reputation for conferring with the private sector, may not simply reflect the quantity of contacts and consultations. Rather, it may be that communication and consultation are not carried out according to traditional corporatist rules and channels, thereby creating a threatening sense of discontinuity and uncertainty. Two members of the Collor government's economic team spoke of their fatigue because of the time and energy spent in communicating with groups of economic actors rather than in policy design, which they saw as their principal responsibility. Some of these enervating discussions may represent the cost of damage control after the fact, the result of an implicitly hierarchical and authoritarian model of determining policy.

Nevertheless, the differences in how business leaders in the two countries see their relations with new democratic governments may have other explanations: one is the simple fact of size—the size of the country, the size of the economy, and the size of the political task.

To allow representation of all interests in Brazil—which has a much larger and more complex economy than Chile—requires communications on a much greater scale; in a large, heterogeneous society, the difficulty of disseminating political policy in a democratic system so as to effect radical structural changes may increase in geometric rather than linear progression. Even with its intermediary associations, the corporatist Brazilian economy may simply be too massive for feasible consultation with business, even to give the appearance of encouraging participation in structural reform. The minister of finance in a country of 13 million people can more readily communicate with private-sector leaders about relatively incremental changes than can his counterpart who seeks a fundamental restructuring of economic and political relationships in a country of 150 million people.

However, the divergent reactions of business in the two countries may also reflect differences in political organization and style. Chile began its transition with a coalition of major parties that created a broad base of representation. Even before the election, the new administration used this support base to negotiate various types of social pacts, both within the coalition and with outside groups, including the business community and the center-right political party that represented it. Astute negotiating under such circumstances may have not only tapped a growing reservoir of national pride and loyalty inspired by an evidently successful transition, but also created a perception of a positive-sum game for most participants. In Brazil, on the other hand, a president described by interview respondents of the same socioeconomic level as a "maverick" without a strong political base, in a nation of weakly identified political parties, simply failed to set up cohesive social negotiations capable of creating even the perception of a positive-sum game as he introduced fundamental structural reforms through a "top-down" process.[76]

Finally, one could argue that liberalization of the Chilean economy in the 1970s, despite its high social costs in bankruptcies, recession, poverty, unemployment, and political repression, may have been structurally simpler than attempting to liberalize the Brazilian economy today. As Chile reallocated resources from inefficient protected industries in the 1970s, those that were adversely affected by liberalization were largely consumer-goods and soft-goods industries that were probably less capital-intensive and less technologically retarded than Brazil's capital-goods industries and durable-goods industries that could be threatened by liberalization today. A 1991 study by the secretary for science, technology, and economic development for the State of São Paulo suggests that the technological gap between Brazilian industry as a whole and the rest of the world grew wider during the 1980s than in previous decades.[77]

Moreover, Chile was able to identify production possibilities, some of which could be called nontraditional, in which it had a natural market advantage and for which international markets were relatively open and growing—for instance, temperate-zone fruit, wood products, fish products, and natural energy sources (methanol). Fortunately for Chile, the technology necessary for effective competition in temperate-zone agricultural products is largely nonproprietary, and because it can apply to farms of various sizes is not conducive to oligopolistic control of national production. Chile's climate, especially in the central valley, is similar to that of central California, where sophisticated agricultural technology has been developed in nonprofit research universities like the University of California at Davis. Well-educated Chileans who pursue advanced studies at such institutions establish necessary contacts for relatively free future access to new information. These are inexpensive technology transfers compared to the cost of such transfers in manufacturing industries, where technology is developed under private contracts and protected by patents.

Whether similar opportunities are available to Brazil to offset the potential damage of complete liberalization to its relatively capital-intensive, import-substituting, industrial sectors is unclear. Nor can anyone predict whether multinational firms that were originally lured to Brazil by the potential size of its domestic market will continue to produce locally for local consumption if liberalized imports prove to be more cost-effective.

Business enterprises make investment decisions on the basis of many factors: interest rates, projected profitability, risk, uncertainty, liquidity, credit rationing, opportunity costs, and so on. Economic theories place different emphases on determinants of capital supply and capital demand and the specific variables in both. Interviews made it clear that business investors also vary in how much weight they give these variables. Before Chile's transition to democracy, some respondents in growth sectors, such as export agriculture, complained about supply-side variables, such as credit rationing by banks and rising land costs. During the growth period after the transition, the same respondents spoke mostly of demand-side variables—for example, international market prospects—but were satisfied with the availability of credit, partly because foreign loans were once again available.

In Brazil, on the other hand, supply-side concerns like high interest rates caused by inflation, uncertainty, and crowding out by government borrowing, were dominant concerns in 1988 for domestic firms, while foreign firms relied upon retained earnings and access to credit through parent companies abroad. By 1991, reduced profit margins in both domestic and foreign firms, cash flow crises, and lack of confidence in government policies simply overwhelmed normal investment expectations and raised the perceived real cost of interest rates, while lowering expected returns when discounted for perceived risk and uncertainty.[78]

So, it is possible that the fear and defensive behavior of Brazilian business people is at least partly a rational response, individually and socially, to liberalization and to the uncertainty and alienation created when new economic rules are imposed within an economic and political system grounded in individualistic behavior. On the other hand, the cumulative success of entrepreneurial initiative, consistent economic policies, and political negotiation and coalition building that has accompanied Chile's transition to democracy has yet to be tested for endurance, either by the need to move to more complex forms of industrial modernization, management, and labor relations or by sustained external economic shocks to which small economies are especially vulnerable. Moreover, Chile's return to democracy has been led by political parties, with social movements, labor unions, business associations, and other organizations playing a much less significant role in the process. Consequently, the fact that Chile's political right is declining in influence might hinder the incorporation of business leaders in the democratic process.

Whether Chile's export economy will continue to be dynamic is also problematic. Much of the value of Chile's exports, even its manufactured products, is still based upon primary products, and it was already evident in the 1991 interviews that the period of rapid growth in commercial agriculture for export was ending and copper prices were weakening at the same time. At the same time, there was an effort to increase returns on traditional primary products by increasing domestic value added, such as through food processing and conversion of wood to furniture for export. This may well be enough to sustain economic growth for a nation of only 13 million. But if growth ultimately requires more complex organization of production, mobilization and training of labor, technology development and transfer, and aggressive marketing, Chile will be tested like its larger and more industrialized neighbors.

A more likely test of the relatively open Chilean economy could be the next external economic shock from an increasingly integrated world economy. Such a blow might be an international financial crisis or recession, or a wave of protectionism in its major foreign markets—the same handful of countries facing import pressures from liberalizing developing countries around the world. According to respondents in Chile's private sector, the test of Chile's political resilience will be whether the public sector can make a smooth transition through forthcoming democratic elections, in which the stabilizing role of the initial center-left coalition is uncertain. So, too, the test of economic resilience in the modernized private sector may well be its ability to effect a smooth transition through the next international recession.

Notes

1. Entrepreneurial spirit is subject to culturally relative definitions, but is used here in a classical liberal sense: the "drive for material progress through profit-minded, competitive, innovating, risk-taking enterprise" along with the requisite managerial, marketing, and technical expertise; see Albert Lauerbach, "Management, Entrepreneurship, and Development Needs," in *Workers and Managers in Latin America*, ed. Stanley M. Davis and Louis Wolf Goodman (Lexington, Mass.: D.C. Heath, 1972), 174.

2. See Hugh H. Schwartz, "The Potential Role of Behavioral Analysis in the

Promotion of Private Enterprise in Developing Countries," *Columbia Journal of World Business*, Spring 1988, 53–56.

3. These elements, of course, need not be independent of one another. Market uncertainty, cultural bias against profit seeking, and lack of access to long-term capital may rationalize the alleged preference of Latin American business people for short-term trading profits rather than long-term productive investment, which is cited as evidence of the scarcity of classical entrepreneurial spirit.

4. See Alejandro Foxley, *Latin American Experiments in Neo-conservative Economics* (Berkeley: University of California Press, 1983).

5. Perceptions are here understood as "the process by which economic agents confronted with technological, market and public policy data 'read' those data, assigning quantitative or qualitative values to them." See Hugh H. Schwartz, "Perception, Judgement, and Motivation in Manufacturing Enterprises: Findings and Preliminary Hypotheses from In-depth Interviews," *Journal of Economic Behavior and Organization* 8 (1987): 544.

6. Although the election of Fernando Collor de Mello was not Brazil's first presidential election after the transition from an authoritarian regime, he was the first elected candidate to assume office, since Collor's predecessor, José Sarney, became president following the untimely death of Tancredo Neves prior to his inauguration.

7. Jaime Gatica Barros, *Deindustrialization in Chile* (Boulder, Colo.: Westview Press, 1989), 38–39.

8. Ibid., 32–36.

9. José Franco Mesa, "Agricultura: El difícil año 75," *Mensaje*, March–April 1976, 105–09.

10. Anne O. Krueger, Maurice Schiff, and Alberto Valdés, "Agricultural Incentives in Developing Countries: Measuring the Effect of Sectoral and Economywide Policies," *World Bank Economic Review* 2, 3 (1988): 255–71.

11. Ibid.

12. Jorge Echenique, "Las políticas agrícolas en el marco del ajuste," unpublished, UN Food and Agricultural Organization, Santiago, 1991, 12–13.

13. See "La hora de Angelini y Matte," *Hoy* 464 (15 June 1986), 29–30; and Rodolfo Contreras M., *Más allá del bosque: La explotación forestal en Chile* (Santiago: Amerinda, 1989), chap. 4.

14. See Maurice Zeitlin and Richard Earl Ratcliff, *Landlords and Capitalists: The Dominant Class of Chile* (Princeton: Princeton University Press, 1988), esp. chap. 4.

15. Echenique, "Las políticas agrícolas," 24–28.

16. Alexander Schejtman, "La transformación productiva del sector agrícola: El caso chilena" unpublished, CEPAL, Santiago, n.d., 16.

17. Ibid., 49.

18. By some estimates employment in agriculture has increased more rapidly

than in other sectors during the past decade. See Echenique, "Las políticas agrícolas," 21.

19. Ibid., 20.

20. Guillermo Campero, "Los empresarios ante la alternativa democrática: El caso de Chile," in *Empresarios y estado en América Latina*, ed. Celso Garrido N. (Mexico City: CLACSO, 1988), 248–49.

21. See Oscar Muñoz, "El papel de los empresarios en el desarrollo: Enfoques, problemas y experiencias," *Colección Estudios CIEPLAN* 20 (Santiago: CIEPLAN, 1986), 95–120; and "El estado y los empresarios: Experiencias comparadas y sus implicancias para Chile," *Colección Estudios CIEPLAN* 25 (Santiago: CIEPLAN, 1988), 5–53.

22. For a sociological analysis of the emergence of the new generation of Chilean entrepreneurs, see Cecilia Montero, "La evolución del empresariado chileno: ¿Surge un nuevo actor?" *Colección Estudios CIEPLAN* 30 (Santiago: CIEPLAN, 1990): 91–120, esp. sec. 4, 102–07.

23. The supportive attitude of the Chilean private sector toward foreign investment is mirrored in Ricardo Zabala, "Inversión extranjera en Chile," *Estudios Públicos* 28 (Spring 1987): 219–77.

24. See Campero, "Los empresarios ante la alternativa democrática," 262; cf. Montero, "La evolución del empresariado chileno," 94–97.

25. The U.S. ambassador to Chile, Harry Barnes, recognized this communication problem and initiated unpublicized and unrecorded private discussions among prominent invitees from the private sector and from the democratic coalition prior to the plebiscite.

26. Alejandro Foxley, *Chile y su futuro: Un país posible* (Santiago: CIEPLAN, 1967).

27. Interestingly, the two names mentioned as hostile to the private sector were not among the seventeen members of CIEPLAN who later were appointed to positions in the new democratically elected government.

28. Campero, "Los empresarios ante la alternativa democrática," 262.

29. Alejandro Foxley, "Entre la estabilidad y el cambio," interview in *El Mercurio*, 6 July 1989, 6.

30. Economic Commission for Latin America and the Caribbean (ECLAC), *Preliminary Overview of the Economy of Latin America and the Caribbean 1990* LC/G.1646 (Santiago, Chile, 1990), table 2, 25.

31. Inter-American Development Bank (IDB), *Economic and Social Progress in Latin America, 1990 Report* (Washington, D.C.: IDB, 1990), 74–78.

32. ECLAC, *Preliminary Overview 1990*, tables 4 and 6, 26–27.

33. IDB, *Economic and Social Progress Report 1990*, 76.

34. Cristián Eyzaguirre J., "Comentarios en torno a la reforma tributaria," Puntos de Referencia, Centro de Estudios Públicos, no. 47 (April 1990).

35. For movements in money supply and exchange rates, see ECLAC, *Eco-*

nomic Panorama of Latin America 1990, LC/G.1638 (Santiago, Chile, 1990), tables 9 and 14, 45, 48.

36. Data in this paragraph from ECLAC, *Preliminary Overview 1990*, tables 2, 4–6, 8, 9, 12, 25–30.

37. *El Mercurio*, 28 February 1991, B1; ibid., 6 March 1991, B1.

38. *Set de Estadísticas Económicas*, no. 78 (Santiago: CIEPLAN, March 1991).

39. Ibid.

40. *El Mercurio*, 6 March 1991, B1.

41. Eduardo Aninat Ureta, "Investment Opportunities in Chile: Results from a Survey of Projects 1990–95," unpublished, Santiago, 1990.

42. Interview with Pablo Baraona, former minister of the economy, *Hoy* 691 (15–21 October 1990), 11.

43. Respondents criticized, for example, negative comments about the present government allegedly attributed to the former finance minister and presidential candidate of the parties on the right, Hernan Büchi.

44. *Set de Estadísticas Económicas*, no. 87 (Santiago: CIEPLAN, December 1991).

45. CIEPLAN, "Chile: Situación económica," *Situacíon Latinoamericana* 1, 5 (Madrid: CEDEAL, October 1991), 97–99.

46. Terrorist assassinations of several prominent conservatives in early 1991, including Senator Jaime Guzman, a leader of the far right Independent Democratic Union party, reignited business fears of political instability as well. See "Terrorism Jolts a Prospering Chile," *New York Times*, 9 April 1991, C1.

47. Rodrigo Baño, "Chile: Situación política y social," *Situacíon Latinoamericana* 1, 5 (Madrid: CEDEAL, October 1991), 111.

48. Ibid., 110–16.

49. CIEPLAN, Carmen Celedón, "Chile: Situación económica," *Situación Latinoamericana* 2, 8 (Madrid: CEDEAL, April 1992), 84–90.

50. Ibid., 91.

51. ECLAC, *Economic Panorama of Latin America 1987* LC/G.1481 (Santiago, Chile: 1987), table 4, 25.

52. IDB, *Economic and Social Progress in Latin America,1988 Report* (Washington: IDB, 1988), 361.

53. ECLAC, *Economic Panorama of Latin America 1988*, LC/G.1531, (Santiago, Chile, 1988), table 4, 28.

54. See, for example, Dionisio Dias Carneiro Netto, "The Cruzado Experience: An Untimely Evaluation after Ten Months," *Texto para discussão 152* (Universidade Católica do Rio de Janeiro, Departamento do Economia, 1987); Eduardo Marco Modiano, "The Cruzado Plan: Theoretical Foundations and Practical Limitations," *Texto para discussão 154* (Universidade Católica do Rio de Janeiro, Departamento do Economia, 1987); Werner Baer and Paul Beckerman, "The Decline and Fall of Brazil's Cruzado," *Latin American Research Review* 24 (1989): 35–64; Antônio Kandir, *Dynamics of Inflation* (Notre Dame: University of Notre Dame Press, 1991).

55. For an extended analysis of varying degrees of competitiveness in the Brazilian auto parts industry, see Caren Addis, "Tactics and Hybrids: The Peaceful Coexistence of Mass and Flexible Production in the Brazilian Motor Industry," Ph.D. diss., Massachusetts Institute of Technology, 1992, chap. 4.

56. See "A Survey of Brazil," *Economist* 321, 7736 (7 December 1991), 18.

57. ECLAC, *Preliminary Overview 1990*, table 2, 25.

58. ECLAC, *Economic Panorama 1990*, table 4, 28.

59. ECLAC, *Economic Panorama of Latin America 1991* LC/G.1680 (Santiago: United Nations, 1991), 25. Other estimates place the value of the frozen private savings as high as US $110 billion. See "A Survey of Brazil," 9.

60. ECLAC, *Preliminary Overview 1990*, table 2, 25.

61. See "Baixar o preço para evitar a concordata," reporting a harsh message to FIESP from Minister of the Economy Zélia Cardoso de Mello in *Gazeta Mercantil*, 25 October 1990, 1.

62. See *Folha de São Paulo*, 25 February 1991, cad. 3, 1.

63. See "O desgaste do tempo," *Veja*, 6 February 1991, 35.

64. *O Estado de São Paulo*, 23 February 1991, cad. "Economia," 1.

65. Edward J. Amadeo and Gustavo H. B. Franco, "Inflação e preços relativos no plano Collor: Avaliação e perspectivas," *Texto para discussão* 250 (Universidade Católica do Rio de Janeiro, Departamento do Economia, 1990).

66. The presidents of Argentina, Brazil, Paraguay, and Uruguay had just signed the Treaty for the Creation of the Southern Cone Common Market. See *O Estado de São Paulo*, 23 February 1991, cad. "Economia," 5.

67. ECLAC, *Economic Panorama 1991*, 25.

68. Ibid.

69. "A Survey of Brazil," 9.

70. Ibid., table 5, 25.

71. Ibid., 25.

72. Luis G. Belluzo and J. Gómez de Almeida, "Brasil: Situación económica y situación política y social," *Situacíon Latinoamericana* 2 (Madrid: CEDEAL, April 1992), 43–44.

73. Ibid., 42.

74. Ibid., 33–40.

75. See Guillermo Campero, *Los gremios empresariales en el período 70–83* (Santiago: ILET).

76. Cf. Adam Przeworski's critique of neoliberal stabilization policies in "Notes after the Budapest Meeting," (unpublished, Chicago, 1991), 13.

77. *Folha de São Paulo*, 23 February 1991, cad. 3, 1.

78. For a similar, more focused analysis, see Luis Carlos Bresser Pereira, "Investment Decision and the Interest Rate in Normal and Exceptional Times" (unpublished, February 1991).

Catherine M. Conaghan

3. The Private Sector and the Public Transcript

The Political Mobilization of Business in Bolivia

In 1984, Carlos Díaz-Alejandro drew attention to one of the most important contradictions brewing in Latin America's debt crisis—namely, the relationship between "public debt and private assets." With his usual acuity, Díaz-Alejandro pointed to the political problem involved in the state's assumption of the debt burden as private-sector actors (many of whom had actively participated in accruing the debt) scrambled to shield their private household wealth from the effects of the crisis by capital flight—investing their assets abroad. Díaz-Alejandro suggested that this behavior by wealthy private citizens not only reduced the legitimacy of government efforts to service the debt, but also "generated a crisis of legitimacy for the role of the private sector in Latin American development."[1]

This chapter examines this crisis of legitimacy and the business community's efforts to respond politically to public challenges to its role.[2] While the analysis focuses specifically on Bolivia, what happened in Bolivia occurred throughout Latin

America in the 1980s. The widespread political activation of Latin American business leaders in this period suggests that the private sector indeed felt caught in a legitimacy crisis, which it sought to resolve through direct political means.

Business groups throughout the region demonstrated new levels of organizational capacity, sophistication, and class consciousness in the 1980s. Moreover this surge in activity was not entirely defensive—that is, aimed at staving off "negative" public policies. Political activity on the part of business broadened to include more concerted efforts to mold the ideological climate so as to enhance the status of business. With the completion of political transitions and the reestablishment of civilian governments, the task of "winning hearts and minds" was of increasing concern to business groups.

The political activation of business in the 1980s raises the perennial question regarding the prospects for "bourgeois hegemony" in Latin America. While the overall ideological shift of the 1980s was clearly in a conservative direction, domestic capitalists have a long way to go before they resolve their longstanding lack of hegemony. There were important challenges to the role of the private sector in the 1980s and into the 1990s. Moreover, the poor economic performance by these capitalists and these capitalist systems means that they still lack the minimal material conditions for hegemony. As Díaz-Alejandro pointed out early in the debt crisis, the economic behavior of individual capitalists frequently undercuts the quest by the entire bourgeois class for political acceptance and a stable social consensus on capitalism.

The Post-1952 Reconstruction

The recent economic and political behavior of Bolivian capitalists is best understood within its historical context. The 1952 revolution launched the emergence of a new capitalist class in Bolivia and set the trajectory for state-society relations that lasted until the 1980s.

Bolivian capitalism was dramatically recast in the wake of the 1952 revolution led by the populist Movimiento Nacionalista Revolucionario (MNR). The revolution began as an armed popular uprising of peasants and miners in response to an attempt by the armed forces to scuttle the election of MNR leader, Víctor Paz Estenssoro, as president.[3] Swept into office by this successful popular insurgency, the MNR government wiped out the last vestiges of the old oligarchy, based in the traditional hacienda system and tin mining, that had dominated the country's political-economic system since the nineteenth century. A substantial agrarian reform was enacted in 1953; the state nationalized the largest privately owned mines and formed the public enterprise, COMIBOL, to oversee their operations. As part of the *co-gobierno* arrangement struck between the MNR and the trade union movement, the Central Obrera Boliviana (COB) was given control over COMIBOL and oversaw workers' control of the mines. The most radical phase of the revolution was short-lived. Facing serious economic difficulties and seeking aid from the United States, the subsequent MNR government led by Hernán Siles forced the COB out of the cabinet and enacted draconian stabilization measures in 1956.

With the most radical elements of labor and the left eliminated from the governing coalition, the dénouement of the Bolivian revolution became apparent. The goal of the MNR-led project was to modernize Bolivian capitalism, not to effect a socialist transformation. But in the absence of an entrepreneurial class, the state was assigned a pivotal role in the modernization process. Reelected to the presidency in 1960, Paz Estenssoro became the author of a state-centered capitalist model of economic development that remained essentially unchallenged until the 1980s.

Paz's successor military governments in the 1960s and 1970s continued to deepen the state's involvement in the economy. The most intense expansion came during the first half of the dictatorship of General Hugo Banzer. By the mid-1970s, the state's domination of the economy, particularly through the proliferation of public enterprises, was evident. Government activities accounted for 33 percent of Bolivia's gross domestic product, 70 percent of all investment, 59 percent of exports and 13 percent of total employment.[4]

This state-centered capitalism did not preclude the development of a private sector—but it created one closely tied to and dependent on the rhythms of state expansion. The new private sector emerged as a highly subsidized creature, extremely dependent on government consumption and investment. By the late 1960s, the contours of Bolivia's new capitalist class were coming into focus. As elsewhere in Latin America, the leading strata of this class were organized into economic groups—that is, diversified conglomerates controlled by family clans or friendship cliques.[5] Private wealth became highly concentrated in these groups. The size of this newly emergent dominant class, composed of the proprietors of modern firms, was minuscule. Alejandro Portes estimates its size as 1.3 percent of the economically active population in 1970, and 0.6 percent by 1980.[6]

One important set of economic groups, headquartered in La Paz, grew up around investments in medium-sized mines. Three firms came to dominate production in this sector: COMSUR, EMUSA, and Etalsa S.A. Through shrewd management and aggressive diversification, the three firms became the principal private producers of all of Bolivia's mineral exports by the late 1980s.[7]

In the eastern department of Santa Cruz, economic groups developed agricultural, agroindustrial, and commercial ventures. Starting with Paz's first presidency, the government channelled significant resources to Santa Cruz in order to develop its infrastructure and agriculture. Forty percent of all agricultural credit between 1955 and 1966 went to Santa Cruz, most of it destined for sugar, cotton, rice, and soybean producers.[8] By the early 1970s, the Santa Cruz region had absorbed 66 percent of all agricultural credit, with about half of it directed to medium-sized and large landholders. A high rate of default on agricultural loans ultimately turned the credit program into an enormous giveaway to the private sector of Santa Cruz.[9]

Investments in financial institutions were an important factor in the diversification of the economic groups. The Banco de Santa Cruz, founded in 1966, became the banking hub that brought together virtually all of the economic groups of Santa Cruz, including the Grupo Monasterios, Roda, Kuljis, Willie, Gasser, and Romero.[10] Other leading banks (Banco Boliviano Americano, Banco Hipotecario, Banco Mercantil, Banco Nacional) similarly fell under the control of La Paz–based economic groups.[11]

For the most part, the small size and the impoverishment of the internal market made manufacturing industries relatively unattractive investments. In the post-1952 period, Bolivian industrial development lagged significantly behind that of its neighbors, including countries of comparable size like Ecuador. Industrial production remained concentrated in nondurable goods—that is, food, beverages, textiles, and footwear. Notwithstanding the overall backwardness of the sector, some notable family fortunes were derived from industrial ventures in La Paz, Santa Cruz, and Cochabamba. On the whole, however, investment in manufacturing was not a prominent concern for most economic groups. Eckstein and Hagopian report that manufacturing enterprises constituted the "lead" firms in only two of the fifteen large economic groups they studied.[12]

The economic boom during the Banzer dictatorship helped to solidify the position of these emerging economic groups. Conditions in the international market and the probusiness stance of the Banzer government created propitious conditions for consolidation of groups. Prices for Bolivia's agricultural and mineral exports surged in the early 1970s, and the state's revenues increased with revenues from petroleum exports. The export bonanza led to real growth rates in the gross domestic product of between 5 and 7 percent from 1971 to 1975. After 1975, the Banzer government was able to prolong the economic boom by aggressive borrowing and deficit spending. Given the extraordinary conditions prevailing in the international financial community, foreign banks eagerly entered the Bolivian market.[13]

Bear in mind that the economic growth that took place during the Banzer period was based on consumption, not new production.[14] Increases in international market prices accounted for Bolivia's improved export performance; production increases registered during this period were modest. The expansion of public-sector employment fueled middle-class consumption which, along with government spending, contributed to an import binge. Construction and real estate ventures flourished in response to new government building projects. This economic growth fortified the position of the economic groups, but it did not represent significant new conquests. Rather, trends of the 1970s only underscored how closely tied the private sector was to public spending.

Exit, Shyness, and Staying Liquid

By the late 1970s, the Bolivian "economic miracle" was screeching to a halt. The termination of the foreign credit cycle coincided with an extended political crisis that began with General Banzer's botched attempt to rig his own presidential election in 1978. From 1978 through 1982, a string of interim military and civilian governments failed to reconstitute a stable political regime or remedy the growing economic crisis. In 1982, the installation of Hernán Siles Zuazo as president signaled the end of military intervention, but poor macroeconomic management continued.[15] By 1985, Bolivia was in the grip of one of the world's worst hyperinflations of the twentieth century. The inflation rate for 1985 was a staggering 8,170 percent.[16]

At least three propensities marked the economic behavior of Bolivian capitalists during the 1980s: (1) recourse to capital flight (or "exit," to borrow Albert Hirschman's term); (2) a reluctance to engage in any new productive investment (Juan Antonio Morales refers to this as investor "shyness"); and concurrently (3) a preference for holding liquid assets (which makes it easier to choose the exit option or defend one's position domestically by transactions in the foreign currency market).[17] These propensities were, of course, not unique to Bolivian business. Capitalists from Argentina to Mexico engaged in similar behavior as the economic crisis descended on Latin America in the 1980s.

In the recent literature on capital flight, *exit* is depicted as both responding to and aggravating the debt crisis of the 1980s. Analysts concerned with the origins of the crisis focus on how domestic capitalists contributed to the debt overload by contracting loans to underwrite the costs of enterprises, while shielding their personal wealth from risk through flight.[18] Other analysts have explained capital flight as a response to the fear of increased taxes as governments assumed responsibility for guaranteeing public and private debt.[19] In retrospect, capital flight from Latin America in the 1980s appears to have been unavoidable. Almost every conceivable economic phenomenon—overvalued exchange rates, high interest rates in the international market—together with political uncertainty made flight seem the most reasonable option for individual investors.

In the Bolivian case, Oscar Ugarteche and others have argued that flight began to take off in the 1970s.[20] During the Banzer government, investors redirected the subsidized loans provided by the state to bank accounts outside Bolivia. The mismanagement of public-sector enterprises also channelled funds illegally to individuals. In a sense, the capital flight from Bolivia in the 1970s was proactive—an aggressive move used by domestic investors to maximize and secure their share of the bonanza conditions in the international credit market. Capital flight in the first half of the 1980s was, in contrast, more defensive—a push to protect resources in an atmosphere of escalating political and economic uncertainty. Poor macro-economic management and increasing social conflict scared off domestic capitalists.

The amount of capital that left Bolivia, judging from errors and omissions in the balance of payments, is estimated in table 3.1. As the table indicates, the flight of capital accelerated in the second half of the 1970s. By 1985, Bolivians held an estimated $400 million in banks in the United States, totaling 10 percent of the country's gross domestic product.[21]

Investors also demonstrated their lack of confidence by a reluctance to make any new productive investments. Figures for the late 1980s demonstrate the continuing problem of investor shyness even after economic stability was restored. As table 3.2 shows, there was virtually no change in the private sector's commitment to investment even after stabilization was achieved.

TABLE 3.1   Capital Flight from Bolivia

	Amount in $ U.S. millions	As % of GDP
1971–1975	$77.3	4.0 (1975)
1976–1981	216.9	6.0 (1981)
1982–1983	106.2	3.0

Source: Juan Antonio Morales and Jeffrey D. Sachs, "Bolivia's Economic Crisis," in Developing Country Debt and Economic Performance, ed. Jeffrey D. Sachs (Chicago: University of Chicago Press, 1990), 2:213.

TABLE 3.2 Investment in
Bolivia as a Percentage of GDP

	Public	Private	Total
1987	6.4	3.9	10.3
1988	8.3	3.9	12.2
1989	8.7	3.1	11.8
1990	8.1	3.8	11.9

Source: International Monetary Fund and
Banco Central de Bolivia; table originally published in "Por qué no hay inversión en Bolivia?" *Epoca* 27 (August 1991).

The post-1985 shyness was a rational choice for investors,
especially considering the bitter lessons taught by the intense
economic stress of the early 1980s. Bolivian business leaders
frequently refer to their experiences during the hyperinflation
of 1984–1985 in dramatic terms: it was *una escuela bárbara* (a
savage school) or *años amargos* (bitter years). Among the immediate lessons learned by business executives during hyperinflation was the importance of staying liquid: for example, demanding immediate payments on delivery in U.S. dollars, and
using assets to engage in currency speculation.[22]
    The success of the 1985 economic stabilization program
notwithstanding, Bolivian capitalists have not rushed in to develop new productive ventures. In a parody on the Gabriel
García Márquez title, one analyst commented of the orthodox
economic program in Bolivia, "El modelo no tiene quien in-
vierta" (No one invests in the model).[23] While a significant
amount of capital was repatriated after 1985 (wooed by high
interest rates), the lion's share was placed in short-term dollar
and dollar-linked deposits in the banking system. An estimated
90 percent of banking deposits (as measured in June 1989)
were located in such accounts. Of the $323 million in such ac-
counts, $175 million were in thirty-day accounts.[24]
    In the second half of the 1980s, Bolivian investors clearly

preferred to keep their assets readily accessible and moveable. The "hot money" character of these deposits became visible in June, July, and August 1989, when uncertainty over the outcome of the presidential election triggered a run on deposits. Approximately 28 percent of all bank deposits were withdrawn from the system between the weeks of 28 May and 4 August 1989, as negotiations over the presidential succession took place in Congress.[25]

Exit, shyness, and staying liquid were three strategies used by Bolivian capitalists in the market to deal with the uncertainties of the 1980s. Politics was another avenue. While acting as individual economic agents in the market, they did not eschew a collective response in the political arena. Defensive economic behavior did not preclude a resort to political voice.

The political mobilization of Bolivian business leaders in the 1980s brought together the regional and sectoral groups. Playing a central role in the process were business organizations and leading personalities connected to the major economic groups. Business mobilized with remarkable energy and ambition; it was a multifaceted effort aimed not just at honing the business lobby per se, but at shaping public opinion and electing individuals associated with business to public office. The following section traces the development of business-led political action and ideological efforts. As influential as the business movement came to be, however, the campaign to promote a probusiness climate in politics and society ran into difficulties—in part because the private sector's own lackadaisical economic performance exposed the distance between its rhetoric and reality.

Public Relations and Politics

The political activation of business in Bolivia began as part of the "resurrection of civil society" during the struggle against military rule in the early 1980s.[26] This mobilization extended through the tumultuous civilian presidency of Hernán Siles Zuazo (1982–1985) as business lashed out against the government's economic policies and the militant Central Obrera Boliviana (COB), the powerful trade union organization. The business mobilization of the 1980s was organized through a preexisting network of organizations. The umbrella organization that incorporates sectoral and regional groups, the Confederación de Empresarios Privados de Bolivia (CEPB), was created in 1962. Among its founding institutions were the Chamber of Industry, the Banking Association, the Chamber of Commerce, and the Chamber of Construction.[27] Also joining the foundation of the CEPB was the Association of Medium Miners that had been reconstituted in 1957.[28] Once founded, however, the CEPB remained skeletal, staffed by a single director and a secretary.[29]

In Santa Cruz, business leaders were organized into three associations. The oldest was the Cámara de Industria y Comercio, founded in 1915. New agricultural entrepreneurs organized the Cámara Agropecuaria del Oriente (CAO) in 1966. The CAO became the umbrella group for the agricultural producers' groups in the region (such as the Federation of Cane Growers, the Association of Cotton Producers, the Federation of Ranchers, etc.), The Federación de Empresarios Privados de Santa Cruz acted as the umbrella representing *cruceño* interests in the CEPB. Similar organizations also developed in the city of Cochabamba. Among the oldest were the Chamber of Industry and the Chamber of Commerce. The Federación de Empresarios Privados de Cochabamba, founded in 1970, linked these local groups to the CEPB.

All these organizations remained relatively quiescent throughout the Banzer period. Because Banzer's policies were generally favorable to the private sector, there was little cause for mobilization. Moreover, when conflicts arose, the dictatorial character of the government made public dissent difficult. Disagreements were voiced behind closed doors.[30]

The political instability of the post-Banzer period prompted business organizations to take a more active role regarding regime transition. The repressive and internationally embarrassing military government of General Luis García Meza (1980–1981) galvanized leaders inside the CEPB to push for a definitive return to civilian rule.[31] Business pressures coincided with broad popular opposition to García Meza. In Santa Cruz, business organizations joined in defiance of the García Meza government as part of the regional civic committee, the Comité Pro–Santa Cruz.[32]

Although the CEPB supported the deal leading to the installation of the Siles government, it swung into action almost immediately to defend business from what it knew would be a center-left administration with labor sympathies. The Siles period became a turning point for all players in Bolivian politics—business, labor, and political parties. Composed of a heterogeneous mix of communists, social democrats, and "independents," the Siles cabinet vacillated between the demands of labor and business in making economic policy. In the process, Siles satisfied neither group. Conflicts over economic policy spilled into the streets as unions and civic committees undertook direct actions to press their claims. According to Roberto Laserna, an average of fifty-three instances of collective action (civic strikes, marches, road blockades) took place monthly during Siles's thirty-three months in office.[33] The number of industrial strikes and work actions also surged. The COB called a total of nine general strikes. This labor militancy was not confined to wage demands. In 1984, the COB issued its "emergency plan," which called for an immediate transition to socialism.

Bolivian business was profoundly threatened by the mobilization of the leftist labor movement during the Siles government. By 1984, the convulsive state of the society and economy placed Bolivia at the brink of what Guillermo O'Donnell has called a "crisis of social domination"—that is, a situation in which disruptions in the capital accumulation process are accompanied by "lower class behavior that undermines the social relations upon which the capitalist order is built."[34] In short, the future of the private sector itself appeared to be at stake. This is how the CEPB characterized their perception of the threat:

The Bolivian private sector, because of cumulative events (some frontal and others carefully furtive), is certain that a systematic offensive exists to weaken it and eventually displace it from the national economy. This operation has its roots in the most radical political sectors that use democracy as an instrument of its ends.[35]

Within this crisis atmosphere, the CEPB was galvanized as a organization and emerged as the voice of a capitalist class seeking to reassert itself. Fernando Illanes served as the CEPB's president during the critical years 1982–1985. Illanes, himself a member of a La Paz–based economic group, was strongly supported by other economic groups in his efforts to transform the CEPB from a shoestring operation into a modern professional lobby. Illanes began by hiring a regular staff that included economists and by installing computers in the office.[36]

The CEPB used its new resources for three related tasks: (1) to mount a lobby capable of countering the COB and generating alternative economic policies; (2) to educate and mobilize its own membership in support of new policies; and (3) to launch a broad public relations campaign to organize support for business. In short, the CEPB and its allied organizations began a conscious effort to shift elite and public opinion away from the state-centered and populist formulas that had dominated policy making in Bolivia since the 1950s. The CEPB wanted to replace the old formulas with market-driven economics and attitudes favorable to the private sector.

Even before Illanes assumed the presidency, leaders inside the CEPB had developed a critique of the state's economic role and were arguing for a greater role for the private sector. The

CEPB commissioned several economic studies between 1978 and 1981 that attacked inefficiencies in the public sector and defended the productivity of the private sector. Once the full-time staff was in place, these efforts to develop a comprehensive set of policy proposals continued. Many of the proposals developed by chief economist Fernando Candia and his staff prefigured the components of DS 21060, the neoliberal package launched under the subsequent government of Víctor Paz Estenssoro in August 1985.

Formulating an orthodox remedy for Bolivia's economic woes was just one dimension of the CEPB's hyperactive style in this period. CEPB leaders realized that the new ideas had to be sold to the public at large and to many of the CEPB's own members who were accustomed to the protection and subsidies provided by Bolivia's hypertrophied state. CEPB leaders recognized that an ideological campaign had to be a component of its overall political strategy. Illanes contracted a public relations firm to correct the "distorted image of the private sector" and commissioned a Gallup poll to tap public opinion on issues of concern to the CEPB.

The CEPB's advertising campaign (which included both newspaper ads and radio spots) pivoted on two themes. First, the ads sought to portray business as an ardent defender of democracy and civil liberties while casting aspersions on the conduct of other (unspecified, but undoubtedly leftist) actors. A contrast was drawn between the democratic commitment of the CEPB and the oppressive nature of the antibusiness opposition. Two such ads read as follows:

What kind of society do you want for yourself and for your children? One in which you choose various work, familial, and religious options? Or one in which everything is imposed on you? DEMOCRACY IS FREEDOM TO CHOOSE.[37]

Do you want a fractured Bolivia—one dominated by violence, arbitrary acts, and hate among brothers? We don't! That's why we support respect for the law, pluralism, and free choice without marginalizing anyone. WE VOTED FOR DEMOCRACY. LET'S DEFEND IT![38]

The other thrust of the ad campaign was to promote a positive image of business by contrasting the "productivity" of the private sector with the inefficiency of the public sector. One ad featured graphs showing that private enterprise accounted for 70 percent of all tax contributions; another claimed that the private sector produced 500,000 new jobs without "deficit spending or inflation."[39] Another juxtaposed the wheels of industry with that of a machine spewing forth money; the bold type in the ad declared, "We live by production, not by emission!"[40] The concluding tag line of this series of advertisements was "Free Enterprise: Pillar of a Productive Democracy."

Meetings and public forums served as important venues for putting forth the ideas of CEPB leaders and developing a consensus within the CEPB on the need for an orthodox restructuring of the Bolivian economy. The activity was intense. In 1983–1984, nine "extraordinary" general assemblies and meetings were called to discuss the deteriorating economic situation and draft policy recommendations to the government. One event reported to have an important ideological impact was a meeting featuring a speech by Alvaro Alsogaray, an ultraliberal Argentine economist. Another was the "Free Enterprise Encounter" held in May 1983. In addition to the meetings, the CEPB began publishing *El Empresario* (The Entrepreneur) to communicate on a regular basis with its members.

The CEPB did not confine its mobilization to meetings. It joined in the street politics characteristic of the Siles period. The CEPB organized two business shut-downs in 1984. A forty-eight-hour strike was held in February to protest government economic policies, followed by a September action to express outrage at the murder of a prominent businessman. The murder was portrayed by the CEPB as an act of aggression against the private sector as a whole.

The number of business groups affiliated with the CEPB ballooned during the Siles period as smaller and medium-sized business looked to the CEPB for leadership and defense. Leaders in the CEPB cultivated ties with small business—and this was reflected in the ad campaign. One of the 1983 ads pictured a young man in a cap (clearly *clase popular*) and declared,

This mechanic is also private enterprise . . . because a mechanic that works in his own shop is a person who undertakes an activity in which he risks the resources that he has.

Private activity benefits the entrepreneur, but it also creates wealth, progress, and work for the whole country.[41]

The CEPB extended its ties to small business by creating a foundation to promote small enterprise in 1984. In 1987, the CEPB invited the Peruvian champion of the informal sector, Hernando de Soto, for a visit.[42] Other groups picked up on the idea of an alliance with the informal sector. In 1988, for example, the Federación de Empresarios Privados de Cochabamba (a regional affiliate of the CEPB) kicked off a campaign called "Empresarios Somos Todos" (We're all entrepreneurs) to promote the idea of free enterprise and pride within the business community.[43]

One more aspect of the ideological ferment is worth noting—namely, the efforts to develop business-oriented educational programs under private control. The CEPB, for example, sponsored IDEA, a program that offered courses to executives on such topics as tax and industrial policy. In Santa Cruz, the effort to develop alternative education went even further. The Cámara de Industria y Comercio, with the support of individuals from Santa Cruz's leading economic groups, founded a private university in 1984. The Universidad Privada de Santa Cruz de la Sierra (UPSA) was conceived as a site to train professionals for private enterprise without the strikes and political agitation that plagued the public system. Fields of concentration are limited to systems analysis, computer science, and communications. It is not surprising that this ambitious project was hatched inside the ranks of the *cruceño* private sector. Santa Cruz business leaders cultivate the image of innovative entrepreneurs and have been successful at tying free-enterprise rhetoric to the emotional appeals of Santa Cruz regionalism. An extensive network of institutions in Santa Cruz articulates a probusiness position. One of the major daily newspapers, *El Mundo*, was founded in 1979 by the Cámara de Industria y Comercio. Moreover, the private television stations are owned by the principal economic groups, as are a growing number of public relations firms. The Cámara, CAO, and the Federación de Empresarios Privados occupy important positions inside the Comité Pro–Santa Cruz, the departmental civic committee that wields enormous political and ideological clout.[44]

As in other Latin American countries, filling a high-profile position in a business interest group became a launching pad for a political career in the 1980s. The new "political business leaders" were major players in the electoral resurgence of the right.[45] In Bolivia, the most important figure to emerge from this process was Gonzalo Sánchez de Lozada (popularly known as "Goni"). Raised and educated in the United States, Gonzalo Sánchez de Lozada is a major shareholder in COMSUR, Bolivia's largest private mining company. He began his political career as an MNR deputy to the 1980 Congress. He became a biting critic of the Siles government and an ardent defender of the positions of the CEPB. He urged his fellows in business to get involved in politics, not simply by participating in the CEPB, but to take action "through individuals."[46]

As the hyperinflation and social disorder spun out of control, President Siles succumbed to calls for advancing the presidential and congressional elections of 1985. Sánchez de Lozada subsequently won a Senate seat for the MNR in the

1985 election; he resigned the presidency of the Senate, at President Paz's request, in January 1986 to take over as minister of planning. He held that position until he launched his own presidential campaign in 1989.[47]

Sánchez de Lozada's involvement in politics had a profound impact on the course of economic policy and the entire ideological climate in Bolivia. He became one of the most effective advocates of the free market and the driving force behind Paz's orthodox stabilization program. The program included measures for downsizing public-sector enterprises, liberalizing trade, and economic deregulation.[48] As the intellectual architect of the program, Sánchez de Lozada was able to translate many of the ideas that had been bubbling inside the CEPB since the 1970s into a concrete plan of economic reform. Moreover, his personal style—built on a disarming sense of humor and "tough but honest" talk—lent credence to the ideas and policies of the Paz government.[49] The success of DS 21060 (at least in halting hyperinflation) gave even further credibility to the discourse of economic liberalism.

By 1989, a remarkable consensus had emerged within the political class regarding the desirability of continuing the market experiment initiated by the Paz Estenssoro government. Along with the MNR, the social democratic Movimiento de la Izquierda Revolucionaria (MIR) and the rightist Acción Democrática Nacionalista (ADN) endorsed economic restructuring. This consensus reflected the relative success of neoliberal business leaders and technocrats in capturing important posts within the parties. In both the MNR and the ADN, neoliberals occupied top party positions and acted as trusted advisors to the party chiefs, Paz Estenssoro and Banzer, respectively. The ascent of neoliberals within the MNR and ADN, however, did not go completely unchallenged. In both parties, the neoliberals found themselves at odds with populists who balked at the idea of reducing the size of the public sector and resented being displaced by the new strata of politicized business people and young technocrats. In the MNR, for example, this conflict crystallized in the competition between Sánchez de Lozada and longtime MNR stalwart Guillermo Bedregal over the party's presidential nomination. The populists lost and Sánchez de Lozada won the party nomination.

The presence of a core of business leaders and technocrats inside the MNR and the ADN was crucial in keeping the initial stabilization and reform effort intact. As minister of planning from 1985 to 1989, Sánchez de Lozada provided strong leadership for the economic team and ensured that the program would not be whittled away by the populist factions inside the government or by popular protests. At the same time, the ADN provided political support for the economic reforms by entering into a pact with the MNR in 1985. This pact ensured that there would be no congressional majority that could act institutionally to block the actions of the executive. The ADN continued its support for neoliberalism when it sealed a subsequent pact with the MIR in 1989.

Spreading the doctrine of economic liberalism and organizing political support for it became the project of business leaders and allied technocrats. It would be a mistake, however, to attribute this spread solely to the energies of business leaders. It is important to keep in mind that the neoliberal project enjoyed unusually propitious circumstances in Bolivia in this period. The catastrophic deterioration of the economy under the direction of the center-left Siles government had undermined the public's belief in leftist prescriptions and had severely undercut sympathy for the COB by 1985. Moreover, the capacity of the COB to project an alternative to economic liberalism faded further as Paz's policies effectively dismantled the COB's constituency—especially the mine workers who were dismissed as part of the cutbacks in the state-owned mining sector. And, by the end of the 1980s, changes in the international climate (such as the collapse of Soviet bloc socialism, the electoral defeat of the Sandinistas) deprived what remained of the left of external referents. Along with the weakening of the left, another factor had a critical effect on Bolivia's ideological climate: the real pressures coming from international public and private financial institutions to restructure the economy and renegotiate the foreign debt.[50] Given these pressures, prevailing conditions in the 1980s were ripe for domestic capitalists to push a neoliberal economic project.

Yet, the political victory of the new neoliberal coalition in Bolivia was not without its contradictions. While Bolivian capitalists celebrated the virtues of the market and staked a claim as authors of "productive democracy," they balked at risk-taking investments. Even after economic stabilization was consolidated in 1986 and the major parties endorsed neoliberalism, Bolivian investors remained "shy." Business leaders have explained this reaction by underscoring the need for further assurances from the government to reestablish fully a climate of confidence. The demands from the private sector now include: (1) systematic privatization of public enterprises; (2) sweeping legal reforms to facilitate both domestic and foreign investment; (3) a more aggressive channelling of "reactivation" credits to the private sector and lowering interest rates; (4) continued reduction of the fiscal deficit. In addition to these specific policy measures, business leaders also stress that politicians must demonstrate their "seriousness" and managerial prowess. The competence of politicians, rather than their ideology, has become the prime concern of the business community. The fears that continue to prevail among business leaders arise from skepticism about the capacity of politicians to act as skillful and sober guardians of the new neoliberal model over the long haul.

Contestation and Credibility

Through its new activism and intensive public relations work, the domestic private sector in Bolivia reinvented itself as a political and ideological force in the 1980s. Yet these efforts did not put an end to public skepticism regarding business's capacity to act as an agent of economic growth and development. While business projected itself as the heroic protagonist of accumulation and growth, other voices contested that image in a variety of ways. Although a complete description of the contestations during the 1980s cannot be attempted here, I will briefly highlight some of the ways in which various actors (including some allies of business) challenged business's political and ideological assertion in this period.

One would expect, of course, a challenge "from below." But business's traditional challenger, organized labor, was not the sole (nor even the most important) voice of opposition. Organized labor, represented by the COB, suffered a major blow with the enactment of Paz Estenssoro's economic stabilization and restructuring program. The "New Economic Policy" (NEP) drastically reduced the number of miners in COMI-BOL, and a liberalized labor code allowed private employers to dismiss workers at their own discretion. By 1988, 23,118 miners had been dismissed from COMIBOL, and 5,371 miners from private firms had been released.[51] An estimated 29,000 industrial jobs were eliminated between 1985 and 1987.[52] The net result of this state shrinking and labor liberalization was a dramatic decline in the ranks of organized labor. An important segment of the labor force was effectively "deproletarianized" as dislocated workers were forced into informal-sector activities or returned to agriculture.[53]

In addition to this reduction in the constituency of organized labor, the COB was further debilitated by the government's use of force in applying the NEP. Paz Estenssoro twice invoked emergency powers to deal with union protest, and his cabinet ministers threatened repressive action on numerous other occasions.

With the power of labor eclipsed, some of the most effective popular resistance to the probusiness agenda came from residentially based groups asserting the rights of the community over that of private enterprise. The most important instance took place in August 1990, when 800 members of indigenous communities from the Beni marched 650 kilometers to press their land claims in La Paz. The protestors were objecting to the concessions extended to six lumber companies and demanded the creation of an indigenous controlled territory in the Chimanes Forest. In an unexpected move, President Paz Zamora acceded to the demands and ordered lumber companies out of the zone by the end of October 1990.[54] In another act of local resistance, the civic committee of Potosí (a poor mining town) organized a series of demonstrations against the granting of a concession for lithium exploration to a North American firm, LITHCO. Protesters argued that the terms of the agreement would bring little in the way of new revenue or jobs to the region, while conceding windfall profits to LITHCO. In this case, Paz Zamora also backed off and withdrew the concession.[55]

Both decisions incurred the wrath of business organizations, including the CEPB. The Chimanes decision was portrayed as an illegal disruption of contractual relations and an attack on the rights of business. In both cases, the CEPB underscored the detrimental effects of action against business on the overall investment climate. The head of the Chamber of Lumber Industries (Cámara Forestal), Edgar Landívar, put it even more bluntly. He declared that such reversals in the "rules of the game" would permanently douse investor interest in Bolivia. Landívar warned that the concession to indigenous groups could trigger parallel demands for mining and agricultural zones under their control. "Next they are going to want to be the owners of the petroleum," he concluded.[56]

President Paz Zamora's capitulations to popular protest were objectionable to the business community at large for two reasons. First, the decisions gave weight to the idea of collective rights. Second, they raised concerns about the commitment of the Paz Zamora administration to "holding the course" on neoliberalism. From the perspective of business, it raised the question of the government's credibility. This brings us to the disruptions created by yet another set of actors—politicians. One lesson that business leaders have been forced to learn in the period since the transition to democracy is that even politicians whom they perceive as "their own" (that is, committed to a probusiness posture) can stray as political calculations warrant. Given the electoral logic that can take over politicians, it is no surprise that they frequently opt to carry out "reform" functions rather than accumulation functions.[57]

Business-government relations in Bolivia remained uneasy even after economic stabilization was secured by the Paz Estenssoro administration. In 1986, a polemic over economic "reactivation" led business leaders and politicians into a game of casting blame on each other for the lack of economic growth. Leaders of the CEPB hammered the government for a rapid disbursement of "reactivation" credit and lowering interest rates. They were quick to dissociate themselves from the economic recession even as the government pointed to the private sector as a part of the problem. Carlos Iturralde, president of the CEPB, repeatedly intoned that "it was not fair or honest to try to transfer the responsibility for economic reactivation to the private sector."[58]

By 1989, business leaders broadened the debate over reactivation by arguing that fundamental reforms (such as privatization of public firms, decentralization, restructuring of the legal code) were required as a signal of the government's good faith before new investment could occur. In other words, business always seemed to be "moving the goalpost"—ratcheting up the conditions that would define what constituted a stable investment climate.

But there was also some notable frustration with the private sector's posture even among some of its ardent spokespersons.

Some of the most pointed criticism came from Hugo Banzer, leader of the conservative ADN and supporter of the neoliberal model. In March 1990, Banzer cautioned business that the security of the investment climate was already assured and that the only missing element was a "courageous participation" by the private sector.[59] Banzer's criticisms continued over the following months. In June, he suggested that investors engage in some "self-criticism" regarding their lack of entrepreneurialism instead of constantly blaming the government.[60] In another speech, Banzer challenged the private sector, "Show your face in this historic moment and invest something in this country— and as in any business, run a risk."[61]

Banzer's biting comments rekindled questions about the character and the commitment of the Bolivian bourgeoisie. Moreover, Banzer's reprimands demonstrate another way in which business discourse is contested in these settings—from inside the ranks of business supporters and conservative ideologues. As much as business leaders try to project themselves as heroes of a dynamic capitalism in the making, it is an image that is not completely believed even by capitalists themselves. Evidence of such inner skepticism frequently emerges in private conversations with entrepreneurs. It also spills out in the public arena in ways that undercut the efforts to project business in a positive light. The recent participation of high-profile business leaders in elections opened the doors for an attack on their values and behavior.

One such attack was made on Gonzalo Sánchez de Lozada during his 1989 presidential bid. Hugo Banzer, his rival for the presidency, launched a negative ad campaign against Sánchez de Lozada that repeatedly raised questions about his business behavior. A number of the negative television spots opened with a clip of a speech by Sánchez de Lozada in which he pronounced, "Bolivians will bring back their money to Bolivia when they have confidence in their country." This was followed by a red screen and black letters that declared, "NO

SEÑOR SÁNCHEZ DE LOZADA." A dramatic voice-over intoned,

Nobody has asked you how you made your money. The only thing the people ask and that you don't want to answer is—how many millions of dollars have you taken out of Bolivia because you have no confidence in Bolivia?

The query was followed by booming music and two male voices reading the names of eight firms incorporated in Panama, Argentina, Brazil, and Peru that are affiliated with Sánchez de Lozada's COMSUR.[62] While it is impossible to draw any firm conclusions about such an attack's overall impact on public opinion, the tactic was targeted to play on deepseated public skepticism about the behavior of the upper echelons of Bolivia's business class. In a political culture steeped in populism, portraying one's rivals as "La Rosca" (literally, the screw—the traditional term for the Bolivian oligarchy) is a well-worn political tactic. Nonetheless, the recurrent use of such imagery by politicians (including those on the right of the spectrum) helps keep populist thinking alive and subverts the notion of a hardworking, sober, and deserving upper class.[63]

Rewriting the Public Transcript?

In certain respects, the politico-ideological mobilization just described should strike a familiar chord among observers of U.S. politics in the 1980s. As David Vogel and others argue, the U.S. business community also moved to reassert its political and ideological clout in the same period.[64] In the 1980s under Ronald Reagan, the celebration of business and business values was in full swing.

In both the United States and Latin America, the political resurgence of business was part of an effort to take the offensive. In the United States, corporate leaders recognized the need for more effective political intervention and favorable public opinion as the power of the public-interest lobby (consumer, environmental groups) grew in the 1970s. The mobilization of business in Bolivia occurred in response to an even more profound type of threat emanating from the labor-left and a collapsing state structure. In both settings, leaders of both corporate and business interest groups responded to the new threats by developing a more sophisticated political apparatus for business, increasing solidarity within the business community, and injecting probusiness values into political culture.

While there are broad similarities in the conditions in the United States and Latin America that have recently provoked new political activity by business, the tasks faced by the respective business communities are extremely different. In the United States, business was attempting to reassert its position in a cultural context that already contains a large reservoir of support for business.[65] By contrast, Bolivian business leaders seek to assert themselves in an environment where there is no such reservoir of goodwill. It should be no surprise to conclude that the search for political and ideological ascendance by these domestic capitalists is and will remain extremely problematic.

The essential "hegemonic" problem for Bolivian capitalists is that they are identified as leaders of an incompetent capitalist system. So far, the Bolivian economy has persistently failed to produce the material base of a sustainable class compromise. As Adam Przeworski and other theorists argue, hegemony is not simply smoke and mirrors—that is, it is not a question of clever manipulations by capitalist leaders.[66] In the advanced capitalist economies, hegemony involved trading workers' compliance for investment and economic performance by capitalists. This is the tradeoff that is missing in the Bolivian case— and in most of Latin America. Certainly, domestic capitalists are quick to offer up an endless inventory of explanations as to why they have not performed ably; these explanations typically focus on the "dysfunctional" state and its irrational interventions. But with the neoliberal model now in place, capitalists can no longer point to the state as the sole source of the problem. With neoliberalism in gear, capitalists will have to bear some of the responsibility for economic performance.

In retrospect, the business campaign in Bolivia looks like an attempt to substitute public relations for the missing economic performance. The selling of capitalist rhetoric without any accompanying "proof of the pudding" in these settings is not easy. It is important to appreciate not only the immediate contradictions involved, but also the difficulties posed by the historical context in which capitalists assert their claims to legitimacy. In Bolivia, popular memories of the oligarchic past remain alive, stoked by populist language and daily experience. Indeed, many domestic capitalists still cling to the seignorial cultural styles associated with that past. Moreover, in this racially divided country, popular alienation from the business elite is further fueled by their identification with white society.

Status anxieties and fears about the loss of control over family firms are also important variables in understanding the investment behavior of Bolivian economic groups; such concerns are often at odds with their attempt to project themselves as authors of a dynamic modern capitalism. The extreme underdevelopment of Bolivia's stock market reflects these fears of loss of control and of associating with anyone outside one's immediate circle of family and confidantes.

Let me conclude with an example taken from a recent interview of how such concerns affect investment behavior in Bolivia. Several years ago, two of the largest economic groups in Santa Cruz expressed an interest in mounting an airline to compete with the state-run Lloyd Aero Boliviano, but were short of capital to start up the project. A local executive consulted by the groups suggested that they tap into the financial resources of "informal-sector" merchants in Santa Cruz. After speaking to a number of these merchants, the executive compiled a list of hundreds of individuals willing to become stockholders. On second thought, however, the economic groups backed away from the project. When pressed by the executive to explain their decision, the group managers confessed their reluctance to get involved in an investment with "people from the street."[67]

In recent years, the growth of a nouveau riche stratum connected to the drug trade has reinforced this tendency by economic groups to fear collaboration with new investors. While such fears may be well founded, the closed character of these economic groups reinforces the image of big business as a closed oligarchic (and white men's) club. In Bolivia, the rocky relations between Max Fernández and the business establishment illustrate the point. Fernández is a businessman from Cochabamba who purchased and refurbished Bolivia's major beer bottling plant in La Paz. It was widely rumored that the start-up capital for this project came from the drug trade. His high-profile approach to business has also included major promotional efforts of his products, philanthropic activities, and more recently launching his own political career.[68] Because of his allegedly unsavory connections, Fernández has been the object of scorn from established business leaders, politicians, and the U.S. Embassy. Yet, if there is anyone who can lay claim to being a popular hero of Bolivian capitalism, it is probably Fernández, who came from a humble background and "made it." By rejecting Fernández so roundly, the established economic groups have distanced themselves from the one figure who can attest (with some measure of authenticity in the public mind) to the opportunities in the marketplace.[69]

Business did make significant gains through its political mobilization. The antistatist attack by business organizations produced greater support for free-market thinking inside the parties and the economic policy-making apparatus. The political victories by conservative forces have been important, but they are not irreversible. Business leaders have learned a great deal about the uncertainty of democracy over the last decade—and they know that their gains can be eroded or completely overturned. As such, business recognizes the need to foment ideological change as part of the overall strategy to recast the policy-making environment.

One can look back at the 1980s as a period in which Latin American business leaders began a definitive push to rewrite the "public transcript" of capitalism in these systems. That is, they attempted to paint a new official portrait of themselves as proficient economic actors and defenders of democratic freedoms. As James Scott argues, any "public transcript" has a number of functions. One of the functions is to make an ideological case for domination that can have at least *some resonance* among subordinate groups. The problem for Bolivian capitalists is that their own track record (at least so far) strips much of the resonance from their public claims that they are acting in ways that promote the general health of the Bolivian economy. A second function of the public transcript is to draw leaders themselves together around common beliefs and rituals. Scott suggests,

If much of the purpose of the public transcript of domination is not to gain the agreement of subordinates but to awe and intimidate them into a durable and expedient compliance, what effect does it have among the dominant themselves? It may well be that insofar as the public transcript represents and attempts to persuade or indoctrinate anyone, the dominant are the subject of its attentions. The public transcript as a kind of self-hypnosis within ruling groups to buck up their courage, improve their cohesion, display their power, and convince themselves anew of their high moral purpose? The possibility is not all that farfetched. . . . If autosuggestion works with individuals it might well characterize one of the purposes of group ritual as well.[70]

On this level, the business campaign of the 1980s was somewhat more successful. It conjured up visions of a flourishing capitalist future—one with a minimalist state and a civil society infused with respect for business and entrepreneurial values ("Empresarios Somos Todos"). For business classes riddled with identity questions and self-doubt, the dream was a welcome relief. It fed class solidarity and laid the basis for the collective political action of the 1980s.

Notes

1. Carlos Díaz-Alejandro, "Latin American Debt Crisis: I Don't Think We Are in Kansas Anymore," *Brookings Papers on Economic Activity* 2 (1984): 379. Díaz-Alejandro's observation is underscored in Miguel Rodríguez, "Consequences of Capital Flight for Latin American Debtor Countries," in *Capital Flight and the Third World Debt*, ed. Donald R. Lessard and John Williamson (Washington, D.C.: Institute for International Economics, 1987), 139.

2. To clarify my use of terms, I am using **business** to refer to **big business**, that is, the leading strata of domestic capitalists. I take the position that while their interests (sectoral concentration, market orientation) often diverge, it is possible to make useful generalizations on the behavior of these capitalists as a whole. Specifically, this chapter examines how new levels of class solidarity and cohesion were promoted by business interest groups.

3. For further discussion of the Bolivian Revolution of 1952 and its aftermath, see James M. Malloy, *Bolivia: The Uncompleted Revolution* (Pittsburgh: University of Pittsburgh Press, 1970); James M. Malloy and Richard Thorn, eds., *Beyond the Revolution: Bolivia since 1952* (Pittsburgh: University of Pittsburgh Press, 1971); and James Dunkerley, *Rebellion in the Veins: Political Struggle in Bolivia, 1952–82* (London: Verso, 1984).

4. Figures are taken from L. Enrique García-Rodríguez, "Structural Change and Development Policy in Bolivia," in *Modern-Day Bolivia*, ed. Jerry Ladman (Tempe: Arizona State University Press, 1982), 176.

5. For a review of the literature on economic groups, see Nathaniel H. Leff, "Industrial Organization and Entrepreneurship in the Developing Countries: The Economic Groups," *Economic Development and Cultural Change* 26, 4 (July 1978): 661–75.

6. Alejandro Portes, "Latin American Class Structures: Their Composition and Change during the Last Decades," *Latin American Research Review* 20, 3 (1985): 22.

7. Manuel E. Contreras and Domario Napoleón Pacheco, *Medio siglo de minería mediana en Bolivia 1939–1989* (La Paz: Biblioteca Minera Boliviana, 1989).

8. Mario Arrieta et al., *Agricultura en Santa Cruz: De la encomienda colonial a la empresa modernizada* (La Paz: ILDIS, 1990), 193.

9. Michael Mortimore, "The State and Transnational Banks: Lessons from the

Bolivian Crisis of External Public Indebtedness," *CEPAL Review* 5 (August 1981): 146.

10. For further information on economic groups in Santa Cruz, see Grupo de Estudios Andrés Ibáñez, *Tierra, estructura productiva, y poder en Santa Cruz* (La Paz: Centro de Estudios Andrés Ibáñez, Comité Ejecutivo de la Universidad Boliviana, 1983).

11. Miguel Fernández Moscoso, "La empresa privada y la reactivación: Apuntes para el debate," in *El rol de la empresa privada en el desarrollo*, ed. Taller de Investigaciones Socio-económicas (La Paz: ILDIS, n.d.), 47.

12. Susan Eckstein and Frances Hagopian, "The Limits of Industrialization in the Less Developed World: Bolivia," *Economic Development and Cultural Change* 23, 1 (October 1983): 81.

13. Robert Devlin, *Debt and Crisis in Latin America: The Supply Side of the Story* (Princeton: Princeton University Press, 1989).

14. Horst Grebe López, "Notas sobre la coyuntura económica y sus perspectivas," Documento de trabajo FLACSO-Bolivia, March 1988.

15. Siles Zuazo gained the presidency as the result of the decision to recall the congress elected in 1980. The congress was never seated because of the García Meza coup. The congress, in turn, elected Siles Zuazo to the presidency. Siles had won the popular vote in the 1980 presidential election by a narrow margin.

16. Juan Antonio Morales and Jeffrey Sachs link Bolivia's hyperinflation to the expansion of seignorage financing by the central government. See their analysis, "Bolivia's Economic Crisis," in *Developing Country Debt and Economic Performance*, ed. Jeffrey D. Sachs (Chicago: University of Chicago Press, 1990), 2:157–268.

17. The reference is from Albert O. Hirschman, *Exit, Voice, and Loyalty: Responses to Decline in Firms, Organizations, and States* (Cambridge: Harvard University Press, 1970). The notions of exit and voice were used by Jeffrey A. Frieden, "Winners and Losers in the Latin American Debt Crisis: The Political Implications," in *Debt and Democracy in Latin America*, ed. Barbara Stallings and Robert Kaufman (Boulder, Colo.: Westview, 1989), 39–58. On investor shyness, see Juan Antonio Morales, "Bolivia's Post-Stabilization Problems," Documento de trabajo, Instituto de Investigaciones Socioeconómicas, Universidad Católica Boliviana, June 1990.

18. See the previously cited work by Carlos Díaz-Alejandro and Miguel Rodríguez. For a discussion of such behavior in the Peruvian case, see Richard Webb, "Internal Debt and Financial Adjustment in Peru," *CEPAL Review* (August 1987): 55–74. For further discussion of the origins and effects of recent capital flight, see Manuel Pastor, "Capital Flight from Latin America," *World Development* 18, 1 (1990): 1–18.

19. Jonathan Eaton, "Public Debt Guarantees and Private Capital Flight," *World Bank Economic Review* 1, 3 (May 1987): 377–95; Jonathan Easton and Mark Gersovitz, "Country Risk and the Organization of International Capital

Transfer," in *Debt, Stabilization, and Development*, ed. Guillermo Calvo et al. (Cambridge: Basil Blackwell/WIDER, 1989), 109–29.

20. Oscar Ugarteche, *El estado deudor: Economía política de la deuda, Perú y Bolivia 1968–84* (Lima: Instituto de Estudios Peruanos, 1986); and Devlin, *Debt and Crisis in Latin America*.

21. Figure is cited by Morales and Sachs, "Bolivia's Economic Crisis," 213.

22. Interviews, Santa Cruz, 27 July 1990 and 29 July 1990.

23. The observation is by Flavio Machicado Saravia, *Sistema financiero y reactivación* (La Paz: ILDIS, 1989), 59. The reference is taken from Gabriel García Márquez's short story, *El coronel no tiene quien le escriba* (Buenos Aires: Editorial Sudamericana, 1969), trans. as "No One Writes to the Colonel," in Gabriel García Márquez, *Collected Stories* (New York: Harper and Row, 1984).

24. Machicado Saravia, *Sistema financiero*, 45.

25. Ibid., 25.

26. The reference is from Guillermo O'Donnell and Philippe Schmitter, *Tentative Conclusions about Uncertain Democracies* (Baltimore: Johns Hopkins University Press, 1986), 48–56.

27. Industrialists had been part of the Cámara Nacional de Comercio until 1931 when they split to form their own Cámara de Fomento Industrial; this was transformed in 1937 into the Cámara Nacional de Industrias. See Cámara Nacional de Industrias, *Breve historia de la industria nacional* (La Paz: Empresa Editora Gráfica, n.d.). The Bankers Association was founded in 1957.

28. The AMM was founded in 1939. For a discussion of the early interest organization that preceded the AMM, see William L. Lofstram, "Attitudes of an Industrial Pressure Group in Latin America: The Asociación de Industriales Mineros de Bolivia," M.A. thesis, Cornell University, 1968.

29. Interview, CEPB, La Paz, 18 February 1986.

30. Interview, La Paz, 11 February 1987.

31. I treat business's role in the transition in "Retreat to Democracy: Business and Political Transition in Bolivia and Ecuador," in *Democratic Transition and Consolidation in Southern Europe, Latin America, and Southeast Asia*, ed. Diane Ethier (London: Macmillan, 1990), 73–90.

32. Gonzalo Flores, "Movimiento regional cruceño: Aproximación e hipótesis," in *Crisis, democracia y conflicto social: La acción colectiva en Bolivia 1982–1985*, ed. Roberto Laserna (Cochabamba: CERES, 1985), 262.

33. Roberto Laserna, "La protesta territorial (La acción colectiva regional y urbana en una coyuntura de crisis democrática)," in *Crisis, democracia y conflicto social*, 203–52.

34. Guillermo O'Donnell, *Bureaucratic-Authoritarianism: Argentina 1966–1976 in Comparative Perspective*, trans. James McGuire (Berkeley: University of California Press, 1988), 24–30.

35. "Discurso de clausura del Ing. Fernando Illanes de la Riva en el encuentro de la libre empresa," *Pensamiento y acción de la empresa privada 1982–1985* (La Paz: CEPB, 1985), 295.

36. Information on the development of the CEPB is taken from numerous interviews conducted with CEPB officials from 1986 through 1990.

37. *Presencia*, 10 April 1983.

38. *El Diario*, 28 May 1983.

39. *Presencia*, 18 August 1983.

40. Ibid.

41. *El Diario*, 29 September 1983.

42. A Bolivian chapter of de Soto's Instituto Libertad y Democracia was founded in 1989 in Cochabamba. See *El Mundo*, 5 January 1989. The institute floundered, however, and by 1991 was moribund.

43. *Presencia*, 28 April 1988.

44. Grupo de Estudios Andrés Ibáñez, *Tierra, estructura productiva, y poder en Santa Cruz*.

45. President León Febres-Cordero of Ecuador, who governed from 1984 to 1988, launched his political career as president of the Guayaquil Chamber of Industries. In Peru, Vargas Llosa's Movimiento Libertad drew a number of high-profile business group leaders into politics who went on to become congressional candidates in the 1990 election.

46. *Presencia*, 6 May 1983.

47. Sánchez de Lozada went on to a narrow win of the popular vote in the 1989 election. In accordance with Bolivia's constitution, the election was thrown into the congress for a final decision since no candidate achieved a majority. A political agreement struck between Banzer's ADN and Paz Zamora's MIR denied Sánchez de Lozada the presidency. The position went to Jaime Paz Zamora.

48. The politics surrounding the launching of the neoliberal project in Bolivia is described in Catherine Conaghan et al., "Business and the 'Boys': The Politics of Neoliberalism in the Central Andes," *Latin American Research Review* 25, 2 (1990): 3–30.

49. For a discussion of "gonismo," see Carlos F. Toranzo Roca and Mario Arrieta Abdalla, *Nueva derecha y desproletarianización* (La Paz: UNITAS-ILDIS, 1989), 58–69.

50. For a discussion of the new pressures exerted by internal institutions, see Miles Kahler, "Orthodoxy and Its Alternatives: Explaining Approaches to Stabilization and Adjustment," in *Economic Crisis and Policy Choice: The Politics of Adjustment in the Third World*, ed. Joan Nelson (Princeton: Princeton University Press, 1990), 33–62. For a discussion of the "Washington consensus" on restructuring, see John Williamson, "What Washington Means by Policy Reform," in *Latin American Adjustment: How Much Has Happened?* ed. John Williamson (Washington, D.C.: Institute for International Economics, 1990), 5–20.

51. These figures are cited in Godofrino Sandoval and M. Fernanda Sostres, *La ciudad prometida: Pobladores y organizaciones sociales en El Alto* (La Paz: ILDIS, 1989), 147.

52. Alvaro Aguirre Badani et al., *NPE: Recesión económica* (La Paz: CEDLA, 1990), 151.

53. For a discussion of this process, see Carlos F. Toranzo Roca, "La desproleta-rización e 'informalización' y sus efectos sobre el movimiento popular," in Toranzo Roca and Arrieta Abdalla, *Nueva derecha y desproletarización*, 115–41. Also see CEDLA, *El sector informal urbano en Bolivia* (La Paz: CEDLA, 1988). For further discussion of the decomposition of the labor movement, see Jorge Lazarte, "El movimiento obrero: Crisis y opción del futuro de la COB," in *Crisis del sindicalismo en Bolivia*, ed. FLACSO-ILDIS (La Paz: FLACSO-ILDIS, 1988), 251–59.

54. See "Ya no son fantasmas: ¿Volverán con territorio y dignidad?" *Informe R* 10, 203 (September 1990); "El fin de una larga marcha," *Informe R* 10, 204 (October 1990).

55. "Congreso extraordinario: Lento pero . . . seguro," *Informe R* 10, 194 (May 1990).

56. Quoted in "La esperanza en el futuro," *Informe R* 10, 204 (October 1990).

57. For a discussion of the tension between reform and entrepreneurial func-tions, see Albert O. Hirschman, "The Turn to Authoritarianism in Latin America and the Search for Its Economic Determinants," in *The New Authoritarianism in Latin America*, ed. David Collier (Princeton: Princeton University Press, 1979), 87–97.

58. "Mensaje a los empresarios por el Presidente de la CEPB, Lic. Carlos Itur-ralde Ballivian, 5 February 1988," in *Memoria anual 1987–1988* (La Paz: CEPB, 1988).

59. *El Mundo*, 24 March 1990.

60. *Hoy*, 27 June 1990.

61. *Hoy*, 2 July 1990.

62. The transcript of the commercial appears in Raúl Rivadeneira Prada, *Agre-sión política: El proceso electoral 1989* (La Paz: Libreria Editorial 'Juventud', 1989), 144–45.

63. For an amusing look at the colorful language of Bolivian politics, see Waldo Peña Cazas, *El lenguaje político en Bolivia: Guia para entender el oficialismo y la oposición* (Cochabamba: Ediciones Runa, 1991).

64. David Vogel, *Fluctuating Fortunes: The Political Power of Business in America* (New York: Basic Books, 1989). Also see Thomas Ferguson and Joel Rogers, *Right Turn: The Decline of the Democrats and the Future of American Politics* (New York: Hill and Wang, 1986).

65. Certainly, strong populist challenges to business have also been a feature of American life. For a discussion of the growth of support for business in the United States, see Louis Galambos, *The Public Image of Big Business in America, 1880–1949* (Baltimore: Johns Hopkins University Press, 1975).

66. Adam Przeworksi, *Capitalism and Social Democracy* (Cambridge: Cam-bridge University Press, 1985), 133–63.

67. Interview, Santa Cruz, 25 July 1990.

68. For a fascinating discussion of Fernandez as head of the party Unión Cívica

Solidaridad, see Fernando Mayorga, *Max Fernández: La política del silencio* (La Paz: ILDIS, 1991).

69. For a discussion of the development of the "burgesía chola" in Bolivia, see Carlos F. Toranzo, "Los rasgos de la nueva derecha," in Toranzo Roca and Arrieta Abdalla, *Nueva derecha y desproletarianización*, 43–75.

70. James C. Scott, *Domination and the Art of Resistance: Hidden Transcripts* (New Haven: Yale University Press, 1990), 67–68. Scott develops the notion of "public" versus "hidden" transcripts in this insightful work. He defines the public transcript as the official discourse of the dominant, while the hidden transcript is the discourse of subordinates that takes place outside of the direct observation of the dominant.

Francisco Durand

4. From Fragile Crystal to Solid Rock

The Formation and Consolidation of a
Business Peak Association in Peru

Since 1980, Latin America has witnessed business efforts in many countries to create and/or consolidate "peak" associations (also known as umbrella organizations or comprehensive organizations) that represent the business sector as a whole. These efforts have coincided with other deep changes taking place in the region: the transition to democracy and the adoption of liberal economic policies. The two phenomena are closely related. Peak associations emerged as business's collective reaction to profound alterations in both the economic and political rules of the game. This reaction, in turn, was possible because a new generation of business leaders seized the opportunity for collective action and sought to develop and strengthen umbrella organizations. It was not easy. Business people had to struggle hard to form them, to consolidate them, and to achieve social recognition from their own peers and others—the state, political parties, and civil society.

This political issue is crucial to understanding collective business action in Latin America because institutions have to be properly built before they can play a positive role in defending interests related to specific policies. In this transitional period when the business umbrella organizations are emerging but still lack consolidation, economic and political dynamics overlap yet should not be confused. There is a struggle around specific issues of economic policy and, at the same time, a struggle over consolidation and recognition of political institutions. The achievement of these two goals depends on the ability of business leaders to act, despite objective economic differences and political disagreements. Internal discipline to mobilize the business sector as a whole, and to avoid interference from other actors who might take advantage of business's lack of cohesion, is seen as an indispensable requirement for a more effective role of peak associations in the political arena.

Peru in this context is a fascinating case. After a ten-year struggle, the Confederation of Private Entrepreneurial Institutions (CONFIEP) was finally founded in 1984. But it took several skirmishes and one final battle with President García (the 1987 nationalization of the banks) to strengthen the organization and obtain internal and external recognition. It is a case where the drama of changing circumstances was fittingly combined with organizational vitality and astute business leadership.

The Peculiar Character of Latin American Business

The emergence of a peak association is a major event in business politics, and in politics in general, for any country.[1] Peak associations emerge when the industrialization process is well under way and business people feel an urgent political necessity for organized collective action. In that moment, several trade associations, representing different sectors and regions, are united under a single representative institution. This institution is unique because it becomes the mouthpiece for the business sector as a whole, an attribute that is recognized by

PERU • 143

other pressure groups (such as labor), political parties, and the state. This recognition, granted according to the rules of the political system, is important and necessary, since the organization represents those who control economic resources. Business peak associations gradually become an essential part of the system of interest representation.[2]

The emergence of business peak associations in the United States and Western Europe (for example, the U.S. National Association of Manufacturers and Italy's Confederazione Italiana Dell' Industria) was a sign of the collective development that began to occur in developed countries as early as 1885 and 1910.[3] That is why scholars can take for granted, as Claus Offe argues, the "solid and undisputable acceptance" of a system of interest representation.[4] Is this the case in Latin America?

The appearance of a modern business elite began late in the region, compared to developed countries, as did business trade associations and peak associations. But, together with the timing of industrialization, there were other more significant distinguishing factors: the economic weakness of native elite groups and their political ineffectiveness. In Latin America, peak associations did not become an expression of business political activism until the 1980s.[5] Between 1935 and 1944, such associations were formed in only two countries, Chile and Venezuela. Paraguay and Bolivia followed in the next two decades, and Mexico, Nicaragua, and Peru in the 1970s and 1980s. In several countries (Argentina, Ecuador, and Colombia), trade associations are still struggling to create a confederation or have attempted to build temporary coordinating organisms.[6] The business associations that have arisen in Brazil have yet to demonstrate notable effectiveness.

Thus, in Latin America, business peak associations are a rather recent phenomenon, and their stature and impact are conditioned by the economic weakness and degree of politicization on the part of native business people.[7] The national private sector in Latin America, unlike that of developed countries, does not play a dominant role in the economy and is rarely unified as a hegemonic political player. These facts deeply affect the nature of the relationship with the state and other actors. The economic weakness question must be understood because it means that business in general, and peak associations in particular, are not particularly important for the state, which is always more interested in powerful investors (but is potentially able to "protect" the weak). Lack of economic hegemony conditions the game played by national business and its organizations. Economic weakness, however, cannot be automatically translated into political weakness, as some scholars would have it.[8] This correlation is too simple to be of any analytical use because national business still represents a political force of some significance and participates, even as a minor partner, in political coalitions. Its relative importance can be enhanced if there is internal unity and if leaders are able to participate in or create coalitions. In sum, economic weakness can be compensated by organizational means, particularly by forming umbrella organizations and participating in broader probusiness alliances.

These developments indeed took place in Latin America in the 1980s, stimulated by overall social changes. In the midst of an economic crisis, the region experienced two major transformations in the 1980s: a transition to democracy and to liberal economic policies. The change away from authoritarian or semiauthoritarian regimes (*democracia limitada*) was not merely one more swing of the Latin American pendulum. The adoption of democracy was accompanied by much deeper legal transformations: many countries adopted new constitutions (or are in the process of changing existing ones), and many laws have been changed or are under revision. The political transition, then, defined a whole new set of rules for political players, business included. At the same time, democracy provided an environment more suitable for and more tolerant of organizational initiatives. It encouraged business people to raise their voices and to bargain more freely than under a military regime. Even though the militarism of the 1970s was more determined to suppress grass-roots organizations and unions than business associations, the latter were also constrained by authoritarian rule, and in some cases such as Argentina, were directly affected.[9] Democracy gave the business sector new opportunities for political participation.

The transition from protectionist economic policies to more open trade policies also had a stimulating effect on business political activism. The new set of policies deeply affected vested interests, with varied results. While industrialists and manufacturers had to face foreign competition and were negatively affected by open trade policies, others, such as exporters and the so-called Groups (diversified economic conglomerates with a special interest in export-import activities and in control of the banking sector), clearly benefited. Despite the diversity of interests and the constant struggle between defenders of import substitution industrialization and advocates of free trade that characterizes much of Latin America, business people felt the need to organize and to mobilize themselves collectively to reject the changes or, eventually, to set the pace and the conditions under which liberal policies were adopted. It must be noted that this economic transition (accompanied by a deep recession) also affected public firms. The decline in the number of public firms owing to privatization weakened those that were left, and as a result the national private sector became an increasingly important investor. The debt crisis also made governments that badly needed investment more sensitive to private-sector demands. The 1980s and 1990s are thus a new era, one that is crucial for understanding the emergence and consolidation of business peak associations in Latin America.

A final caveat is necessary here. Studies have correctly pointed out critical units of analysis—constituents, internal cohesion, representation, types of demands, modes of influence, and expectations and reactions of those who deal with peak associations (the state, labor)—that are all acutely important.[10] As a step toward contextualizing such units, we should examine how associations are formed and how business is politicized—that is, the "logic of consolidation" of umbrella organizations and the business sector as a political actor.[11] The nature of the units of analysis just mentioned depends on the growth and organizational development of peak associations. A feeble peak association, with low levels of representation, cannot deal with the state on key issues in the same way as a strong and highly representative association.

In the transitional period, when peak associations are consolidating and moving toward a strong position, they begin to acquire a defined location in the new institutional universe. As a result, relations between peak business associations and other private and public institutions undergo a change.

Origins of Peru's Peak Association

The 1980s and early 1990s have seen deep changes in the system of interest representation in Peru that are reflected not only in social actors' initiatives but also in the nation's overall political and economic performance. The country moved to a democratic regime in 1980, after adopting a new constitution in 1978. In the 1980s, there were several attempts to change economic policies as social actors and political institutions tried to assess the costs and benefits of these changes. Economic liberalism in general and free trade policies in particular were initially advocated by the Morales Bermudez government (1975–1980) and continued during Belaúnde's administration (1980–1985); however, the opposition was able to stop this trend momentarily, and during García's government (1985–1990) Peru moved back to nationalist and protectionist policies. In 1990, president Fujimori adopted stabilization plans and deepened the liberalization of the economy.

These policy changes were attempted in a context of continuing economic crisis and rising political violence that became the trademarks of the decade. In the 1980s Peru suffered two great depressions: in 1983 when the annual growth rate of GDP plummeted to −12.3 percent, and in 1988 and 1989 when GDP fell to −8.3 percent and −11.6 percent, respectively. Inflation was another constant element in the troubled economic scenario: between 1983 and 1990 the inflation rate has always exceeded 78 percent and reached a record high in 1990, with an annual growth rate in consumer prices of 7,482 percent.

Policy experiments, combined with negative economic trends, provided a fertile ground for those willing to bet on revolutionary armed struggle. Two guerrilla movements (the Shining Path and the Tupac Amaru Revolutionary Movement) started to operate in 1980 and 1983, respectively, generating a wave of political violence from below and from above. Between 1981 and 1989, 1,819 police and military officers were killed, while 6,808 guerrillas died in the same period, a fact that did not prevent escalating terrorist attacks: 17,358 from 1980 to 1989. In this context of instability, recession, and violence, economic interest groups experienced deep changes. Grass-roots organizations and unions were negatively affected by high rates of unemployment and declining standards of living, while business organizations experienced a surge of political activism.

Several factors help to explain the politicization of business. The state was severely weakened as an economic agent, and foreign credit and investment declined sharply. Both facts enhanced the political importance of the national private sector and showed that the relationship between the state and civil society was being transformed. It is in this context that Peru's peak business association was created. A comparison between state-business relations in the 1970s and in the 1980s sheds light on this process.

Peru's new system of interest representation emerged as follows. In 1968, under Velasco, Peru was governed by a military populist regime that developed an interventionist state. In the early 1970s, unions and "popular" organizations developed quickly, partly because the state, seeking to create social bases of support, sponsored them and partly because of the autonomous dynamism of civil society. A strong state (*dirigiste* and authoritarian) also dealt with business trade associations according to their stance (positive or negative) toward the government and the "structural reforms" being implemented (agrarian reform, nationalizations, the industrial communities). In 1969 the government first eliminated the rural trade association—the National Agrarian Society—to facilitate extensive expropriations of land. Then, after 1970, the government moved to isolate those trade associations that rejected reforms—the National Industrial Society—and openly favored those who supported dialogue with the state.[12] But the state, no matter how hard it tried, never succeeded in imposing its rule over a civil society, bourgeois or proletarian, that jealously guarded its tradition of "autonomy."

In the 1970s, business associations remained autonomous but divided, unable to participate actively in policy making and limiting themselves to "dialogue" with the state or to angry reaction against decisions taken without any prior consultation. Attempts to break out of isolation and act cohesively, when business interests were threatened by nationalizations or when policy changes affected their interests, failed twice. The first attempt occurred in 1974 when the National Industrial Society tried unsuccessfully to create a United Front for the Defense of Private Property in order to oppose the nationalization of the fishing industry. Most trade associations, feeling economically and politically weak, did not dare to challenge Velasco and opted for silence to avoid trouble or to win particular favors from the state. Later, in 1977, when General Morales Bermudez, Velasco's successor, decided to shift the course of the military revolution and "reform the reforms" (to cope with a severe economic recession and the effects of the external debt crisis), a new peak association emerged. The Private Business Union of Peru (UEPP) was formed by seven trade associations, but it did not last long. UEPP was dissolved six months later after its leaders failed to maintain internal unity or to adopt a common position with regard to radical policy changes implemented under pressure from the International Monetary Fund. The sharp division of interests within the private sector (for and against economic liberalization) helped bring about the demise of UEPP. In addition, state officials consciously reinforced internal divisions by favoring exporters and isolating industrialists, in order to neutralize them as political players.[13]

It is important to remember that the factors that prevented the formation of a business peak association in the 1970s had to do with business's internal problems and with state obstacles to class cohesion. Blocking the formation of a peak association were the prevailing divisions among trade associations and business people in general, not only because of differences in economic interests but also because of political differences. In particular, disagreements arose over how business people should unite and how to ensure democratic procedures in the selection of leaders. Business also feared confronting an authoritarian government. The first United Front failed in 1974 because trade associations were unwilling to fight a powerful government and instead opted for accommodation. In the second attempt, when the UEPP was formed in 1977, policy makers tried to exacerbate internal divisions by granting special favors to exporters and economic power groups while seeking to isolate the industrialists.

But outcomes in Peru of the 1970s cannot be measured only in terms of failure to form a business peak association. A unified organizational project was still pursued by business leaders, who decided to evaluate their experience and to find a better time to found a peak association. Gian Flavio Gerbolini, a textile industrialist and leader of Action for Development, an important entrepreneurial institution, used to say, referring to their political experience, "We learn the hard way." Indeed, the learning process had already begun and had lasting consequences in the next decade. The legacy of the 1970s was the growth of business leadership and the ability to learn from failure.

In the late 1970s and 1980s, the system of interest representation changed dramatically under several influences. A new constitution was approved in 1979, granting trade associations the right to organize freely and reestablishing the rights to private property. The constitution introduced a new bargaining concept, typical of the 1980s, known as "concerted action." Economic interest groups (business and labor) and the state could agree on policy changes in order to develop plans for economic development (*planificación concertada*).[14] Additionally, the powers of the executive were enhanced. The constitution authorized the cabinet and the president to issue decree laws under several legal modalities.[15] These new rules of the game influenced the behavior of economic interest groups, who tried to adapt themselves to the new constitution.

Civil society remained even more autonomous in the 1980s, after political liberalization, but the balance among economic interest groups differed greatly from the previous decade, not only because of political changes but also because of changing economic trends. During the Great Depression of the 1980s, unions and peasant organizations were weakened and had less bargaining power, while scattered "informal-sector" organizations and "survival" organizations flourished to cope with the crisis. But even these gains were limited because beginning in 1990 the Shining Path, a violent guerrilla movement, began to attack and dismantle these groups. With regard to business associations, the trend was the opposite. Their activity increased, as a reaction to macroeconomic policy changes and a constantly increasing rate of political and social violence.[16]

In 1984, a business peak association, the Confederation of Private Entrepreneurial Institutions (CONFIEP), was finally formed and legally recognized by the state and by the International Labor Organization.[17] In this period, the state was severely weakened by the fiscal crisis, the private sector's effective political offensive, and external forces pressing to reduce its role in the economy.[18] A hectic period of policy changes started, aggravated by the continuing economic crisis. Some policy steps taken in the early 1980s, without consultation and issued by the executive in most cases, were supported by the private sector: labor laws and moves to weaken the state, for instance. Others, such as tariffs, floating exchange and interest rates, affected industrialists and were criticized by several trade associations. As the crisis deepened, it affected all business sectors, making the economic differences among business groups less significant. In 1984, the Peruvian bourgeoisie demanded the adoption of "emergency" policies to avoid general bankruptcy and overtly struggled against open trade policies; by so doing, it began to organize itself collectively.

The formation of CONFIEP was thus stimulated by a changing economic and political environment, particularly by three main sources of instability: continuing stagflation, rising terrorism, and policy shifts. Peru had become unpredictable in the 1980s, and the response of the business sector to extreme uncertainty was expressed in organizational developments. That is why one of CONFIEP's first claims did not have to do with specific policy issues but with demands to put an end to *inestabilidad jurídica*—that is, continually changing policies and policy orientations. Business organizations reacted positively to a particularly hectic, unstable environment, trying to offset unpredictability by increasing their political influence, hoping to make politics and policies less erratic.

In sum, political and economic changes clearly encouraged

the formation and determined the character of Peru's first business peak association. More specific analysis, however, is necessary to explain the politicization of the Peruvian bourgeoisie and to identify the critical factors that led to the creation of a peak association. The formation of CONFIEP, more concretely, occurred for the following reasons:

1. The active role played by a cadre of politically experienced business leaders. The leaders were known in business circles as *gremialistas*—that is, those who defended trade associations and fought for the formation, consolidation, and recognition of a comprehensive business organization. The *gremialistas* acknowledged the importance of internal divisions and rivalries among trade associations and knew that policy makers were unwilling to go along with *concertación* because it limited their autonomy. The leaders were fully aware that high state officials sponsored separate dealings with individual trade associations as a way of interfering with their internal unity. In the 1980s, the *gremialistas* took full advantage of a democratic climate to demand participation in the policy-making process despite resistance from state officials.

2. The growth of business unity in 1983–1984. Class cohesion tended to prevail over divisions among individuals and/or economic sectors, favoring united action. The leaders seized the opportunity in 1984 when the general economic crisis forced all segments to mobilize and when the government's unpredictability became a serious worry. The business sector was able to exploit a unique opportunity for forging extensive unity. Even if differences resurfaced later on, the confederation could arbitrate conflicts among business factors and mobilize core action.

3. The demonstration that collective action by business produces tangible results. CONFIEP was formed in November 1984, three months after a group of trade associations united against the government's attempt to impose a new tax raising

the cost of credit transactions from 8 to 17 percent. This became a public political confrontation known to the press as *el lío del 17%*. Business unity and mobilization successfully forced the government to limit the tax increase to 10 percent. This first battle ended in a tangible victory for the united front. It became a "demonstration of mutual advantages" obtained by collective action.[19]

Finding a Place in a New Organizational Universe (Hacerse Sitio)

The emergence of a peak association modifies both relations among trade associations and those linking business to the state, political parties, and labor unions. When the newly founded organization emerges, a new point on the institutional map appears and the lines joining organizations and classes are gradually redrawn. The system of interest representation is affected as the business peak association struggles to consolidate itself, to be seen by "others" as an institution that not only enjoys formal recognition but also seeks social recognition. In Peru, business leaders refer to this issue as CONFIEP's need to become *un interlocutor válido*, that is, to be recognized by the state and others as a valid representative of collective business interests. The process by which CONFIEP gradually gained an invitation to the bargaining table to hold dialogues, consultations, and negotiations with the state was neither immediate nor easy.[20]

The political game was altered as CONFIEP emerged, because how business influenced the state was being conditioned by the process of institutional consolidation. For CONFIEP, the idea was not only to be a member of a club of organizations but also a member with the prestige and recognition granted by its peers and by others as the single spokesman for the private sector. This means that, in order to exist, CONFIEP could not afford to be ignored. The process of institutional consolidation will be illustrated with reference to two types of political battles: the struggle to achieve recognition from the García government and disputes over the nomination of business leaders to serve on government commissions. CONFIEP's first battle is particularly illustrative. In 1985, Alan García's government received strong support from the business sector and CONFIEP because García temporarily eliminated one worrying factor: he shifted from recessionary neoliberal to protectionist and demand-stimulation economic policies.[21] García, however, was reluctant to admit CONFIEP as a permanent member at the bargaining table. A loose political alliance with business based on its support for an administration that changed economic policies in a direction desired by most business segments was one thing, but it was quite another to expect García to share policy-making decisions with business organizations.

García did not feel he had to reduce his room to maneuver in order to please the members of the ruling coalition. On one occasion, he told one of Peru's top business leaders, Juan Francisco Raffo, "Leave politics to me." By that, García meant that he expected the business sector not to involve itself in politics and not to interfere directly policy making.[22] Many policy makers (*técnicos*) shared García's concern because they were reluctant to divulge information and to be constrained by CONFIEP, which demanded real recognition as the mouthpiece of the private sector and consultation over policy decisions taken by the executive, a branch empowered by the new constitution.

In its first meeting with García, after he was elected president (May 1985), CONFIEP demanded *concertación institucionalizada*, including negotiations with labor confederations, to deal with a number of issues. García dismissed the proposal on the grounds that the Communist labor confederation (CGTP) was too problematic. CONFIEP, however, pressed this key issue because the problem was not only that labor was being ignored: the question of recognition was critical. In 1986 and 1987, the author conducted personal interviews with all sixteen leaders of trade associations belonging to CONFIEP and with the peak association's first two presidents.[23] The issue of recognition was raised by all of them. The issue was perceived as more important than specific policies being discussed, such as labor laws, taxes, custom duties, price controls, the external debt, and investment incentives.

CONFIEP's first clash with García came in late 1985. In a move typical of Peruvian policy makers, accustomed to acting on their own but conscious of potential reactions from civil society, the government approved, without any prior consultation, a decree law (DS 362) modifying tax incentives for investments in all economic sectors. The measure was approved on December 27, a day when protest was not expected—two days after Christmas, four before New Year's Eve, and one day before the end of the 1986 legislature.[24] CONFIEP's first reaction was cautious, avoiding an open display of displeasure. Nevertheless, it pressed hard to suspend the decree law until discussions about its implications for the business sector were held.[25] The government, reacting to business pressure, decided to hold a dialogue.

In early 1986, CONFIEP leaders and several ministers met and agreed to create a commission to discuss DS 362, but the commission failed to materialize owing to the administration's lack of interest. When CONFIEP sensed that the commission was basically a diversionary move, it started a mail campaign, sending letters that were never answered. Later, frustrated by the ineffectiveness of that tactic, CONFIEP's leaders started to send telexes directly to the prime minister, but weeks passed and the government remained silent. Finally, after all other initiatives failed, a meeting with García himself took place in mid-1986. But the process just started all over again: promises of commissions that were never formed! It was now clear that it was the president himself who had devised this tactic. The dialogue, held first with cabinet members and later with the president, did not lead to negotiations as CONFIEP expected, but these events contributed toward a process of organizational consolidation that must be understood in a larger perspective.

The issue at stake was not so much taxes but what the peak association perceived as a negative attitude of *políticos* and *técnicos* toward dialogue, consultation, or negotiation about policy decisions. As Edgardo Palza, manager of CONFIEP, stated: "This was a question of principles, not taxes."[26] CONFIEP's position was backed by all trade associations, but there was some hesitation about going further because it could endanger the whole alliance with García. The general interests of business prevailed in two senses: the need for collective action and the need for caution to maintain the alliance with García. "We agree on twenty out of twenty-one policy decisions," CONFIEP leaders used to say, trying to emphasize business support for policy measures, but they insisted that "this one" (DS 362) implied lack of consultation and unwillingness to accept concerted action. CONFIEP was not willing to give up because the consolidation of the peak association was clearly at stake, as well as the definition of the rules of the game.

Other battles followed. The appointment of business leaders to government councils has traditionally been the state's prerogative, but CONFIEP wanted to put an end to arbitrary selection of business leaders by high state officials. CONFIEP's reasoning was clear: if trade associations now count on a confederation that represents them collectively, and if CONFIEP speaks for the private sector, then the state has to consult with CONFIEP before appointing business representatives. This second battle had several rounds. First, the minister of economy and finance formed an advisory committee in 1985 and decided to appoint to it one leading businessman (Dionisio Romero, a powerful investor) and CONFIEP's first two presidents (Julio Piccini and Miguel Vega Alvear). Both CONFIEP members accepted the nomination because the state implicitly recognized the existence of CONFIEP, but they politely insisted that it would be better if the minister would ask CONFIEP itself to nominate "representative leaders" (*empresarios gremiales representativos*). A second round came in 1986, when the National Planning Institute created a consultative commission and appointed a number of individual entrepreneurs and trade association leaders, including CONFIEP's president. The same line of action followed: CONFIEP accepted the appointments, but reminded the government that it would prefer to be consulted first. CONFIEP's first victory came in 1987 when in a newly created organism, the Institute of Foreign Trade (ICE), a consultative commission, was formed. In this third round, ICE leaders and CONFIEP agreed on the composition of the committee.

Lack of Class Cohesion: A Permanent Danger

Internal divisions are among the most difficult problems afflicting a business peak association. Besides market competition among firms belonging to the same economic sector, differences in size and types of economic activity (manufacturing industry, agriculture, banking, etcetera), can negatively affect the cohesiveness of the business sector until particular interests (for example, the defense of the internal market) makes it impossible to defend general interests (the overall influence of business on the political and policy process). These divisions, at the same time, give rivals or enemies a political advantage; they can be used politically to reinforce the divisions and neutralize or reverse business-sector action.

A peak association emerges when the business sector can distinguish between general and particular interests, when it learns to mediate conflicts among members, when it becomes politically capable of speaking with a single voice and avoiding outside interference. Nevertheless, a business peak association has one disadvantage when compared to labor unions: it does not have binding rules. Business peak associations, on the other hand, are not influenced by political parties, as are labor unions.[27] The Peruvian business peak association, for example, is fairly independent from political parties, but internal cohesion is difficult to achieve and maintain. The two following cases illustrate this point.

The issue that tested the resolution of CONFIEP, DS 362, also explains the causes and consequences of internal divisions. As noted above, member trade associations supported CONFIEP's position against reducing tax incentives for investors for two reasons: first, because the measure touched the interests of all trade associations; second, because they considered that CONFIEP had the right to demand dialogue, consultation, and negotiation—a right that was not fully recognized by García's government. Business unity, however, was more solidarity among leaders of member trade associations rather than a solid class unity.

The *gremialista* leaders at work in CONFIEP knew that it was a poor idea to raise issues that were not supported by all or most members. The need for consensus was based on their earlier collective political experience and reflected an internal agreement: CONFIEP could act only when leaders of all member trade associations agreed. In addition to the consensus rule, the founders also decided that CONFIEP's president could not be reelected and that all trade association leaders had to rotate in the presidency. Finally, it was also informally agreed that CONFIEP spoke only on general matters, letting individual trade associations deal with issues involving particular interests.

García's government was not disposed to open a dialogue about DS 362 because it assumed that policy decisions (decree laws) approved by the executive did not require consultation. But there was more than that, and this case reveals why the government did not care to listen to CONFIEP's complaints. It is true that all trade associations were against DS 362—and they acted accordingly, using CONFIEP as the spokesman of the private sector—but individual capitalists were not equally affected. According to the Peruvian Industrial Law of 1983, foreign corporations and larger national firms are entitled to sign a "tax stability contract" with the state for a given period.

When the government issued DS 362, policy makers knew they could get away with it despite CONFIEP's pressures because "the big ones" were not touched by it. This fact was even publicly recognized by the minister of industry, Manuel Romero, who asserted: "The vast majority of large firms . . . signed stability contracts with us at the end of 1985, so later laws [DS 362] do not affect them."[28] CONFIEP's strong institutional pressure was weakened because a handful of powerful firms were not interested in modifying DS 362. It is clear, then, that lack of class cohesion weakened CONFIEP's role.

The danger of internal divisions also arises from rivalries among business institutions and the state's subtle interference in class unity. The case to be analyzed concerns this issue and also sheds light on how the system of interest representation is reordered once a new organization is added to the mix.

The actors in this conflict are CONFIEP and the Peruvian Institute of Business Administration (IPAE), an educational entity founded in 1962 to train middle managers and to disseminate the ideas of "scientific management." Before CONFIEP emerged, trade associations lacked cohesion and acted without coordination, but through IPAE they could hold an informal collective dialogue with the state. Every November IPAE organized a highly publicized conference (Conferencia Anual de Ejecutivos, CADE) to discuss management problems and business issues. When the military government closed Congress in 1968, IPAE continued to hold the conference and, since all formal mechanisms of access to the state were closed, it decided to invite the military leaders to discuss economic policies at its annual meeting. Since then, the CADE conference has become the major business-government event of the year.

IPAE, comprised only of individual firms and entrepreneurs, not trade associations, organized a forum (*tribuna de diálogo*) to which entrepreneurs from all sectors were invited. Business people were attracted because CADE conferences were usually attended by cabinet members and, on the last day, by the president himself. For the government, CADEs were important for obtaining useful information about business. They were also occasionally used by the government to announce new measures, to foster dialogue, and to consult informally about policy changes with progovernment business leaders. But the CADE meeting, by definition, was not a bargaining table. The only organization allowed to "represent" the business sector and bargain on its behalf was a peak association. Since CONFIEP was not founded until 1984 and trade associations were usually divided, most business people tolerated the CADEs because this was the only option available to approach the military government and obtain information.[29]

CADE conferences continued over the years, despite policy and political changes, and gradually became a tradition. CADE's prestige as the *tribuna de diálogo* contrasted with that of trade associations, which used to object loudly whenever the government adopted policy measures without their knowledge. CADE and IPAE, as compared to trade associations like the National Industrial Society, had a "positive" outlook, not a "negative" one. This image also reflected the interests of IPAE's leaders, mainly from big national and multinational firms, who were interested in more informal, less institutionalized, channels of access to political power.[30]

The CADEs were the only point of contact between entrepreneurs of all economic sectors and state officials, and CONFIEP was originally conceived at a CADE meeting. The first step was taken when business leaders decided to act collectively. At CADE 1983, IPAE and trade association leaders agreed to work on a National Plan for Economic Development to be presented at CADE 1984. The objective was to produce a document that reflected the views of the business sector as a whole, so the government could know in advance the collective interests of business. The hectic economic and political environment of the mid-1980s makes this rather unusual initiative understandable: it was a collective reaction to overall social changes designed to make politics and policies more predictable. The idea of elaborating this document was justified on the grounds that the new constitution allowed social groups to present proposals based on concerted action.

A business collective dynamic started (reinforced by the economic and political circumstances of this critical moment) and achieved unforeseen results: business leaders could not determine how far events would push business toward unification. Meetings held by those charged with elaborating the economic development plan created strong bonds among them. Once their common problems became clear, because of the generalized and sharp economic decline of 1984, they decided to act collectively to protest the 17 percent tax increase, an initiative already explained. When they won the battle over credit taxes, the initiative to form CONFIEP was taken. Policy decisions could be stopped or negotiated by a threat of unified action, and permanent unity could be facilitated only through a peak association.

IPAE, then, helped to nurture CONFIEP, but CONFIEP was soon to develop its own dynamic and, eventually, compete with IPAE. The whole system of interest representation was being redefined. In the beginning, IPAE went on organizing its CADE annual conferences and CONFIEP concentrated on building its organization by incorporating new members. As of November 1984, CONFIEP had eight members. As of March 1985, two more trade associations enrolled, and a year later six more joined its ranks.[31] In two years, by 1986, CONFIEP had doubled its membership, increasing its representativeness significantly. It was ready to hold its ground against the state, as the conflict over DS 362 convincingly revealed.

García's government, however, was determined to exploit the business sector's internal divisions, relying on differences between IPAE and CONFIEP and counting on its leaders' vulnerability to temptation whenever the president offered special access to political power. In November 1985, at the CADE conference, García announced his intention to "dialogue in a permanent way" with business leaders and urged CADE organizers to form a "*CADE permanente.*" The initiative came at a moment when CONFIEP was beginning to claim that dialogue with the state was now institutionalized, that CONFIEP now "represented" the private sector.

In CADE 1985, García chose to ignore CONFIEP and to favor continuing dialogue with IPAE leaders, even if the *CADE permanente* did not represent any trade association. *CADE permanente* was a direct challenge to CONFIEP, but IPAE's president, Octavio Mavila, decided to publicly and enthusiastically support García's "historic decision."[32] In so doing, IPAE and Mavila did not bother to consult with CONFIEP. CONFIEP's reaction was to criticize Mavila quietly and to hold private meetings with IPAE leaders to reaffirm its status as the true representative of business. IPAE tried to defend its position, arguing that the dialogue was an opportunity to establish "a permanent channel of communication" with the state that could not be dismissed. IPAE also assured CONFIEP that it was not interfering with it. According to Mavila, the dialogue was limited to individual entrepreneurs who did not claim collective representativeness.

One consequence of the clash between IPAE and CONFIEP was that it helped to set the boundaries between both organizations: IPAE now knew that any interference with CONFIEP would create problems because CONFIEP was ready to defend its jurisdiction. Since IPAE was better known to the public,

CONFIEP tried to obtain further public recognition and to gain legitimacy within the business sector. After the clash, CONFIEP decided to organize an annual congress to discuss policy problems and agree on issues to be discussed with the state, collectively setting the agenda of business-government relations. The first congress, held in August 1986, effectively consolidated CONFIEP's position. The debate was publicized in the press, and the number of entrepreneurs attending it exceeded participation in the CADEs. President García was invited to give the closing address, but he declined and sent a minister instead. But the president could not ignore CONFIEP indefinitely. Once the conclusions of the congress were printed in the press and sent to the president (including the call for "concerted action" with "representative institutions"), García invited CONFIEP leaders to the presidential palace before the press started to make an issue of their misunderstandings.

IPAE did not dare to interfere with CONFIEP again, and both organizations continued to organize annual meetings. CONFIEP was finding a place in the new organizational universe, and the state and other institutions were beginning to recognize its existence. Political parties, for instance, began dialogues with CONFIEP whenever they needed to discuss business issues, and labor confederations became more concerned with the effectiveness of business pressures organized by CONFIEP.

The Battle of the Banks and CONFIEP's Final Consolidation

According to the "investment mandate" approach, because business commands key resources, the state establishes a privileged relationship with the private sector.[33] This approach, however, refers to the business class as a whole; it does not account for internal differences. If the control of key resources explains privileged business access to political power, then the most powerful business segments (or class fractions) tend to establish a more privileged relationship than weak segments. This distinction is important because it is generally accepted among scholars that a major distinction among businesses is size—between large and small firms—and that it can be expressed politically and organizationally.[34] Relations with the state need not be the same for all firms because large firms are in principle more important to the government than small ones. In Latin America a "weak national bourgeoisie" has not usually enjoyed special access and has had little influence on policy making. This situation was probably reinforced by the political weakness of the national bourgeoisie, which was internally divided, unorganized, and unable to gain allies to support its cause.

Is the situation changing in the 1980s and 1990s? We have argued that the formation of a peak association is one step toward the political mobilization of the business sector. In addition, as stated, private capital plays a more important role today because the state is incapable of leading the process of capital accumulation, as in the past. In Peru during the García administration (1985–1990), the government could not count on the public sector to reactivate the economy and had no external financial support because of its nationalist stance on payment of the external debt. Therefore, attention to the national private sector was critical despite its relative economic weakness. The national bourgeoisie was part of the government coalition and backed the new policy orientation, particularly those segments that were threatened by bankruptcy or affected by free trade policies.

Although CONFIEP was an element in this complex connection between business and the García administration, policy makers tried to ignore it or to block its consolidation because they correctly feared that CONFIEP would sooner or later interfere with the policy-making process. But the government was willing to take concerted action with large investors, owners of economic conglomerates known as Groups, to promote investment.[35] By doing so, the administration once more ignored CONFIEP, and García dared to admit openly that he dealt only with the big ones, "con los que mandan." The phrase reflects part of CONFIEP's problems, indicating that big business was willing to play another game, a game from which CONFIEP could be excluded. CONFIEP's representativeness in terms of capital was relatively low because the largest Groups could establish a private privileged relationship with the state, leaving CONFIEP in the cold.

CONFIEP dealt with this challenge in the cautious but firm way already manifested in earlier battles for institutional recognition. CONFIEP could not force the Groups to abandon special concerted action, but it could try to avoid further damage to class cohesion by tolerating the private deal and, at the same time, letting García know that it was not the proper way to approach the issue. CONFIEP also sent the message to the leaders of the twelve Groups who were engaged in this dealing that a failure in negotiations could lead to a confrontation between the Groups and the state. If the press named these powerful investors the "twelve apostles," CONFIEP leaders renamed them the "twelve prisoners" because of their political vulnerability in investment negotiations. In other words, the unpredictability of government behavior required not only caution on the part of business leaders but also a safety net that only a collective association could provide.

The struggles with the state and internal class disagreements reinforced a sense of political precariousness in the early stages of organization building, a precariousness that was perceptible among CONFIEP leaders. One of its presidents, Julio Piccini, once defined CONFIEP as a "crystal" that had to be handled with care.[36] The erratic nature of government behavior also affected business's relations with government. Business leaders in Peru talked constantly about the charming but audacious, unpredictable nature of the president (known as "Crazy Horse").

The following revealing statement illustrates the point. The various policy alternatives President García was considering became public knowledge in 1986 in a speech given on Peru's national holiday, 28 July:

One possibility for us, as some sectors propose, is to proceed with the nationalization of firms owned by Groups. However, that would generate the distrust and apprehension of the middle class, the economic agents, and would inevitably lead to a greater bureaucratization of our economy. . . . We offer a different alternative . . . through productive investment of Groups' economic surplus, according to national goals. In this way, they will not be the center of accumulation and power, or accomplices of dependency, but rather factors of support and stimuli to national development.[37]

The Groups were fairly aware of the danger and decided to play a double game: to attend CONFIEP meetings and keep in touch with trade associations who belonged to CONFIEP but to continue with the special concerted action scheme designed by García to negotiate private investment. García himself stepped up political pressure on investors because his government badly needed to maintain economic recovery. (For that reason, 1987 was officially labeled the Year of Investments).

The Groups' approach was criticized by the *gremialista* leaders who were particularly sensitive about matters of recognition, but they could not afford to fight the powerful conglomerates. A fight between CONFIEP and the Groups could have meant the end of business's precarious unity and a blow to the existence of the newly founded confederation. CONFIEP leaders, therefore, decided to introduce organizational innovations and create "special committees" that included some Group leaders. A "problem-solving" logic was applied to CONFIEP's political learning process. In that way, CONFIEP had an institutional device to exchange opinions with the Groups about policy and political matters.

Industrialist Carlos Verme, one of CONFIEP's founders, stated that the conglomerates viewed CONFIEP as a "cheap shield" (*escudo barato*) because they did not take part in the struggle to found it, but could still make use of it in case of danger. And indeed CONFIEP became a cheap shield for the Groups. In July 1987, one year after the president's enigmatic speech about different policy scenarios, the nationalization of the banks was announced without warning.[38] It is not possible here to analyze the causes and the political dynamics that led to the nationalization. Suffice it to say that the alliance was broken, and since private property was at stake and CONFIEP was available, class unity could be rapidly activated. The nationalization was not only a question of the Groups' rights as owners of the banks, but as CONFIEP put it, "a question of principles"—that is, of general interests. Business had the right to defend private property, and the constitution provided an effective legal defense for opposing nationalization.

García, unable to understand CONFIEP's role and the nature of business political activation, badly miscalculated class divisions within business when he announced the nationalization of the banks. He tried to present the measure as beneficial to small and medium-sized firms because nationalizing the banks could "democratize credit," but CONFIEP, fearful of more nationalizations and already doubtful about the president's sincerity, decided to support the conglomerates. CONFIEP seized the opportunity and used this battle to achieve final institutional consolidation. First, it welcomed the Groups, strengthening organizational unity. Second, it coordinated the protest of trade associations and individual firms against nationalization, seeking to broaden this support to include the middle class and informal entrepreneurs. Third, it started a legal battle in the judicial system to declare the measure unconstitutional and to lobby in Congress against it.

Three months after García's dramatic announcement, the project was approved in Congress but largely modified. The modification was a desperate but ineffective effort by García and his party, APRA, to cope with their increasing isolation from the business sector. Once it was approved, it was never fully implemented. García lost the political will to continue with bank nationalizations, and the state, weakened by a severe fiscal crisis, could not even formally take over the banks by compensating the owners. It was a major political victory for CONFIEP, and for Peru's business class a historic turning point. The battle of the banks demonstrated to entrepreneurs and other social groups that internal business unity, institution building, and clever political leadership could defeat the government. The rewards were immediate: seven trade associations joined CONFIEP in 1987, for a total of twenty-three as of November 1987 (see table 4.1). Its political success, and the fear of further nationalizations, convinced other trade associations that it was better to be under CONFIEP's umbrella, just in case.

Another clear indicator of CONFIEP's strengthening also has to do more with politics than policy making. Since 1987, CONFIEP has become the acknowledged mouthpiece of the private sector in a number of matters. The fact that many of CONFIEP's suggestions were not acted upon (because of open confrontation with García) did not mean that the peak association was weak and politically ineffective. On the contrary, it played a role—a political role. From then on, society paid attention to CONFIEP's public communiqués, and the business sector felt collectively represented by the peak association. In 1988, four years after its founding and hardened by many political battles, CONFIEP obtained real recognition. Ricardo Vega Llona, president of CONFIEP at the time of the nationalization, was pleased to say, "Today CONFIEP is not a crystal any more, it is a rock."[39] In the 1990 presidential elections and after the Fujimori administration came to power, CONFIEP played a key role in voicing the interests of the business sector. This time it was the president who sought CONFIEP's support.[40]

TABLE 4.1 Foundation and Membership of Private
Entrepreneurial Institutions in Peru

Trade Association	Date Founded	No. of Members
As of November 1984:		
National Industrial Society	1896	1,654[a]
Association of Exporters	1974	952[a]
National Mining and Petroleum Society	1896	120
Peruvian Chamber of Construction	1954	1,048[a]
Lima Chamber of Commerce	1888	4,000
National Confederation of Merchants	1945	100,000
National Fishing Society	1952	108[a]
Association of Radio and Television	—	—
As of March 1985:		
Peruvian Association of Shipowners	1919	10
Peruvian Association of Insurance Companies	1904	22[a]
As of March 1986:		
National Confederation of Chambers of Commerce and Production	1970	—
Association of Banks	1967	15[a]
Association of Hotels and Restaurants	1943	800
National Agrarian Association	1980	250,000
National Chamber of Tourism	1971	130
Association of Airplane Companies	1979	15
As of November 1987:		
Peruvian Association of Car Manufacturers	—	—
Association of Construction Engineers	—	—
Association of Insurance Producers	—	—
Peruvian Chamber of Realtors	1984	56
Peruvian Association of Aviculture	1953	560
National Association of Pharmaceutical Laboratories	1965	67[a]
National Association of Pharmacy Owners	—	—

Source: Other data are approximate and, for the most part, are taken from Luis Abuggatas, "Crisis de transición, asociaciones empresariales y partidos políticos: El caso peruano," presented at the annual meeting of the Latin American Studies Association, Boston, October 1986, p. 35.
a. Data obtained from membership lists provided by trade associations.

Business Politicization in Times of Crisis

Michael Useem, in his study of U.S. and British business, argues that trade associations play a particular function: to train business people in political matters and to contribute to leadership formation.[41] This is also the case with CONFIEP, but we might add that the political climate of Peru in the second half of the 1980s and early 1990s was so intense and hectic that it accelerated the learning process for business.

One of the most important consequences of the battle of the banks was the politicization of the business sector.[42] Business leaders were more concerned with politics and the danger of social chaos (continuing economic recession and widespread social and political violence) than with policy matters. CONFIEP and IPAE became centers of political activism, and in the midst of the battle of the banks, a new political organization (Libertad) with business connections was formed. CADE 1987 sought to find political solutions to the crisis, assessing different political alternatives for business and debating the ways to *hacer política*, to become involved in politics.[43] A sign of changing business attitudes was the (admittedly naive) declaration by a young industrialist, José Chlimper, who stated at the CADE 1987 conference that the historic mission of business was "to become a ruling class." Chlimper touched a sensitive issue because an economically weak and politically divided national bourgeoisie could not consider itself a "ruling class," but new political developments seemed to provide a chance for social leadership.[44]

The increased political activation of Peruvian business is evident in its active connection with political parties.[45] The Democratic Front, founded in early 1988 and headed by Mario Vargas Llosa, was the result of the unity among Popular Action, the Christian Democratic party, and Libertad.[46] This unity, according to several interviews, was fostered by business people who urged political parties to unite themselves: "We will not give any money for parties that are unwilling to create a front," stated Julio Piccini.[47] Business thus conditioned the formation of the Democratic Front and, at the same time, opened a door for the personal involvement of business leaders in party politics.[48]

Business leaders could become directly involved in politics in two ways: to create a new party or to join existing political parties. Both options were tried in the 1990 general elections with varied results. Four business leaders decided to form a new independent organization, Somos Libres, but it failed to become widely known and none was elected. Five trade association leaders (three of them former presidents of CONFIEP) ran as the Democratic Front's senatorial candidates and three were elected (those related to CONFIEP).[49] In general, CONFIEP provided the opportunity for business people to become not only peak association leaders but public leaders as well, another important sign of the rise of business political activism.

During the Fujimori administration (1990–1991), CONFIEP's leaders had opportunities to participate in public life, not only as members of political parties, spokespersons of business institutions that have obtained social recognition, but also as cabinet members. Four business leaders of the *gremialista* generation formed in the previous decade (Jorge Camet, Arturo Woodman, Alfonso Bustamante, and Efrain Goldenberg) have filled important executive positions. Jorge Camet, CONFIEP's president in the 1990–1991 period, was at first minister of industry; later, since January 1993, he has held the most powerful cabinet position as minister of economy and finance. Alfonso Bustamante was first called to replace Camet in the ministry of industry and in 1994 was prime minister for a short period. Efrain Goldenberg became minister of foreign relations and prime minister in 1994. Arturo Woodman was elected to be the first executive director of the National Social Fund (FONCODES) in 1993 and, when he retired, became CONFIEP's president in 1994–1995.

Conclusion

This analysis of the Peruvian case shows the conditions under which a structurally young, economically weak, and politically divided business sector was able to form and consolidate a peak association that became the single spokesman for the private sector. The business confederation, CONFIEP, struggled for recognition among its peers and from others: the state, political parties, labor unions. The peak association realized the dangers of lack of coordination in the business sector and business's vulnerability to state leaders' efforts to manipulate internal divisions. In the process of institutional consolidation, because of the political nature of this struggle, business leaders became national figures, some of whom later intervened in public life.

This process was the result of a positive combination of factors that emerged in the 1980s. Economic changes, particularly Peru's struggle to adopt open trade policies and their impact on business, stimulated the need for a collective response to defend business interests and to accommodate to changing circumstances. Political changes, the transition to democracy and the modification of the constitution, facilitated the formation of a business peak association and redefined the rules of the game between the state and Peru's business sector. The executive branch enhanced its constitutional power capabilities and new mechanisms of policy-making participation (concerted action) were adopted. But the emergence and subsequent consolidation of the business peak association resulted from the active role played by a new generation of business leaders dedicated to organization building. They learned from their first unification experiences in the 1970s by identifying the internal and external causes of their early failures. In the 1980s, the peak association was formed and strengthened, particularly when it became the shield that protected business from the attempt at bank nationalization. In the 1990s, political parties and government leaders recognized the existence and role of the peak association.

When this happened, the system of interest representation was modified, because it included an organization that claimed representativeness as the single spokesman for the private sector, and others granted this recognition. This "logic of institutional consolidation" had political implications that developed as CONFIEP's struggle to influence the policy-making process progressed. The consolidation of a business peak association changed the ability of business to influence policy and political decisions because business people could now act in unison and defend general interests whenever necessary.

Notes

1. See John Turner, ed., *Businessmen and Politics* (London and Exeter: Heineman, 1984), 7; John P. Windmuller and Alan Gladstone, eds., *Employers' Associations and Industrial Relations* (Oxford: Oxford University Press, 1984), iii; and David Becker, "Business Associations in Latin America," *Comparative Political Studies* 22, 1 (1991): 114.

2. Philippe C. Schmitter and Wolfgang Streeck, *Private Interest Government* (London: SAGE Publications, 1985), 2–4.

3. Harmon L. Zeigler and G. Wayne Peak, *Interest Groups in American Society* (Englewood Cliffs, N.J.: Prentice-Hall, Inc., 1972), 227; and Alberto Martinelli and Tiziano Treu, "Employers' Associations in Italy," in *Employers' Associations*, ed. Windmuller and Gladstone, 265.

4. Claus Offe, "The Attributions of Public Status to Interest Groups: Observations on the West German Case," in *Organizing Interests in Western Europe*, ed. Suzanne Berger (Cambridge and London: Cambridge University Press, 1981), 151.

5. Alain Touraine, *Actores sociales y sistemas políticos en América Latina* (Santiago de Chile: PREALC, 1987); Sylvia Maxfield and Ricardo Anzaldúa Montoya, "Government and Private Sector in Contemporary Mexico," Center for U.S.-Mexican Studies, Monograph Series no. 20 (University of California at San Diego, 1987), 5; and Agustín Cueva, *Las democracias restringidas de América Latina* (Quito: Editorial Planeta, 1988), 39.

On peak associations in the region, see Centro de Investigación Económica de América Latina (CIEDLA), *El empresariado latinoamericano* (Buenos Aires: CIEDLA-Fundación Konrad Adenauer, 1984); and *Empresarios y estado en América Latina*, ed. Celso Garrido N. (Mexico City: CIDE-UAM/A-UNAM/Instituto de Investigaciones Sociales–Fundación Friedrich Ebert, 1988). For Argentina and Brazil, see Carlos H. Acuña, "Empresarios y política. La relación de las organizaciones empresarias con regímenes políticos en América Latina: Los casos argentino y brasileño," *Boletín Informativo Techint* 255 (November–December 1988): 35. For Chile, see Guillermo Campero, *Los gremios empresariales en el período 1970–1983: Comportamiento sociopolítico y orientaciones ideológicas* (Santiago de Chile: ILET, 1984). For Mexico, see Roderic A. Camp, *Entrepreneurs and Politics in Twentieth-Century Mexico* (New York: Oxford University Press, 1989). For Peru, see Francisco Durand, *Los empresarios y la concertación* (Lima: Fundación Friedrich Ebert, 1987) and his "The National Bourgeoisie and the Peruvian State: Coalitions and Conflict in the 1980s," Ph.D. diss., University of California, Berkeley, 1990. Venezuela is a rather exceptional case because FEDECAMARAS has been part of the institutional landscape for several decades. That is why studies about its role and a debate about its influence are more abundant: see Samuel Moncada, *Los huevos de la serpiente. Fedecamaras por dentro* (Caracas: Alianza Gráfica, 1985); René Salgado, "Economic Pressure Groups and Policy-Making in Venezuela: The Case of FEDECAMARAS," *Latin American Research Review* 22, 3 (1987): 91–105; and Becker, "Business Associations in Latin America."

7. The economic weakness assertion has been explained elsewhere (Durand, *Los empresarios y la concertación*, 44–45). The same argument has been used to explain the peculiarities of two Western latecomers, Italy and Canada. See Tom Bottomore and Robert Brym, eds., *The Capitalist Class* (New York: New York University Press, 1989), 110–77.

8. Nathaniel H. Leff equates economic weakness with political weakness. See "Capital Markets in the Less Developed Countries: The Group Principle," in *Money and Finance in Economic Growth and Development*, ed. R. McKinnon (New York, 1976), 97–122.

9. Acuña, "Empresarios y política," 35.

10. Windmuller and Gladstone, *Employers' Associations*, 2.

11. Philippe C. Schmitter and Wolfgang Streeck, "The Organization of Business Interests," Paper IIM/LMP 81-13 (Berlin: Wissenschaftszentrum, 1981), have emphasized the importance of studying two "logics" that govern the life of business peak associations in Western Europe: the logic of membership" and "logic of influence." See also Acuña, "Empresarios y política," 27.

12. See Thomas Patrick Bamat, "From Plan Inca to Plan Tupac Amaru: The Recomposition of the Peruvian Power Bloc," Ph.D. diss., Department of Sociology, Rutgers University–State University of New Jersey, New Brunswick, 1978); and Anthony Ferner, *La burguesía industrial en el desarrollo peruano* (Lima: Escuela Superior de Administración de Empresas, 1982).

PERU • 175

on

13. Durand, *Los empresarios y la concertación*, 12–15.

14. In many Latin American countries, the idea of concerted action between the state and interest groups became particularly strong with the transition to democracy. See Mario Dos Santos, *Concertación y democratización en América Latina* (Buenos Aires: Centro Latinoamericano de las Ciencias Sociales-CLACSO, 1987).

15. Enrique Bernales B. and Marcial Rubio C., *Perú: Constitución y sociedad política* (Lima: Centro de Estudios Promoción y Desarrollo–DESCO, 1981).

16. César Germaná, "La oposición burguesa ¿Hasta dónde va?" *Sociedad y política* 12 (Lima, August 1981): 7–19.

17. On the formation of CONFIEP, see Durand, *Los empresarios y la concertación*. On the recognition of CONFIEP, see Alejandro Demaison, "Las instituciones empresariales en el Perú," *Análisis Laboral* (Lima, October 1985): 47–48.

18. A useful overview of policy changes and the reaction of the business sector to them at the beginning of the 1980s is provided by Luis Abuggatas, "Crisis de transición, asociaciones empresariales y partidos políticos: El caso peruano," presented at the Latin American Studies Association meeting, Boston, October 1986.

19. This idea is developed by Windmuller and Gladstone in *Employers' Associations and Industrial Relations*.

20. See Harry Eckstein, *Pressure Group Politics* (Stanford: Stanford University Press, 1960), 22–25.

21. See Javier Iguiñiz, "La crisis peruana actual: Esquema para una interpretación," in *Las crisis económicas en la historia del Perú*, ed. Heráclio Bonilla (Lima: Centro Latinoamericano de Historia Económica y Social–Fundación Friedrich Ebert, 1986), 229–364; and Carol Wise, "Peru's Political Economy, 1980–1987. Responses to the Debt Crisis: From Neoliberalism to New Orthodoxy," presented at the Latin American Studies Association meeting, New Orleans, March 1988.

22. *Peru Report*, "The Peruvian Financial System at the Time of the Expropriation," Peru Reporting E.I.R.L. (1987).

23. On these and other interviews with business leaders, see Durand, "The National Bourgeoisie and the Peruvian State."

24. *Peru Económico*, May 1986, 5.

25. *Industrial Peruana*, January 1987, 11.

26. Personal interview with Edgardo Palza, Lima, November 1986.

27. Martinelli and Treu, "Employers' Associations in Italy," 269.

28. *Peru Report*, "The Peruvian Financial System."

29. Edgardo Palza, manager of IPAE (Instituto Peruano de Administración de Empresas) for fifteen years, defined CADE during the 1970s as an "informal parliament." According to him, the CADEs became a tradition without government interference because it was a way of sending signals to the business community without having to compromise on policy matters. It was a forum, not a bargaining table between trade associations and the state (personal interview, Lima, November 1986). See also Francisco Durand, "La 'batalla' de los empresarios," *Quehacer* 56 (Lima, January 1989): 24–27.

30. Ferner, *La burguesía industrial*; Durand, "La 'batalla' de los empresarios."
31. Durand, "The National Bourgeoisie and the Peruvian State," 222.
32. *Gerencia*, December 1985, 2.
33. Charles Lindblom, *Politics and Markets* (New York: Basic Books, 1977).
34. Wyn Grant and Wolfgang Streeck, "Large Firms and the Representation of Business Interests in the UK and West German Construction Industry," in *Organized Interests and the State*, ed. Alan Cawson (London: SAGE Publications, 1985), 145–73; and David Vogel, *Fluctuating Fortunes: The Political Power of Business in America* (New York: Basic Books, 1989).
35. For information on specific policy proposals on this issue see Luis Alva Castro, "El desafío del cambio," *Gente* 26 (February 1987), 35–42.
36. Interview with Julio Piccini, CONFIEP's first president, Lima, February 1987.
37. Alan García Pérez, "Mensaje a la nación," Sistema Nacional de Comunicación Social, Lima, 28 July 1986.
38. A list of the banks, insurance companies and financial firms potentially affected by the nationalization attempt is found in the *Peru Report* (1987).
39. Personal interview, Lima, February 1988.
40. On relations between business and the Fujimori administration, which decided to adopt open trade policies with the support of most trade associations and CONFIEP, see Manuel Castillo Ochoa, "Realineamientos, sorpresas y responsabilidades de la clase empresarial," *Quehacer* 66 (Lima, September–October 1990): 46–52, and Ochoa, "Empresarios: Promesas incumplidas," *Quehacer* 70 (Lima, March–April, 1991): 20–22. On collective business support for Fujimori, despite the adverse effect of liberalization on some segments still active at the beginning of the 1990s, see IPAE, *CADE 90. Anales de la XXVIII conferencia anual de ejecutivos* (Lima: IPAE, 1990) and IPAE, *CADE 91. Anales de la XXIX conferencia anual de ejecutivos* (Lima: IPAE, 1991). It must be noted that Fujimori's "presidential coup" against Congress and the courts, launched in April 1992, had the solid backing of the business sector, raising the question of the commitment of Peruvian entrepreneurs to democracy.
41. Michael Useem, *The Inner Circle: Large Corporations and the Rise of Business Political Activity in the US and the UK* (New York: Oxford University Press, 1984), 104–05.
42. Fernando Rospigliosi, "Empresarios en política," *Caretas*, 4 November 1991, 25.
43. IPAE, *CADE 87. Anales de la XXV conferencia anual de ejecutivos* (Lima: IPAE, 1987). I attended this conference.
44. Francisco Durand, "La nueva derecha se organiza," *Quehacer* 50 (Lima, January–February 1988): 20–23.
45. Mario Vargas Llosa's own account of the political activation of Peruvian leaders, business people included, is found in "A Fish out of Water," *Granta* 36 (Summer 1991): 15–75.

46. See Movimiento Libertad, *Libertad. Primer ciclo de conferencias*, 2 vols. (Lima: Pro-Desarrollo, 1988).

47. Informal interviews were conducted at CADE 87 and in CONFIEP's second congress in 1988. Personal interview with Julio Piccini, Lima, February 1988.

48. CONFIEP's second president, Miguel Vega, became a powerful senator of the 1990–1995 legislature representing the Democratic Front.

49. *El Comercio*, 8 January 1990, A5.

Blanca Heredia

5. Mexican Business and the State

The Political Economy of a
Muddled Transition

In the late 1970s and early 1980s, authoritarian regimes throughout Latin America experienced severe and, in most cases, unmanageable stress. The most pivotal factors working against authoritarian stability were intensified conflict in state–private sector relations, along with growing politicization on the part of domestic entrepreneurs. In most cases, in fact, the collapse of authoritarianism and the transition toward democratic forms of rule tended to be strongly associated with ruptured relations between the state and the private sector, as well as with new and more diverse forms of business involvement in social and political life.

As elsewhere in Latin America, business-government relations in Mexico deteriorated sharply in the early 1980s, and political activation of important segments of Mexican business increased likewise. In contrast to the changes in most other authoritarian regimes in the region, however, conflict in Mexican state-business relations stopped short of rupture, and business leaders' political activation failed to facilitate a full-fledged transition to democracy. While democracy may evolve in the future, business leaders have thus far succeeded only in ushering in partial and segmented political liberalization that has tended to reinforce, rather than erode, the basic pillars of authoritarian rule.

To explain the role of Mexican business in what remains a "muddled" political transition, I will focus on the strategic interaction between economic and political leaders. Such a focus highlights the essential interdependence of the choices that determine whether or not business leaders withdraw their support from authoritarianism. This approach is also appropriate from a comparative vantage point, since it explores how political leaders' choices and resources shape the political and economic behavior of business people.

This chapter argues that Mexican entrepreneurs failed to play a role similar to that of other business leaders in authoritarian settings in the early 1980s because the government was better able to withstand and respond effectively to their demands; it could do so because it commanded greater economic and political resources than other Latin American authoritarian regimes.

Key among such resources was state ownership of the main source of foreign exchange—oil—as well as a number of peculiar features of Mexico's political system: the prohibition against presidential reelection, highly inclusionary structures of corporatist control over popular sectors, official party dominance in the electoral sphere, along with considerable technocratic insularity and competence in key economic policy-making institutions. These advantanges largely explain why Mexico's leaders were less vulnerable to business opposition and better able to rebuild an alliance with major economic groups than most other authoritarian leaders in the region.

The chapter first examines the conditions that led to conflict in state–private sector relations and the growing politicization of Mexican business leaders during 1970–1982. The second section analyzes how the government managed to deal with and rapidly undermine business opposition after 1982.

Business-Government Relations Under Stress

After long decades of relatively good cooperation between the state and Mexico's private sector, opportunities for conflict arose in the 1970s because of the social transformations caused by thirty years of rapid and sustained economic growth and by Mexico's integration into the liquid international financial markets of the day.

From 1940 to 1970, the Mexican economy grew at an average annual rate of over 6 percent and manufacturing production at around 8 percent. Throughout the period, and especially from 1954 to 1970, rapid growth was accompanied by low rates of inflation, a stable exchange rate, and relatively small fiscal deficits.[1] Industry, primarily in private hands, increased its share in GNP from 24 percent to 34 percent,[2] and private investment as a percentage of total investment went from 51 percent to 67 percent during the same period.[3] The number of industrial establishments jumped from 31,195 in 1945 to 120,802 in 1975, and the number of private commercial firms experienced a similar growth.[4]

As a result, the size and strength of the private sector grew steadily. Through the expansion of middle sectors, rapid and sustained economic progress also gave business leaders new and extremely important potential allies in their relations with government. Equally significant were the effects of a long period of economic growth on the internal diversification of the private sector. However, greater diversity in the size, location, and economic sector of private firms turned out to be a mixed blessing in political terms. On one hand, it created incentives and opportunities for more explicit forms of collective action on the part of business. On the other, it tended to undermine the historical role of large business firms as the sole political representatives of the private sector. Greater diversification generated new sources of instability in government-business relations, as well as new and different ways for business to exert political influence.

Thirty years of high economic growth was also extremely important for government. Political institutions created during the 1920s and 1930s in an essentially rural and agricultural country were now forced to deal with an increasingly complex urban and industrial society. The sharp inequalities in income and unequal growth in regional terms had intensified social demands.[5] Strict budgetary and monetary policies since 1954 had significantly reduced social spending, thus further accelerating the growth of social and political pressures caused by a highly skewed structure of income and wealth.

Hence the long period of rapid, sustained economic growth altered the balance of forces on which cooperation between business and government had been premised. Growth gave added economic and social weight to business, while simultaneously placing urgent challenges and demands on the government's agenda. The resulting tension was inevitable.

Changes in the world economy also generated conflict in state-business relations in Mexico in the 1970s and early 1980s. Especially salient was Mexico's rapid integration into the highly liquid financial markets of the 1970s. Ready access to low-cost foreign credit had two important effects on private sector–government relations. First, it substantially increased the short-term financial autonomy of government and, therefore, it was less vulnerable to the demands of the most powerful segment of the Mexican business community: private bankers. Second, it made capital more mobile than ever before and significantly limited the state's ability to influence the allocation of private investment. By simultaneously increasing the financial autonomy of the state and the mobility of capital, easy access to international financial markets eroded some of the key mechanisms that had assured reciprocal restraint and cooperation in the past. Private financiers were less able to constrain economic policy makers, and state leaders had less power to channel private funds—through both incentives and controls—into long-term productive investment.[6] By the late 1960s, the remarkably dynamic Mexican economy appeared to be losing momentum. Behind the stable growth of previous decades, tensions had steadily accumulated. Agricultural production had become virtually stagnant, an inward-oriented trade regime had become increasingly incompatible with the maintenance of a fixed nominal exchange rate, and the growth of the budget deficit since the mid-1960s, along with wage raises not matched by productivity increases appeared to be threatening price stability.[7] Equally problematic were the increasing number of bottlenecks produced by lags in infrastructure investment, higher deficits in the current account, and the trend toward declining private investment.

Rather than pursuing costly though badly needed microeconomic reforms, after 1972 the government embarked on a course of rapid fiscal expansion. Since repeated attempts at fiscal reform had failed, increased government spending had to be financed by a rapidly growing public foreign debt and rising inflation. High liquidity in international credit markets, along with very substantial revenues from oil exports after 1978, allowed the government to pursue such a course.[8] Affluence worked against undertaking politically costly structural reforms, while it generated the illusion among policy makers that budget constraints had somehow disappeared. Though different in terms of their political objectives and thus in their political effects, populist policies during the Luis Echeverría (1970–1976) and José López Portillo (1976–1982) administrations were premised on the continuing availability of abundant financial resources.

Populist macroeconomic policies throughout most of the

1972–1982 period brought high, though unstable, rates of economic growth. However, the formidable expansion of the public economy in those years had harmful effects on government finances as well as price stability. Because microeconomic reforms were postponed, populist economic policies magnified many of the structural constraints that prevented balanced and self-sustained economic growth.

In economic policy making, financial abundance contributed to the ascent of a new generation of statist-oriented technocrats who challenged the traditional control over policy by fiscal conservatives. The rising influence of statist orientations and developmental agencies in economic policy making during 1973–1982, however, never fully undermined the fiscal conservatives' grip on the Finance Ministry and the Central Bank. Instead, the two warring factions competed, leading to decreasing levels of policy coherence and effectiveness.[9] The violent expansion of the public economy as a whole, on the other hand, meant a steady erosion of the executive's ability to manage its own bureaucracy.

The rapid expansion of the public economy, shown in table 5.1, the reduced power of financial conservatives over policy, growing incompetence in the policy-making apparatus, and the exclusion of large financially based economic groups from the policy process exacerbated conflict between government and business. With the wider social changes produced by a long period of rapid economic growth, these developments precipitated unprecedented business-state confrontations during the Echeverría administration and in López Portillo's last year. However, relations were not consistently antagonistic throughout the period, suggesting the influence of other equally important factors. Particularly significant were the changing political constraints and opportunities that government and business leaders faced in dealing with each other.

TABLE 5.1   Public-Sector Economic
Indicators in Mexico (as percent of GDP)

	Oil Revenues	Total Expenditures	Financial Deficit
1970	—	22.4	3.8
1971	3.0	20.5	2.5
1972	2.8	22.9	4.9
1973	2.6	25.8	6.9
1974	3.4	27.0	7.2
1975	3.3	31.9	10.0
1976	3.3	32.0	9.9
1977	3.8	30.0	6.7
1978	4.5	31.4	6.7
1979	5.6	33.0	7.6
1980	7.3	33.5	7.5
1981	7.3	39.7	14.1
1982	9.9	44.5	16.9

Source: Bazdresch and Levy, "Populism and Economic Policy
in Mexico," table 8.2.

The Political Economy of Government-Business Relations, 1970–1982

Acrimonious conflict from 1972 to 1976, reconciliation and close cooperation from 1977 to 1981, and renewed confrontation in 1982—this evolution indicates that despite similarities in economic policy and structural constraints, business-government relations evolved along very different lines during the administrations of López Portillo and Echeverría. Key features of Mexico's political system and the political challenges facing each administration account for these differences.

Among the mechanisms that give the Mexican political system its remarkable resiliency, paramount is the prohibition against presidential reelection. This is one of the few, and clearly the most important, formal constraints on executive power.[10] Because presidents cannot be reelected, the system includes significant political mobility and periodically adjusts to new configurations of power. Losers in one six-year term can reasonably assume that they may be better compensated during the next presidential period. This reduces the incentives for defection while favoring continued cooperation.

The *sexenio* has tended to stabilize the regime by generating a pattern of "delayed responsiveness." Nonreelection, along with the formidable legal and informal executive powers, makes Mexican presidents virtually unaccountable for their behavior and insensitive to the long-term costs of their decisions or omissions. It gives them significant incentives for embarking on policies with short-term gains, and it pushes them to delay decisions that are costly in the short run. Hence incoming presidents are systematically burdened with the problems and tensions accumulated during the previous term. But it also creates incentives for dealing with inherited problems as fast as possible, both because they are urgent and because they allow the new president to assert his autonomy from his predecessor. This last is particularly important in a system in which the president almost singlehandedly chooses a successor. This key feature of the Mexican political system helps to explain the very different political constraints that Luis Echeverría and José López Portillo faced upon assuming office. The distinct political challenges produced very different approaches toward business.

The Echeverría Administration: Conflict and Political Activism

Luis Echeverría inherited two main challenges when he became president in December 1970. First was the political cost of the previous administration's violent repression of the

1968 student movement, in addition to mounting political and social tensions resulting from the highly skewed pattern of economic growth. Second, he faced a number of economic problems, all of which centered on sustaining previous rates of growth.

The Echeverría administration dealt with these challenges by adopting populist macroeconomic policies and initiating political reform. The combination of the two strategies enabled the government to reconcile demands caused by pressing political tensions while promoting continued economic growth.

Political stress during this period was particularly acute. Social groups questioned the regime's commitment to democracy and revolutionary ideals. These criticisms came primarily from members of the previous administration as well as disaffected and radicalized students, independent trade union leaders, and rural leaders. The regime silenced its opponents with subsidies and payoffs, made possible by renewed economic dynamism and an expanded public budget.[11] By creating new channels of political participation and political inclusion, the regime further defused opposition. Political reforms and changes in economic policy were accompanied by equally significant shifts in official rhetoric: government discourse became increasingly populist and nationalistic. The new rhetoric reflected both changes in the composition of government (that is, the rise of statist-oriented technocrats and the incorporation of "leftist" and progressive opponents into the administration) and a determination to rededicate the government to its revolutionary origins. The regime also adopted a more active, diversified, and militant foreign policy. It emphasized bilateral relations with other developing countries and assumed a visibly confrontational position toward the developed world.

The regime's strategies successfully defused opposition from leftist groups, but its political and economic reforms exacerbated conflict with the private sector. Business leaders resented and feared the rapid expansion of the public economy. The state had heretofore assumed an important but essentially subsidiary presence in the economy. Major business groups viewed the state's heightened role as violating the rules of the game on which previous cooperation had depended—profits for business and political power for regime leaders—and as a clear threat to their long-term interests.

Business leaders also feared the Echeverría administration's nationalistic, populist, and "revolutionary" appeal, seeing its discourse and its incorporation of "leftist" political opponents as a direct assault against the private sector.[12] They viewed the growth of guerrilla activity and particularly the assassination of major business figures such as Eugenio Garza Sada (the top representative of the powerful Monterrey group) as clear indications that the government was either unable to control or was actually promoting attacks on business. The administration's Third World orientation in foreign policy, particularly its active support of socialist president Salvador Allende in Chile, further reinforced these perceptions and strengthened the deeply entrenched anticommunism found in most of the Mexican business community.

In this highly charged political and ideological environment, radical antigovernment groups within the private sector increased their activities, strength, and visibility. Behind these movements was a new generation of regionally based business leaders from midsized firms.[13] In contrast to the anticommunist ideology of big business groups, this new group developed more sophisticated ideological convictions and political programs. They did not view political involvement as purely instrumental.[14]

The group enjoyed strong social support because of the proliferation of these midsized firms outside the traditional centers of industrial development, especially in the North.[15] They also joined the expanding urban middle classes and their struggle for increased citizen participation. These links increased opportunities for sustained political involvement.

During this period, strategies that had been seen as relatively marginal to business interests became increasingly salient. For example, business undertook to develop and diffuse new political and social ideas. From 1970 to 1980, business organizations created or strengthened their departments devoted to ideological production and diffusion and to research on culture and society.[16] In addition, business funded private institutes engaged in such research,[17] as well as private universities.[18] Business organizations also developed highly popular courses for executives that included political doctrine along with technical training.[19]

During the Echeverría years, private entrepreneurs became active in various ways in the PAN (National Action party).[20] Members of the pro-PAN business movement from large enterprises tended to assume a more instrumental attitude toward the party, providing behind-the-scenes financial backing rather than open political support. Midsized regional entrepreneurs, in contrast, were often much more willing to affiliate openly and to run as PAN candidates in elections. The increasing influence of business leaders within PAN during these years accelerated the internal transformation of the party, giving new weight to the more liberal and combative currents within it—currents, that is, ideologically closer to business and more eager than the traditional party elite to transform the PAN into a true electoral alternative to the PRI.

Business people's political activism during the 1970s was marked, however, by the multiple tensions generated by cleavages at various levels. Differences in size, sectoral and geographic location of private firms, their varying dependence on state protection, and the diversity of ideological orientations among the most vocal representatives of the private sector, often made communication and sustained collective public action extremely difficult. As long as the confrontation between big business and government remained high, unity was possible. As soon as the confrontation abated, however, internal fragmentation resurfaced.

President Luis Echeverría's term ended during a major economic crisis. The initial success of expansionary policies was soon followed by accelerating inflation (above 20 percent in 1973–1974) as well as a sharp deterioration of the balance of payments. In 1976 the peso was devalued for the first time since 1954, and both inflation and capital flight reached unprecedented levels. Mounting government-business tensions escalated astronomically when Echeverría made a virtual last-minute decision to expropriate land from private owners in the North.

The López Portillo Years:
Reconciliation and Confrontation

In contrast to his predecessor, the first priority for López Portillo was to stabilize the economy and restore private-sector confidence. During its first year, the new administration reached an agreement with the IMF and adopted orthodox stabilization measures. Eventually, however, the government abandoned these orthodox strategies and resumed the pattern of escalating public spending. This resulted from the discovery of abundant oil reserves and new access to foreign credit. Both public and private investment soared after 1977, producing an unprecedented annual growth rate of 8 percent between 1979 and 1982.

López Portillo's conciliatory stance toward business, along with the formidable opportunities for profit making provided by the oil boom, allowed the new government to quickly mend fences with major economic leaders. Prior tensions could easily be attributed to Echeverría's incompetent economic management and strident antibusiness rhetoric rather than to the authoritarian regime as a whole. Business leaders even accepted

López Portillo's brand of populism stripped of "leftist" and nationalistic overtones and oriented toward rapid and seemingly cost-free economic gain. Below the surface, problems accumulated. Public-sector foreign debt[21] and inflation[22] spiraled. Fiscal and current account deficits also rose steadily.[23] The conflict between statist-oriented policy currents and fiscal conservatives grew increasingly intense. When oil prices began to fall in mid-1981 and interest rates rose in 1982, both the economy and the government's capacity to manage it were vulnerable.

In 1982, after three years of spectacular prosperity, GNP dropped to –0.5 percent. Inflation, traditionally quite low, reached 99 percent. The peso during that year was devalued by 466 percent, and the government increased its foreign debt by almost $6 billion. By the end of 1982, the fiscal deficit stood at a record 18 percent of GNP, the total foreign debt reached $84 billion (89 percent of GNP), and interest payments absorbed 44 percent of the total value of exports.[24]

In an effort to deal with the worst economic crisis in the country's modern history, the government resorted to desperate measures. In September 1982, López Portillo used his discretionary facilities to expropriate the assets of private bankers and holders of dollar-denominated assets and imposed a strict system of foreign exchange controls.[25]

The reconciliation between big business and the government ended, almost totally discredited. Yet the antigovernment business group had been greatly weakened during the reconciliation period. Antigovernment business activists who had flourished during the Echeverría years had lost their critical base of support from large economic groups. However, rather than retreat, many of these leaders had gone ahead with their political, ideological, and organizational activities, albeit at a slower pace and in a more subtle way than before.

The expropriation of the private banking system had the unintended consequence of catapulting these leaders back onto center stage. They had, after all, repeatedly warned the business community about the dangers of unrestrained authoritarianism. Their prophetic admonitions, their enduring opposition to the regime, and the considerable influence they acquired within major private-sector organizations enabled them to lead the mobilization against the government in 1982.[26] Indeed, it was this group of business leaders, rather than the expropriated bankers, who organized and led collective action. Expropriated bankers remained politically cautious so that they would receive adequate compensation from the government.

In protesting the expropriation measure, business leaders for the first time explicitly incorporated the demand for democracy into their discourse.[27] Rather than condemning the administrative errors of one president, they questioned the political system itself. They construed their opposition to expropriation as part of society's defense against arbitrary rule. By identifying the needs of the private sector with those of civil society, business leaders merged antistatism and antiauthoritarianism and portrayed themselves as leading a broad national movement against the authoritarian state.[28]

Appeals for political democracy in a context marked by expanding antiauthoritarian sentiment, especially among the urban middle classes, gave this group of mostly regional business leaders an unprecedented opportunity to forge wider social coalitions in support of business interests. More business people openly backed the PAN and became PAN candidates in regional and national elections.[29] Business leaders, while not homogeneous ideologically, were critical to raising the political awareness of people in business, strengthening private-sector organizations,[30] building cross-class electoral and civic coalitions, and giving Mexico's private sector extraordinary ideological, political, and social visibility.

The long decade of erratic relations between political and economic leaders culminated in open confrontation. Business confidence in the regime plummeted. Capital flight assumed perilous proportions. And active opposition against the government regained its lost momentum.

Political Economy of Reconciliation

It took the de la Madrid administration (1982–1988) five years of determined effort to fully reestablish a working relationship with the Mexican private sector. Given the intensity of the 1982 confrontation, as well as the severe and protracted economic crisis, this was not very long. However, considering how easy it had been to mend fences with business groups in the past and the cost of failing to do so earlier, five years seem to be an excessively long period. Hence, while the eventual reconciliation is important to understand, the de la Madrid government's power to withstand business's prolonged political and economic recalcitrance during a major economic crisis is equally significant.

The de la Madrid Administration: Challenges and Constraints

When President Miguel de la Madrid assumed power in December 1982, the economy was on the brink of collapse. Inflation was about 100 percent, the public deficit was the highest in postrevolutionary history, private and public debt had reached unprecedented levels, and the government suddenly found that foreign credit was no longer available.[31] The acute balance-of-payments crisis generated by the drop in oil prices, the rise in interest rates, and the virtual drying up of foreign financial resources forced the Mexican government to declare a temporary moratorium on interest payments in August 1982 and to adopt, a few months later, one of the most severe IMF-sponsored austerity programs in the region. What initially appeared to some, both within and outside the new administration, to be a short-term liquidity crisis soon became a structural crisis of unprecedented proportions. What began as a short-term stabilization program and a vaguely defined attempt to alter the country's developmental strategy soon opened a new chapter in Mexico's economic and political history. In the electoral and partisan terrain, the ruling party also faced new challenges. The increasing visibility of elections and stronger opposition parties (particularly the PAN), both partial outcomes of the regime's political reformism of the 1970s, also reduced the regime's room to maneuver. Finally, a new U.S. administration, firmly committed to recovering hegemony in world affairs, placed additional constraints on the new government's behavior. The Reagan administration's growing intolerance for Mexico's relatively independent foreign policy, particularly toward Central America, along with heightened alarm about its capacity to deal effectively with the economic crisis, limited the policy choices available to the de la Madrid government.

Almost from its inception, de la Madrid and his economic cabinet emphasized the opportunities for economic change inherent in the crisis: it could be a way of overcoming the obstacles to further growth. In particular, they hoped to destroy the conditions that had made possible the economic excesses of the two previous administrations.[32] At first, the nature of this transformation was only very vaguely defined. By 1985, however, the administration had taken on a distinctively promarket orientation and began carrying out in earnest a program of structural change.

Before stabilization and structural adjustments could be effectively pursued, however, business and the state had to be reconciled. The legacy of distrust generated by the expropriation of the private banking system, the climate of uncertainty naturally associated with the economic crisis, along with the virtually irreversible effects of the private sector's politicization, however, made such reconstruction lengthy and difficult.

President Miguel de la Madrid had to deal with a deeply

mistrustful, resentful, and politically active private sector. In 1982, for instance, the presidents of three of the most important private-sector organizations (the Mexican Employers' Association, COPARMEX; the National Confederation of Commercial Chambers, CONCANACO; and the Consejo Coordinador Empresarial, CCE) came from the ranks of the most actively politicized and antigovernment currents within the business community. Business leaders of the same political orientation had made important inroads into other business organizations as well, especially at the regional level.

Vocal opposition to the government was also widespread among local entrepreneurs, especially in the rich northern states of Chihuahua and Nuevo León. Closer ties among the PAN, regional business leaders, and Catholic groups added strength to the complex mosaic of pressures coming from the private sector.

The owners of the largest economic groups were less openly hostile in their relations with the de la Madrid administration, but their attitude was permeated with deep mistrust. While reluctant to engage in open opposition, they tended, at least ini-

TABLE 5.2 Business Leaders' Economic Behavior in Mexico

	Capital Flight (in $ billions)	Private Investment (annual rate of growth)
1982	6.5	−17.1
1983	2.7	−22.1
1984	1.6	7.9
1985	0.7	12.2
1986	− 2.2	−10.4
1987	0.3	4.3
1988	1.11	3.6

Source: Nora Lustig, *Mexico: The Remaking of an Economy* (Washington, D.C.: Brookings Institution, forthcoming).

tially, to both sympathize with and provide behind-the-scenes financial support for organizations and leaders that did.

Equally significant and costly to the government was the economic behavior of business leaders (see table 5.2). Though capital flight lessened after 1983, it continued throughout the period. Private investment stagnated. While both phenomena could be attributed to adverse economic conditions, business also failed to respond to positive signals when they arose, thus demonstrating the enduring costs of business leaders' loss of confidence in government. As a result, from 1980 to 1990 private savings as a percentage of nominal GNP fell from 15 to 11 percent, and the value of the net acquisition of foreign assets by Mexican business as a percentage of GNP increased from 2.5 to 5.7 percent.[33]

Enduring Resistance and Rebuilding Support

Capabilities The de la Madrid administration could both stabilize and restructure the economy, as well as withstand and eventually reverse the economic and political resistance of business, for several important reasons. Salient among them were Mexico's macroeconomic structure and some key features of its political system.

As Jaime Ros persuasively argues, Mexico's macroeconomic structure, especially its large income from oil, initially moderate inflation rate, and considerable room to maneuver in setting wages, were significant assets to policy makers in their efforts to stabilize the economy.[34] Particularly significant was the large foreign exchange surplus from massive oil exports.

Like copper revenues in Chile and coffee export tariffs in Colombia, oil revenues in Mexico (as in Venezuela) turned the exchange rates adjustments required to close the external gap into an automatic mechanism of fiscal adjustment. The importance of this feature can hardly be exaggerated: the 1982 devaluations almost fully explain the increase in Mexico's public savings in that year, as a consequence of the real revaluation of the government's external surplus by 2 percent of GDP; by comparison, without any similar export/fiscal revenues, in the same year currency depreciations in Argentina and Brazil expanded the fiscal deficit, by 5 percent and 2 percent, respectively, as a proportion of GDP.[35] The Mexican state's direct control of the main source of foreign exchange is of paramount importance. At least initially, the government achieved a major fiscal adjustment by simply devaluing the currency. Moreover, in terms of business-government relations after 1982, this control had some very positive results. First, the quick and substantial fiscal adjustment allowed the government to comply with the IMF agreement, retain the support of international financial institutions, reassert its reliability, and thus both send a positive signal to private investors and lessen the administration's vulnerability to them.

Second, the government's ability to close the external gap and simultaneously reduce the fiscal one through exchange rate adjustments allowed it to subsidize the repayment of private foreign debt without stimulating inflation, since it did not face a sizable public foreign exchange surplus.

Third, this mechanism enabled the de la Madrid administration to mitigate the inflationary costs of adjustment and reduce its negative effects on the middle sectors. This helped the government to retain the critically important backing of those groups and, once again, lessened its vulnerability to business's refusal to cooperate.[36]

Key political institutions and practices were also extremely important in directly and indirectly helping the de la Madrid administration to cope with resistance from business. They also enabled it to gradually restore its alliance with the dominant segments of the private sector.

As in the past, the constitutional prohibition against presidential reelection both allowed and forced the government to adjust rapidly to new political and economic conditions. In de la Madrid's administration, however, an explosive economic crisis came at the beginning of a new presidential term. The sheer magnitude of the crisis created the opportunity to change the means by which new administrations traditionally departed from past practices. Nonetheless, the changes did not undermine the continued representation of major political forces and policy currents.[37]

The new administration did drastically reduce the power of different social factions within the upper echelons of government. Technocrats associated with public financial institutions gained a virtual monopoly over the "commanding heights" of the executive branch.[38] Almost half of the new ministers came from the Ministry of Budget and Planning, headed by de la Madrid from 1979 to 1981. The rest came mostly from the Finance Ministry or from the Central Bank.[39]

The close ties between the president and his appointees, along with their remarkable professional and ideological homogeneity, was one of the most valuable political resources of the de la Madrid administration. These strengths reflect, no doubt, the costs of the acute war of attrition among rival policy currents in the state's economic bureaucracy during the previous administration, as well as the virtually complete loss of prestige by statist and developmentalist policy orientations during 1982. The result was a radical redefinition of the balance of forces within the government as well as a forceful comeback for groups associated with the state's most powerful policy-making institutions: the Central Bank and the Finance Ministry.

The return of public financial institutions to a central role in formulating policy was further bolstered by acute financial scarcity and the need to reestablish relations with international creditors. The rise of institutions that had traditionally been much less open than developmentalist agencies to the specific demands of many social groups also made it possible to introduce sharp cuts in government spending. In fact, this helps explain why the administration was able to turn a primary budget deficit of 9 percent of GNP in 1982 into a primary budget surplus of 4 percent in 1983 and to retain a positive primary balance throughout the period.[40]

Public financial institutions' traditionally close ties with major economic leaders also helped them reestablish communication with ex-bankers and other powerful business groups. Their promarket stance, remarkably consistent policy positions, and receptiveness to the demands of big business were powerful assets in facilitating the initial rapprochement and gradually restoring business confidence.

Three other institutional factors played a major role in helping the government to rebuild ties with the private sector: (1) the government's corporatist controls over labor; (2) its quasi-corporatist relations with key business organizations (particularly those representing private industrialists); and (3) the electoral hegemony of the official party.

Mexico's official union structure gives state officials numerous ways to control workers and their organizations.[41] From 1982 to 1988, these instruments allowed the government to pursue an adjustment program that, while relatively less costly than other programs in the region in inflationary terms, nevertheless was extremely costly in its impact on wages and economic growth. During those years, real minimum wages were cut in half, and average annual growth for the whole period was zero. Thus, while labor and the popular sector in general bore the cost of adjustment, corporatist controls safeguarded the government against explosive social rebellions.

However, because the de la Madrid administration hoped to ensure continued cooperation from official union leaders (who control one of the three sectors in the dominant party), the administration reversed its initial tolerance toward the growth of opposition parties. Although the reversal generated heightened opposition from a number of regional business leaders actively involved in the PAN, it proved quite useful in maintaining support from labor leaders.

Strategies The de la Madrid administration's commitment to mending fences with the private sector was evident from the very beginning. Soon after assuming office, de la Madrid provided generous compensation to the expropriated bankers and returned their nonbanking assets (such as industrial commercial firms, brokerage houses, and various other financially related concerns). In addition, the government allowed private investors to buy up to 34 percent of the nationalized banking sector.

Three factors proved decisive in the administration's success in regaining the support of large business: the government's 1983 rescue plan for highly indebted private firms; the dramatic expansion of the nonbanking financial sector; and the adoption of market-oriented reforms, especially the privatization of state firms.

The rescue plan was designed to assist those private firms whose economic viability had been jeopardized by heavy borrowing during the cheap foreign credit binge of the 1970s. From 1976 to 1982, the total foreign debt of the Mexican private sector had jumped from $6.2 to $21.9 million.[42] In 1982, two major devaluations along with the explosion of the crisis led to virtual bankruptcy for many firms. In an effort to forestall a wave of bankruptcies and defaults, the Central Bank created a program to assist private firms in their efforts to repay their foreign obligations. The program involved several financial relief mechanisms. For example, it helped firms renegotiate deadines for meeting their debt obligations. It further gave highly indebted firms various credit schemes in pesos to enable them to continue servicing their foreign-denominated debts. By converting dollar debts into pesos, the government ended up assuming the cost of the exchange rate differential between the moment at which credit was granted and the time payments were due.[43] The main beneficiaries of the government's debt relief scheme were the largest firms in the country, since they had the highest foreign debts.

The formidable expansion of private (or nonbanking) financial markets during 1983–1987 facilitated a rapprochement in government-business relations for two basic reasons. First, it created high profit outlets for private investors. Second, and most important, it stimulated the rapid emergence of a new financial elite within the private sector, indebted to the government for its existence. By the end of de la Madrid's term, this new elite became what the private banking community had been up to 1982: the most powerful economic group in the country and the most important ally of the government within the business community.

The return of nonbanking financial firms to their ex-owners created a financial system in which the private financial sector coexisted with the government-owned financial sector. The growth of the former resulted from the government's need both to raise credit domestically (due to the end of foreign credit flows) and to curb capital flight. Government treasury bills became the main mechanism. Since private brokerage houses had the exclusive right to trade those bonds in the primary market, both the stock exchange and the brokerage houses expanded phenomenally.

From 1982 to 1990, the participation of brokerage houses in the overall flow of funds managed by the financial system increased 587 percent while that of the banking system decreased by 40 percent.[44] From 1983 to 1988, on the other hand, the capital assets of brokerage houses grew almost 600 times.[45] It is important to note that the brokerage houses that experienced the highest rates of expansion were not owned by former bankers but rather the—at least at that point—few new investors.

The expansion of the private financial system became self-reinforcing because it provided extremely attractive short-term financial gains in a context in which productive investment seemed excessively risky. As a result, during 1982–1988 the number of investors in the segment of the market controlled by brokerage houses increased fivefold.[46]

The large gains generated by the exponential growth of the private financial sector were concentrated in a very small number of firms. Those profiting most directly were brokerage houses themselves. The reduced number of firms registered in the stock exchange also obtained large profits through both speculation and access to lower cost credit.[47] The gains obtained in the booming stock exchange allowed a few individuals and groups to buy out a large number of private firms, as well as to acquire many of the public enterprises sold by government during the administrations of both de la Madrid and Salinas (1988–1994).

The program of market-oriented reform, launched during the mid-1980s and expanded during the first half of the Salinas government, provided the third most important strategy by which the government reconstructed the business-state alliance. Particularly salient in this regard was the privatization of many public firms.

Most of the investors in these firms came from the ranks of new private financiers who had risen to power during the financially volatile 1980s. The reprivatization of the banking system had both increased their visibility and further consolidated their power. Most of the major banks sold by the government in 1991 were bought by financial groups whose economic power at the end of the 1970s was negligible. One case in point is the Acciones y Valores brokerage house, which bought the largest bank in the country—Banco Nacional de México—in 1991. Equally significant in the context of privatization was the acquisition of Teléfonos de México by the economic group CARSO, whose head, Carlos Slim, had started out as an independent stockbroker in the 1970s.

The emergence and rapid consolidation of a new private financial elite significantly reduced the economic weight of (understandably mistrustful) ex-bankers, while simultaneously providing the government with a fresh, loyal, and extremely powerful ally within the private sector. Though ultimately crucial in the regime's efforts to rebuild cooperative linkages with the business community, the private sector's internal recomposition did not occur overnight.

To understand how relations between economic and political leaders evolved after 1982, one must explore the government's political strategies. Through these strategies, the government restored business leaders' confidence in the economy and itself and overcame political opposition organized by important segments of the private sector.

As pointed out earlier, when de la Madrid assumed office in 1982, he confronted a newly recalcitrant and vocal private sector. The government was particularly vulnerable to the radical antigovernment business leaders who led major private-sector organizations such as the Consejo Coordinador Empresarial. It was also sensitive to the political activation of growing numbers of regional business leaders. The government used several strategies to deal with this potentially paralyzing state of affairs. For example, it actively attempted to reestablish a working relationship with major business leaders and did so relatively quickly through both political and economic means. Along with providing financial assistance to large economic firms, the government and the heads of key ministries renewed the practice of meeting frequently with the owners of those firms. The government used the Mexican Council of Businessmen, which represents the country's largest entrepreneurs, as the structure for these meetings. Becaue of the highly informal and closed character of this association, the government could reestablish contact with these groups outside the larger, more public and, during those initial years, highly politicized private-sector organizations such as the CCE, CONCANACO, and COPARMEX.

This gradual weakening of radical antigovernment business leaders that this process entailed was further aided by the government's traditionally close ties and extensive controls over private industry. Both the National Confederation of Industrial Chambers (CONCAMIN) and its largest member chamber (CANACINTRA, which represents essentially small and middle-sized industrial firms) provided, in fact, a critical source of support to the government during the early years of de la Madrid's administration.[48] This backing balanced the lack of support from other very important private-sector organizations.

Also significant in both marginalizing antigovernment currents and regaining the political support of business were the administration's active efforts to influence the selection of leaders in private-sector organizations. Equally important was the government's use of inducements and constraints to lure opponents back into a cooperative game and to punish those who continued to actively resist the government.[49] Such devices proved considerably effective because, as one of my interview subjects pointed out, "Saying no to the government is virtually impossible for any individual businessman in Mexico."

A more general feature of the de la Madrid administration's strategy toward business, and one that allowed it to be extraordinarily effective, was its flexibility. Flexibility made it possible for the government to treat individuals and groups within the private sector very differently and adjust to—and profit from—the rapid changes in the constellation of forces within the Mexican business community.

Rapid shifts in the balance of power among various groups and sectors within the business community resulted from a protracted economic crisis as well as radical changes in the rules of the economic game associated with both stabilization and structural reform. The abrupt break in 1985 with the inward-oriented and state-led growth strategies that had been followed since the 1940s was crucial, since it shifted the balance of power away from those sectors that had most profited from protection and increased opportunities for outward-oriented firms. The expansion of private financial markets and its effects on the composition of the private financial community proved equally important contributing factors.

A flexible strategy vis-à-vis business allowed the government to modify its alliances within the private sector in response to the changing constellation of forces. Up to 1985–1986, the government relied on the support of inward-oriented industrialists while simultaneously seeking to rebuild its pre-1982 ties with large economic groups through subsidies of various kinds. When oil prices fell in 1986 and structural reform was accelerated, however, it began to rely increasingly on newly rising export-oriented firms and groups.[50]

The de la Madrid administration's repeated attempts to regain the support of the Mexican private sector culminated during the negotiation of his government's last stabilization package: the Economic Solidarity Pact (PSE), a tripartite agreement involving the government, the private sector, and labor in a concerted effort to control inflation. It was an agreement to adopt orthodox fiscal adjustment measures (that is, reducing the budget deficit and adjusting public-sector prices), "concerted" income and price controls, and accelerated trade liberalization (begun in 1985).

The open commitment of powerful business leaders and all major private-sector organizations to cooperate with the government in implementing the PSE was the first visible indicator that de la Madrid's active and persistent efforts to mend fences with business had finally succeeded. Such a public commitment also signaled the beginning of a new period of close and remarkably unabashed collaboration between major economic leaders and the authoritarian regime.

When, in the July 1988 presidential elections the PRI won by only a slim majority for the first time, the PAN performed relatively poorly, and the left-of-center coalition led by Cuauhtemoc Cárdenas made a spectacular showing, big business became firmly convinced that it should shore up its support for the PRI.

The Balance:
Continuity and Change in Business-Government Relations

The government's ability to reconstruct an alliance with dominant economic leaders did not entail, however, simply a return to the status quo ante 1970. Mexico's economy, society, and businesses had undergone major transformations that made such a return impossible. A once relatively small and predictable public sphere had been infused with new voices, new issues, and novel and more autonomous forms of collective action. Electoral contests for the first time became open and increasingly competitive. Popular quiescence was replaced by new and more diverse forms of social and political participation.

Private entrepreneurs were neither immune to nor detached from these changes. Business political activism, which began in the early 1970s, receded in the latter part of the decade, and reappeared with vigor at the beginning of the 1980s, was an outgrowth of those transformations.[51] Even though the intensity and orientation of the business community's political involvement were affected by government behavior, particularly relations with the state, the growth and development of that involvement sprang from a wider and more complex process that neither government nor large business groups could control.[52]

In spite of the growing rapprochement between government and dominant economic leaders, then, and in sharp contrast to the past, important segments of the Mexican business community continued to engage in a wide range of political and civic activities throughout the 1980s.[53] Active and open involvement in partisan politics, civic associations, and cultural, educational, and philanthropic endeavors, continued to expand.

Business's participation in electoral contests—especially at the regional level—expanded likewise. Business leaders were particularly involved in local elections in states like Baja California Norte, Chihuahua, Nuevo León, San Luis Potosí, Guanajuato, and Yucatán. However, their participation has included *both* PAN and PRI activities. Though the former tends to rouse more attention, the direct involvement of both local and national business leaders in the PRI has increased and has become more visible than in the past.[54]

The PRI has adopted strategies to deal with those states where links between the PAN and the business community are strong. It seeks the support and endorsement of dominant regional economic leaders by promoting candidates who are either entrepreneurs themselves or have important ties to local economic groups.[55] This strategy appeared to result from PAN's victory in the 1983 municipal elections in the state of Chihuahua. This victory was due in no small part to the active participation of business and its opposition to the government. Soon after that election, the government actively sought to divide regional entrepreneurs and to regain the support of the most powerful economic groups in the region. By the time gubernatorial elections took place in 1986, it had essentially succeeded. This strategy allowed the PRI to both regain the capital city from the PAN and defeat the popular PAN candidate, Francisco Barrio, in the election for governor.[56]

In addition, since the early 1980s business support for various civic associations and movements has continued unabated. This support, like that of PAN, has come primarily from entrepreneurs in mid-sized firms. Business groups have developed and strengthened their ties to politically active middle-class and lay Catholic groups through their involvement in antiabortion, ballot-defense, and education-related movements.[57]

Business involvement in philanthropy has also openly increased and at an unprecedented pace. Numerous charitable associations have been created in the areas of health, education, culture, environment, and community development. The greatest contributors are owners of the largest private concerns in the country.[58]

All of these trends, and especially the enduring participation and support of important segments of the business community for the PAN, have contributed to the opening up of new spaces for political and social participation in Mexico. Their impact on the political system as a whole has been moderate and deeply segmented. Continued political participation by business has been a decisive factor in the PAN's growing electoral strength in various regions, but it has failed to push for a full-fledged transition to democracy.

In many ways, in fact, these processes have contributed to an overall political liberalization within existing political institutions, rather than outside. This has ensured political stability but has simultaneously reproduced some of the key mechanisms that have historically shored up authoritarian rule.

A particularly revealing example of how this process works is the evolution and role of the PAN within the political system during the Carlos Salinas administration (1988–1994). Changes in electoral and party politics over the past few years have included two basic components: the incorporation of opposition parties—most notably PAN, and subordination of the PRI to the executive in the areas of public goods and services. The inclusion of PAN in the electoral arena has proceeded via negotiations between PAN leaders and high-level government officials and has resulted in what amounts to a virtual market-sharing arrangement—an arrangement, however, that excludes the presidency, assures a majority for the official party in Congress, and depends on negotiated electoral results rather than the actual counting of votes.[59]

The incorporation of PAN into the electoral arena is clearly not the result of a generous concession from government. The PAN has won a strong presence among the urban middle class in a number of regions over a long period. The government has learned, especially after July 1988, that it is more costly to ignore PAN's strength than to accept it. Furthermore, despite its success PAN has proved to be both a loyal player and relatively nonthreatening contender in what remains essentially a one-prize political system.

PAN's limitations as a truly national contender in presidential elections are not solely due to allegedly insurmountable difficulties in expanding its social base. Its inability to consolidate links with large business groups has also apparently been decisive.[60] PAN's growth, for example, was the result of a serious crisis in relations between the state and big business. Moreover, its electoral success has depended on strong backing from local business leaders.[61] Thus, if PAN were again to gain support from business leaders—regardless of their number—it would become a more powerful contender.

The Salinas administration's negotiation of PAN's incorporation into the electoral arena as a subordinated partner of government was, in many ways, the result of both the successes and the costs of economic policy making during President de la Madrid's government. For the regime, the greatest liability in this area was PAN's ability to capitalize on the widespread discontent generated by economic reform among middle-sized and small regional entrepreneurs. The costs that stabilization and structural adjustment entailed for large numbers of middle-sized and small firms accelerated and consolidated a process of politicization that began in the 1970s. By becoming the vehicle of such discontent, PAN acquired a crucial asset in regional electoral contests and thus a major bargaining chip in its relations with the government.

The negotiation terms with PAN were also decisively influenced, however, by the reconciliation between big business and the state. That reconciliation—well under way by the time Salinas entered office—deprived PAN of support from big business. And it relied on that support to become an effective national contender. Thus, support for PAN grew among middle-size regional entrepreneurs and urban middle classes because of the blows they sustained as a result of economic restructuring. This gave PAN the power to negotiate a larger slice of the electoral pie. Yet the government's ability to reestablish cooperative relations with major economic groups constrained PAN's further growth at the national level. As a result, the government proved capable of incorporating and subordinating PAN into the electoral system.

In contrast to the past, politicized business leaders did not retreat once the government and major economic leaders restored close ties. The restoration, nevertheless, significantly diminished the impact of opposition from within the Mexican business community on authoritarian stability.

Conclusions

Conflict in state–big business relations in Mexico in the early 1970s and early 1980s created a propitious environment for the political activation of growing numbers of private entrepreneurs. This activation, however, was part of a larger process of social change resulting from decades of rapid economic growth, severe crisis, and economic policies adopted to resolve that crisis.

In dealing with a new adversarial business community during the early 1980s, authoritarian leaders in Mexico enjoyed resources unavailable to their counterparts in other countries of the region. Those resources enabled the regime to survive the prolonged political and economic recalcitrance of business that damaged other authoritarian regimes. Moreover, eventually these resources were instrumental in regaining the full support of Mexico's dominant economic leaders.

Despite the restoration of close relations, the regime has not remained intact. Confrontation in business-state relations has started a process of partial and segmented political liberalization. In the short term, this change has strengthened the presidential system and incorporated and subordinated PAN in electoral politics. The longer-term consequences, however, are far from clear.

Notes

1. In the "stabilizing development" period of 1954–1970, annual inflation averaged 3.8 percent. See Edward F. Buffie and Allen Sangines Krause, "Mexico 1958–86: From Stabilizing Development to the Debt Crisis," in *Developing Country Debt and the World Economy*, ed. Jeffrey D. Sachs (Chicago: University of Chicago Press, 1989), 142.

2. Robert E. Looney, *Economic Policymaking in Mexico: Factors Underlying the 1982 Crisis* (Durham, N.C.: Duke University Press, 1985), figures based upon IMF and Central Bank data.

3. Instituto Nacional de Estadística, Geografía e Informática, *Estadísticas históricas de México* (Mexico City: INEGI, 1990), 2:629.

4. INEGI, *Censos Industriales*, various issues.

5. According to one of the most reliable studies on the subject, "Whatever measure of inequality is observed and whatever indicator of relative position is used, whether income or expenditure, the main conclusion . . . is that the income distribution structure of the country remained basically unaltered between 1950 and 1977." Pedro Aspe and Javier Beristain, "Towards a First Estimate of the Evolution of Inequality in Mexico," in *The Political Economy of Income Distribution in Mexico*, ed. Pedro Aspe and Paul Sigmund (New York: Holmes and Meir, 1984), 54.

6. On the effects of international financial integration on business-government relations in Mexico, see Sylvia Maxfield's excellent study, *Governing Capital: International Finance and Mexican Politics* (Ithaca: Cornell University Press, 1990), esp. chaps. 1, 4.

7. Carlos Bazdresch and Santiago Levy, "Populism and Economic Policy in Mexico, 1970–1982," in *The Macroeconomics of Populism in Latin America*, ed. Rudiger Dornbusch and Sebastian Edwards (Chicago: University of Chicago Press, 1991), 235.

8. The annual average rate of growth of government's foreign debt jumped from 16 percent in 1955–1972 to 29 percent during the 1973–1981 period. Secretaría de Hacienda y Crédito Público, *Deuda externa pública mexicana* (Mexico City: SHCP/Fondo de Cultura Económica, 1988), 18, 24.

9. On the policy orientations of the two currents, see Rolando Cordera and Carlos Tello, *México: La disputa por la nación* (Mexico City: Siglo XXI, 1981), chap. 3. On the policy effects of the mounting confrontation between them, Judith A. Teichman, *Policymaking in Mexico: From Boom to Crisis* (Boston: Allen and Unwin, 1988), chap. 5.

212 • BLANCA HEREDIA

10. On the importance of presidential nonreelection, see Daniel Cosio Villegas, *El sistema político mexicano* (Mexico City: Joaquín Mortiz, 1982), 22–35.

11. From 1972 to 1976, employment in the public sector doubled and the participation of total public-sector spending in GDP increased from 20.5 percent to 30 percent (Buffie and Krause, "Mexico 1958–86," 145). Public investment as a percentage of total investment also grew significantly, and the number of public firms increased from 491 in 1970 to 845 in 1976. See Alejandro Carrillo Castro, "La empresa pública y la reforma administrativa," *Empresas Públicas* (Mexico City: Presidencia de la República, 1978), 17.

12. Personal interviews with: Lorenzo Servitge (president of the Grupo Bimbo and one of the most prominent leaders and ideologues of the Mexican private sector), Mexico City, 15 February, 1990; Bernardo Ardavín (president of COPARMEX from 1986 to 1988), Mexico City, 19 February 1990; Emilio Goicochea Luna (president of CONCANACO from 1982 to 1984), Mexico City, 17 May 1990; and Roberto Guajardo Suárez (president of COPARMEX from 1960 to 1973), Mexico City, 6 June 1990.

13. On the generational question, see Rogelio Hernández Rodríguez, "La reconciliación con el empresariado en el gobierno de Miguel de la Madrid," unpublished manuscript, 1989.

14. Relevant members of this group include, among others, Bernardo Ardavín, Manuel Clouthier, Francisco Barrios Terrazas, Emilio Goicochea Luna, Jorge Ocejo, and Ernesto Ruffo Appel.

15. For a more detailed treatment of this issue, see Blanca Heredia, "Politics, Profits and Size: The Political Transformation of Mexican Business," in *The Right and Democracy in Latin America*, ed. Douglas Chalmers, Atilio Borón, and Maria do Carmo Campello de Souza (New York: Praeger, 1992). For empirical data on the evolution of middle-sized firms, see Rogelio Hernández Rodríguez, "Los problemas de representación en los organismos empresariales," unpublished manuscript, 1990.

16. The CCE created the Centro de Estudios Sociales (1977). CONCANACO created the Coordinación de Ideología e Imagen (1980) which is currently the División de Pensamiento Empresarial. BANAMEX created the Fomento Cultural Banamex (1971), and Unidad de Estudios Sociales (1977), which was originally part of the Departamento de Estudios Económicos and later (1982) became an independent Departamento de Estudios Sociales.

17. Two examples are the Instituto Mexicano de Estudios Políticos (1970) and the Instituto de Banca y Finanzas (1980).

18. A good indicator of the rapid growth of private higher education is the absolute and relative evolution of student enrollment. In 1970 the total number of students enrolled in private universities was 32,160, which represented 13.7 percent of the national total. By 1986 the number had risen to 154,862 students, representing 18.8 percent of the total at the national level (ANUIES, *Anuario Estadístico*, 1986).

19. Especially CONCANACO's 'Operación Impacto'—Impulso al Comercio y Turismo Organizado, and COPARMEX's 'Curso de Liderazgo Empresarial.'

20. For a more detailed treatment of this question, see Ricardo Tirado, "Los empresarios y la política partidaria," unpublished manuscript.

21. Long-term public foreign debt increased from 25.6 billion dollars in 1978 to 51.9 billion dollars in 1982. Banco Interamericano de Desarrollo, *La deuda externa de América Latina: Antecedentes y perspectivas* (Washington: BID, 1984), 82.

22. Annual rates of inflation grew from 15.8 percent in 1976 to 58.9 percent in 1982 (Bazdresch and Levy, "Populism and Economic Policy in Mexico," 232).

23. The fiscal deficit jumped from 5.2 percent of GNP in 1977—after the one year of financial discipline that had brought it down from 7.5 in 1976—to 16.9 percent of GNP in 1982 (Banco Interamericano de Desarrollo, *Deuda externa*, 186). The current deficit also experienced a steady rise during the period, increasing from 2.6 billion dollars in 1978 to 12.5 billion dollars in 1982 (ibid., 82).

24. Presidencia de la República, *Las razones y las obras, Crónica del Sexenio 1982–1988, Sexto Año* (Mexico City: Unidad de la Crónica Presidencial/Fondo de Cultura Económica), 19, 25.

25. Though a wide consensus exists concerning the decisive importance of Lopez Portillo's nationalizing the banks, interpretations about its true goals vary profoundly. For the president's views on this issue, see José Lopez Portillo, *Mis tiempos* (Mexico City: Fernández Editores, 1988), 1227–49. For the analysis of one of Lopez Portillo's key supporters during those critical times, the Director of the Central Bank, see Carlos Tello, *La nacionalización de la banca* (Mexico City: Siglo XXI, 1984). For an excellent and more balanced account that portrays the decision as an attempt to restore the power of the state, see Hernández Rodríguez (1989). For an interpretation that reflects the private sector's views of the subject, see Roberto Newell G. and Luis Rubio F, *Mexico's Dilemma: The Political Origins of Economic Crisis* (Boulder: Westview Press, 1984), chaps. 9, 10.

26. Personal interview, Mexico City, 3 March 1990, with Carlos Abedrop, former owner of Banco del Atlántico, president of the Asociación de Banqueros de México during the bank nationalization, and one of Mexico's most important businessmen.

27. For examples of this new discourse, see business leaders' speeches in *Decisión*, October–December 1982.

28. See Matilde Luna, Ricardo Tirado, and Francisco Valdés, "Businessmen and Politics in Mexico, 1982–1986," in *Government and Private Sector in Contemporary Mexico*, ed. Sylvia Maxfield and Ricardo Anzaldía Montoya, Monograph Series no. 20 (San Diego: Center for U.S.-Mexican Studies, University of California, San Diego, 1987), 13–43; Maria Amparo Casar, "Empresarios y Democracia en México," in *México: El reclamo democrático*, ed. Rolando Cordera et al. (Mexico City: ILET/Siglo XXI, 1988), 165–74.

29. See Tirado, "Los empresarios y la política partidaria"; and Graciela

Guadarrama, "Entrepreneurs and Politics: Businessmen in Electoral Contests in Sonora and Nuevo León, July 1985," in *Electoral Patterns and Perspective in Mexico*, ed. Arturo Alvarado, Monograph Series no. 22 (San Diego: Center for U.S.-Mexican Studies, University of California, San Diego, 1987), 81–110.

30. A good indicator of this process was the expansion of COPARMEX during the 1980s. In 1978, the organization had twenty-two *centros patronales* (regional units). By 1990, the number of those units had risen to fifty-eight *centros patronales* in provincial Mexico and six *delegaciones* in Mexico City. Personal interview with Guillermo Velasco, Mexico City, April 1990, general secretary of the organization from 1978 to 1988 and current director of the Instituto de Proposiciones Estratégicas.

31. Presidencia de la República, *Las razones y las obras*, Crónica del Sexenio 1982–1988, Primer Año (Mexico City: Unidad de la Crónica Presidencial/Fondo de Cultura Económica), 14.

32. A good example of this general orientation can be found in the constitutional reforms initiated by president de la Madrid only four days after he assumed power. These reforms constitutionally defined the roles and function of the public, social, and private sectors. Though the measures failed to satisfy anyone—the left argued that the state was in fact building its own straitjacket, while the most radical fractions of business argued that the reforms simply confirmed the trend towards greater and more obtrusive state intervention—their basic intent, to regulate state intervention explicitly so as to limit the margins for discretionary action, was clear. See Miguel de la Madrid Hurtado, *El marco legislativo para el cambio*, vol. 2 (Mexico City: Dirección General de Asuntos Jurídicos de la Presidencia de la República Mexicana, 1983).

33. Jaime Ros, "On the Political Economy of Market and State Reform in Mexico," presented at the conference on "Democracy, Markets and Structural Reforms in Contemporary Latin America," North-South Center, University of Miami; and CEDES, Buenos Aires, 25–27 March 1992, table 1.

34. Ibid., 7.

35. Ibid.

36. I am indebted to Carlos Elizondo for pointing out the significance of this last issue.

37. On the issue of political turnover in Mexico, see Peter Smith, *Labyrinths of Power: Political Recruitment in Twentieth Century Mexico* (Princeton: Princeton University Press, 1979).

38. Robert Kaufman, *The Politics of Debt in Argentina, Brazil, and Mexico: Economic Stabilization in the 1980s* (Berkeley: Institute of International Studies, University of California, Berkeley, 1988), 83.

39. Rogelio Hernández Rodríguez, "Los hombres del presidente de la Madrid," *Foro Internacional* 109 (July–September, 1987), 5–38.

40. The primary budget balance (that is, income minus spending *excluding* interest payments) reflects actual fiscal efforts by the incumbent administration.

Primary Budget Balance (as percent of Mexico's GNP)

1982	–7.6	1986	1.7
1983	4.0	1987	.9
1984	4.6	1988	7.6
1985	3.3	1989	8.3

Banco de México, *Informe Anual*, various issues.

41. A thorough examination of the various means through which the state and the ruling party have controlled organized labor can be found in Ilan Bizberg, *Estado y sindicalismo en México* (Mexico City: El Colegio de México, 1990). Also useful is Angelina Alonso and Roberto Lopez's case study of the oil union, *El Sindicato de Trabajadores Petroleros y sus relaciones con PEMEX y el estado, 1970–1985* (Mexico City: El Colegio de México, 1986).

42. Presidencia de la República, *Las razones y las obras*, Crónica del Sexenio 1982–1988, Primer Año (Mexico City: Unidad de la Crónica Presidencial/Fondo de Cultura Económica),104.

43. Though information about the overall cost of FICORCA is not publicly available, analysts have estimated that by 1987 the program had effectively assumed 21.3 million dollars of the private sector's foreign debt. *Expansión*, 27 April 1987, quoted in Cristina Puga and Constanzo de la Vega, "Modernización capitalista y política empresarial," in *Testimonios de la crisis*, ed. Estela Gutierrez Garza, vol. 4, 253 (Mexico City: Siglo XXI, 1990).

44. *La Jornada*, 6 January 1992, 27. (Figure based on Central Bank data).

45. Secretaría de Hacienda y Crédito Público, *Cuadernos de Renovación Nacional: Restructuración del sistema financiero* (Mexico City: Presidencia de la República, 1988),143.

46. Ibid.

47. According to Sylvia Maxfield, "Financing obtained through the parallel financial system, by selling stock or commercial paper, was as much as 20 percent less expensive than that available through the banking system. However, access to this source of financing is limited to the 200 Mexican corporations which are registered on the stock exchange" ("International Economic Opening and Government-Business Relations in Mexico," Paper presented at the Workshop on Mexico's Alternative Political Futures, San Diego, Center for U.S.-Mexican Studies, 1988, 19).

48. See Carlos Elizondo, "Property Rights in Business-State Relations: The Case of the Bank Nationalization," Ph.D. diss., Oxford University, chap. 7.

49. Inducements included subsidies and special concessions of various kinds, and constraints ranged from fiscal auditing to failure to support employers in their dealings with workers, as well as simple law enforcement. This last feature is particularly important because the high levels of tolerance for illegal practices and behavior provide the government with an extremely powerful instrument in dealing with political opponents.

50. Ibid.

51. On the nature of these transformations, see Héctor Aguilar Camín, *Después del Milagro* (Mexico City: Cal y Arena, 1988).

52. For an analysis of the growth of the PAN along these same lines, see the excellent essay by Leticia Barraza and Ilan Bizberg, "El Partido Acción Nacional y el régimen político mexicano," *Foro Internacional* 123 (January–May, 1991), 418–45.

53. On business elites' political and ideological activism in the course of the 1980s, see Ricardo Pozas and Matilde Luna, eds., *Las empresas y los empresarios en el México contemporáneo* (Mexico City: Grijalbo, 1991), pt. 1.

54. In the August 1991 congressional elections, for instance, 17 percent of the PRI came from the ranks of the business sector. Equally significant has been the growing presence of private entrepreneurs among PRI candidates in regional electoral contests and private-sector financial support for PRI electoral campaigns, both at the national and the regional level. *Proceso* 800 (2 March 1992): 21.

55. Since the late 1980s private-sector financial committees have been created by the PRI in 24 states. José Ignacio Rodriguez Reyna, "Nuevo empresariado: La política como inversión," *Este País* 10 (January 1992): 3. These committees include the largest economic firms in the various states, some of which are also among the most powerful entrepreneurs in the country. Such is the case of the state of Nuevo León, where members include the owners of groups such as VISA, CEMEX, and PROTEXA.

56. On this process, see Alberto Azia Nassif, "Neopanismo and neopriismo en Chihuahua," in *Las empresas y los empresarios*, ed. Pozas and Luna, 217–32.

57. On this question, see the issue of *El Cotidiano* devoted to some of its most salient dimensions, July–August 1988.

58. Salient among them stand Lonrenzo Servitge, owner of BIMBO, the ninth largest economic group in the country; Roberto Hernández Ramírez who, along with Alfredo Harp Helu, bought the Banco Nacional de México in 1991; Carlos Slim, owner of the recently privatized Teléfonos de México; Agustín Legorreta, ex-owner of BANAMEX and currently shareholder in various holdings; and Andrés Marcelo Sada from CYDSA. *Proceso* 798 (17 February 1992): 22–25.

59. A clear example can be found in last year's electoral process in the state of Guanajuato where widespread allegations of fraud resulted in the resignation of the PRI gubernatorial candidate right before assuming office. A good showing on the part of Acción Nacional led to what appears to have been an arrangement between the government and the party whereby the PAN mayor of the capital of the state was appointed—by the local congress—as interim governor.

60. Theoretical support for this argument can be found in Edward Gibson's very important contribution to the study of conservative electoral movements in Latin America, "Conservative Parties and Democratic Politics: Argentina in Comparative Perspective," Ph.D. diss., Department of Political Science, Columbia University, 1991.

61. See Barraza and Bizberg, "El Partido Acción Nacional."

Leigh A. Payne

6. Brazilian Business and the Democratic Transition

New Attitudes and Influence

Scholars generally view business leaders' commitment to democracy as essential to democratic stability.[1] Accordingly, they often view the rejection of democracy by Latin American business leaders in the 1960s and 1970s as ominous signs for the democratic transitions currently under way in that region. For example, O'Donnell and Schmitter warn:

Should the mobilization of regime opponents seem to go "too far," however, then authoritarian rule may again be judged to be indispensable, if unfortunate. Moreover, as was suggested by the study of the breakdown of democracy, an authoritarian inflection by a large part of the bourgeoisie is usually accompanied by another symptom of impending danger: the mobilization of middle sectors in favor of a coup that will bring "order" to society.[2]

This statement suggests three generally accepted, yet untested, assumptions about business leaders' attitudes toward democratic transitions. First, full democracy threatens business interests. Second, as during the 1960s and 1970s, business leaders (along with the rest of the coup coalition) possess both the desire and ability to derail a democratic transition. Third, business leaders believe that an authoritarian political system is more likely to protect their interests than a competitive democracy.

My research on Brazilian business leaders during the New Republic government of President José Sarney (1985–1989) and President Fernando Collor de Mello's administration (1989–1993) challenges these assumptions. While Brazil's business leaders played a critical role in destabilizing the democratic government of João Goulart (1961–1964) and today face threats similar to those encountered in the 1960s, they have not endorsed an authoritarian reversal. I contend that this is owing to their altered perceptions of the costs of authoritarian rule compared to its benefits, and their ability to influence political outcomes within a democratic framework.[3] These changes have led to greater tolerance for democracy among the business elite, which is likely to engender greater democratic stability. Nonetheless, they have also made it easier for business to limit social and economic distribution, thus constraining the democratic process. I conclude by suggesting how the democratic leadership might sustain business's acceptance of democracy while limiting its obstacles to expanded liberalization.

Methodological Note

The research findings presented in this chapter are based largely on interviews with 155 industrial leaders from both Brazilian and multinational firms conducted between 1986 and 1988, primarily in São Paulo, the industrial center of Brazil. The interview subjects included: (1) directors of key business associations; (2) presidents, directors, and managers of industrial firms who had been outspoken on political issues or involved in political activities during the 1964–1988 period and therefore were frequently cited in newspaper or magazine articles, business association archives, or secondary literature;

and (3) industrial leaders who were not necessarily in the public eye but who were considered by other interview subjects to be leaders within the industrial community.

The interview questionnaire I developed included specific questions primarily about the background of the industrialist and the firm. I also asked in-depth open-ended questions that explored industrialists' opinions on a broad range of issues, including changes in labor relations; current debates in the Constituent Assembly, trade unions, and business associations; and particular presidential administrations and political issues. Because I promised my interview subjects anonymity, when their remarks appear in the text, they are identified only by relevant background information.

The research on Brazilian landholders was conducted simultaneously with that of industrialists and extended into 1992. It involved an additional short research trip to Brazil to interview leaders of the rural Democratic Union (UDR) in August 1992.

Threats to Business Leaders During the New Republic

During the New Republic, business leaders faced perils that had also existed before the 1964 coup: economic crisis, changes in capital-labor relations, and the expropriation of private (rural) property.[4] Despite these threats, and discrediting many common assumptions, they did not mobilize against the democratic transition.

Economic Crisis

There is no doubt that the deteriorating economy President Sarney inherited from the military regime, as well as his inability to resolve that crisis, threatened business interests. As table 6.1 indicates, although the first two years of the New Republic brought economic growth, inflation and debt remained high. Moreover, Brazil's economy began to decline at that time. In-

TABLE 6.1   Economic Indiators in Brazil, 1974–1989

	Rate of Inflation (%)	Change in GDP (%)	Current Accounts ($U.S. millions)	Industrial GDP (%)
1974	27.6	9.7	−7.562	8.3
1975	29.0	5.6	−7.008	4.7
1976	42.0	9.7	−6.554	11.7
1977	43.7	2.9	−5.112	3.1
1978	38.7	4.9	−7.036	6.3
1979	52.7	6.8	−10.478	6.6
1980	82.8	9.3	−12.806	9.1
1981	105.6	−4.4	−11.751	−9.1
1982	97.8	0.6	−16.312	0.0
1983	142.1	−3.5	−6.837	−6.3
1984	197.0	5.1	0.420	6.2
1985	226.9	8.3	−0.273	8.9
1986	145.2	7.6	−4.477	11.2
1987	229.7	3.6	−1.275	0.6
1988	682.3	−0.3	—	—
1989	1287.0	—	—	—

Sources: International Monetary Fund, International Financial Statistics; United Nations' Economic Commission for Latin America and the Caribbean, Statistical Yearbook for Latin America.

dustry in particular suffered and reacted by blaming the government. One director from the São Paulo Federation of Industries (FIESP) stated that Sarney had failed to guarantee the minimum needs of industry: profit, a market, affordable credit, stable rules, and solid institutions.[5] Industrialists especially criticized the government for its erratic economic policies and price and wage controls.

Unpredictable Economic Policies Economic policy was highly volatile during the New Republic. In his five years in office, Sarney appointed four different finance ministers (Francisco Dornelles in 1985, Dilson Funaro in 1985, Luíz Carlos Bresser Pereira in 1987, and Mailson Ferreira da Nóbrega in 1987), who issued five different economic programs (Cruzado Plan I in 1986, Cruzado Plan II in 1986, the Bresser Plan in 1987, the Social Pact in 1988, and the Summer Plan in 1989), as well as numerous modifications. These ever changing economic programs not only failed to resolve the economic crisis but actually made it more unpredictable. For example, the Brazilian currency was changed twice (from the cruzeiro to the cruzado in 1986, and to the novo cruzado in 1989) and price and wage controls were periodically implemented and repealed. Moreover, the government did not warn industrialists about anticipated policy changes, and even when it made assurances to business, it ignored them when they proved inconvenient.[6] In short, industrialists could not predict the short- or long-term economic future with any certainty. The following statements from industrialists illustrate this point:

Private initiative needs a clear signal from the government regarding the paths that it will take, so that it knows where to put risk capital. . . . If we're going to run the risk of making long-term investments, we need the certainty that the rules are not going to change in the middle of the game.[7]

The most terrible thing in the world for business people is uncertainty. We business people live with risk and we know how to manage it. But this history of freezing prices for nine months, unfreezing, refreezing, now regulating, deregulating tomorrow, indexes, disindexation . . . constitutes an intolerable level of uncertainty which prevents us from investing and planning our future. I repeat: any rule is better than no rule at all.[8]

In a histrionic plea for economic predictability, FIESP's president, Mario Amato, claimed that as far as the business community was concerned, the government "could be socialist, or even communist. The important thing is that there are rules that the business community can count on."[9]

In response to the unpredictability of economic policies, industrialists demanded participation in, influence over, and information about economic decisions. They sought an end to the government's practice of developing policies in the isolated "laboratory in Brasília."[10] Nevertheless, industrialists had more influence over these economic policies than other social groups did. For example, two of the four finance ministers (Funaro and Bresser Pereira) were from the Paulista business elite. In addition, Sarney personally met with industrialists and even occasionally solicited their opinions on economic policy.[11] Further, the government occasionally modified its policies to reduce the burden on the Brazilian private sector.[12] Finally, many business leaders used certain resources to protect themselves from, and even to benefit from the economic crisis—in particular capital flight, the "overnight," and speculation.

Price and Wage Controls Brazil's industrialists argued that the price and wage controls implemented by the New Republic government to contain inflation hindered their ability to produce, invest, and make profits. For example, when the government froze retail prices, it did not always control the prices for industrial inputs. Thus the costs of producing a given item sometimes exceeded its government-mandated retail price.

Businesses used various strategies to protect themselves from profit losses caused by price controls. Some reduced the contents of their packages without reducing the price, thus defrauding consumers.[13] Others simply ignored the price controls and charged exorbitant black market prices.[14] Still others withheld their products from the market until the government allowed them to raise prices, which caused product shortages.[15]

In addition to these individual strategies, business associations repeatedly demanded that the government remove price controls. For example, on two separate occasions FIESP president Mario Amato threatened to organize business groups to carry out civil disobedience unless the government realigned prices.[16] This threat was never carried out, even though the government did not repeal the price controls.

Business leaders also opposed the recessionary effects of wage controls. After an initial consumer boom under Cruzado Plan I, workers suffered serious wage losses, which industrialists believed reduced consumer demand and, therefore, industrial sales and profits. At that point, the real minimum wage had reached a level comparable to that of the 1950s. Nearly all the industrialists I interviewed (81 percent) considered the minimum wage in 1987–1988 to be insufficient. The following comments illustrate this concern:

> We cannot live in a country of 130 million people of which 82 percent do not consume anything. This might seem like a PMDB or PT [leftist] discourse, but I am a businessman, concerned with the internal market.[17]

> In 1987, wage increases were below inflation. There were no jobs. There was a drop in consumer power. And a fall in the internal market. The president forgot the internal market. He squeezed wages to pay the international debt. Workers are starving to death.[18]

Industrialists responded to the wage controls in various ways. Some paid their workers more than the minimum wage. For example, only 3 percent of the industrialists I interviewed paid their least skilled workers the minimum wage, while the vast majority (79 percent) paid above it: 70 percent paid two to four times the minimum wage, and 8 percent paid five to seven times that amount.[19] Moreover, industrialists sometimes granted wage increases above the stipulated level. For example, when finance minister Bresser Pereira recommended in 1987 that employers offer no more than a 10 percent increase in wages, at first individual firms and then FIESP as a whole rejected his proposal and granted 46 percent increases.[20] Some petitioned the government for more flexibility in setting wages.

For example, after the Bresser Plan was implemented, FIESP predicted that average real wages would fall by about 10 percent and recommended that the government allow a wage bonus to reduce the impact of wage losses on industrial production.[21] Some called on the government to allow the market to determine wages and prices. Finally, some industrialists threatened to join workers in their general strike against the wage controls of the Bresser Plan.[22]

However, the business associations did not consistently challenge the government's economic policies. For example, in October 1987, at the height of industrialists' vehement protests against the Bresser Plan, FIESP publicly declared support for President Sarney. A FIESP director defended this position, stating, "The President of the Republic needs respect to begin to take charge of the political structure in the country and to establish economic rules that restore confidence and stimulate investment."[23] By vacillating between support for and opposition to the government's economic program, FIESP failed to mount a strong opposition. Many of FIESP's members accused the association of taking an accommodating position toward the government—perhaps to encourage personal favors—rather than defending the business community's broad interests and articulating its demands.

The foregoing discussion of business leaders' reaction to the economic crisis of the 1980s illustrates that, as in 1964, nearly all industrialists were dissatisfied with the "democratic" government's capacity to resolve the crisis. However, unlike the precoup period, three conditions prevented them from mobilizing against the government. First, they retained some influence over economic policies through the selection of finance ministers and Sarney's attention to their opinions and needs. This influence led some business associations to believe that they could achieve maximum results by cooperating with, rather than confronting, the government.

Second, they attempted to offset negative economic policies (such as capital flight, speculation, defrauding consumers, and black market prices) individually. Indeed, those industrialists who enjoyed various production, marketing, or financing options tended not to fear the economic crisis during the New Republic.[24] As a result of these first two factors, there was not sufficient motivation within the business community to mobilize against Sarney.

Third, in general industrialists did not believe that an authoritarian reversal would solve their problems. Although some industrialists continued to romanticize the "economic miracle" period, most realized that Brazil was paying the price of the military regime's development strategy—international debt, a devastated internal market, and expansive, ineffective, and costly state enterprises. Instead, industrialists viewed the prospects of an open and direct presidential election in 1989 as a means of replacing economic policies and policy makers without altering the political system. An article in a 1988 FIESP publication illustrated industrialists' hopes for a democratic solution to their economic problems:

The dark clouds accumulating on the horizon at the turn of the year will only be dissipated with an authentic and democratic government. A weak government without credibility . . . will not be able to do anything to change the economic picture for this year—that is, recession, inflation, unemployment.[25]

Thus, like their counterparts in advanced industrial democracies, Brazilian industrialists' dissatisfaction with the economy does not necessarily lead them to endorse a change of regime. Instead, they use their considerable political resources (significant economic power and social ties to key economic decision makers) to influence economic policy from within the existing political framework.

TABLE 6.2   Strikes in Brazil, 1985–1989

	Total No. of Strikes	Total No. of Strikers
1985	712	5,916,905
1986	1,148	4,871,400
1987	1,201	7,797,649
1988	656	7,275,422
1989	1,702	16,597,585
Total	5,419	42,458,961

Source: Departamento Intersindical de Estatística Estudos Sócio-Econômicos (DIEESE), *Boletim*, 1985–1990.

Note: When DIEESE lacked information on the number of workers who participated in a strike, that strike was not included in the total number of strikes, causing an underestimation of strikes, often by as much as 30 percent.

Capital-Labor Relations

Relations between business and labor underwent significant changes during the New Republic. Strong and independent trade unions and labor federations reemerged. Strikes erupted anew and escalated in number (see table 6.2). Employers were forced to negotiate directly with striking workers, rather than relying on the authoritarian state to intervene and end strikes. Changes in labor legislation allowed for shop floor committees, the right to strike, and a reduction in the maximum work week from forty-eight to forty-four hours.

Despite these significant and costly changes (FIESP complained that they raised employers' costs by 30 percent), few employers seemed threatened by capital-labor relations during the New Republic. Sixty-four percent of the industrialists I interviewed expressed satisfaction with labor relations in their firms. Only 21 percent of those who felt threatened during the New Republic mentioned labor as a source of their fear. Employers did not feel threatened because they had substantial control over changes in collective bargaining and legislation, and they perceived that radicalism and the strength of the Brazilian labor movement were limited.

Control over Changes in Labor Relations Employers recalled their first experiences with direct negotiations—during the massive 1978 strikes—as disastrous. They felt that employers had yielded to workers' demands to end the disruption in production. As a result of these experiences, however, FIESP organized a system for collective bargaining and strike resistance. It established guidelines for negotiating with strikers and set up a telephone communication network to gather and disseminate information on strikes. FIESP also formed permanent negotiating teams, led by experts, to centralize bargaining sessions. The most powerful negotiating team was the Group of 14, which negotiated on behalf of the metal, mechanical, and electrical firms in São Paulo.

Industrialists had mixed reactions to FIESP's system of labor relations. Most industrialists during the New Republic (61 percent) believed that centralized negotiations with labor through FIESP was optimal. Those who held this view most strongly were from the oldest, most traditional firms and belonged to FIESP and other prominent business associations.[26] They believed that FIESP's teams simplified labor negotiations and strengthened employers' power by providing a united bargaining front. The following excerpts from my interviews illustrate this view:

Employers started negotiating in their firms. These firms started to give up a lot—make a lot of concessions to labor—too many. FIESP realized that this situation of negotiations was going to continue, and industrialists couldn't keep giving away so much. So FIESP got tough. It tried to centralize negotiations to end firm-by-firm negotiations and put a brake on concessions.[27]

Without the Group of 14, industry would be faced with a domino effect. Unions would get something from one industry and then go on to another, and eventually win all of their demands from all of the industries, and industries would have to give in to avoid a strike.[28]

On the other hand, a significant minority of business leaders (39 percent) advocated—and, at times, engaged in—negotiations without the intervention of the government or business associations. Some believed that FIESP's labor relations specialists were more willing to accede to labor demands than were the owners of firms. As two industrialists commented:

The labor relations experts give away too much because they have learned so much about labor and labor conditions—they're too sympathetic. Industrialists want to go back to the old days when they negotiated with labor because the experts give up too much.[29]

It is better to get in front to discuss things with workers instead of using intermediaries, which weaken the position of employers.[30]

Others felt that FIESP's efforts impeded direct negotiations and the successful resolution of strikes. They believed that FIESP was too intransigent with regard to labor demands, thereby prolonging strikes and costing employers more in production losses than they would have otherwise lost through increased wages.[31] For example, one industrialist described his firm's relationship with FIESP as follows: "We're under pressure from the FIESP Mafia to keep from paying higher wages. We do pay better wages and provide better benefits, but we don't want that to get out, because the FIESP Mafia will be after us."[32] One might expect industrialists who prefer firm-level negotiations to be from larger enterprises that could more easily absorb the higher cost of labor. However, as the following comment illustrates, small firms also felt constrained by FIESP's intransigence.

[The leaders of FIESP] are traditional . . . right-wing . . . against direct negotiations in small firms. They support their own monopoly over labor relations. They inhibit the process of change. They are against modernity. They are retrograde. They do not work on behalf of the small firm. They put a wall up. They force negotiations through the Group of 14. And the smaller firms have just ignored the Group of 14 and done things their own way.[33]

Whether industrialists chose to negotiate through FIESP's teams or their own firm-level bargaining, they generally seemed satisfied with their ability to control production losses and wage increases through collective bargaining.

Another forum for business leaders to assert control over labor was in the Constituent Assembly, the legislative body charged with writing the 1988 constitution. In contrast to their success in collective bargaining, most members of the business community were dissatisfied with their influence in the Assembly. They had failed to defeat key labor provisions, specifically the reduction in work hours, shop floor representation, and the unrestricted right to strike. However, for several reasons these issues did not pose significant problems for employers. For example, although most industrialists opposed the reduction in the work week, the majority of those I interviewed (74 percent) had already agreed to a forty-four-hour (or lower) work week in collective bargaining before the constitution was ratified. Several prominent business leaders publicly stated that they could tolerate this reduction.[34] Employers retained control over shop floor representation and strikes when they defeated the job security measure in the 1988 constitution, which would have provided guarantees against arbitrary dismissal. Business leaders and their advocates in the Centrão, a conservative block in the Constituent Assembly, replaced that measure with an indemnity clause allowing employers to fire employees at will as long as employees were compensated.[35] Thus business leaders remained free to dismiss individual workers who led strikes or participated in other activities perceived as threatening to the firm.

Labor Radicalism and Strength Employers might have viewed the emergence of an independent trade union movement able to endorse constitutional provisions successfully and lead strikes during the New Republic as radical and threatening. Yet this was not the prevailing opinion. Only a minority of the industrialists I interviewed considered workers in their firms to be radical. As table 6.3 indicates, most classified the workers in their firms as moderate left or center, and a significant number even put workers on the right. Only four considered workers in their firm to be on the extreme left.[36]

While most industrialists did not perceive the workers in their firms to be radical, some viewed trade union leaders in such a light. The following excerpts from my interviews with industrialists illustrate the view that certain groups (for example, the Workers' party, PT; the labor federation associated with PT, CUT; the progressive church; and trade union leaders) attempted to radicalize the labor movement, often through intimidation: "Some strikes in the industrial sector are being provoked by the Workers' party [PT] with the assistance of the

TABLE 6.3 Ideological Ratings Chosen by the Industrialists Interviewed for Workers in Their Firms

	No. of Interviewees Choosing Rating	%
Extreme left	4	3
Moderate left	37	29
Center	59	46
Moderate right	25	20
Extreme right	3	2
Total	128	100

Source: Interviews with Brazilian industrialists held in 1986–1988.

church. . . . PT's action is becoming more effective given the lethargy that has overcome the other parties with respect to their activities in the union area."[37] Another individual stated: "CUT and PT are trying to destabilize the economic situation. They want a country run by workers . . . to be owners of production and politics."[38]

Although most industrialists I interviewed (77 percent) perceived CUT and PT as on the extreme left,[39] I did not find any statistically significant relationship between industrialists' perceptions of PT or CUT ideology and their fear of labor during the New Republic. Industrialists generally perceived the labor movement as nonthreatening after several recent changes in labor relations.

First, a capitalist or pragmatic unionism, called the *sindicato de resultados* or goal-oriented unionism, evolved during the New Republic and challenged CUT's and PT's philosophy and tactics. Luiz Antonio de Medeiros (president of the São Paulo metalworkers trade union) and A. Rogério Magri (president of the São Paulo electrical energy trade union) spearheaded this new approach. They discouraged the involvement of trade unions and their leaders in national lobbies, campaigns, strikes, and protests, and instead advocated negotiation and bargaining as the most effective ways to achieve workers' goals. My survey data confirm that many industrialists viewed Medeiros and Magri as representatives of the true conservative interests of the Brazilian working class.[40] As tables 6.3 and 6.4 illustrate, most industrialists considered both Medeiros and the workers in their firms to be centrists.[41] Indeed, a large percentage of industrialists (48 percent) placed workers and Medeiros in the same position, while 29 percent placed Medeiros to the left and 22 percent placed him to the right of workers in their firms.[42]

Experiences under military rule and changes in the international left also appear to have altered industrialists' perceptions of a threat from labor. Several leaders I interviewed com-

TABLE 6.4   Ideological Ratings Chosen by
the Industrialists Interviewed for Luiz Antonio
Medeiros

	No. of Interviewees Choosing Rating	%
Extreme left	9	7
Moderate left	54	40
Center	47	35
Moderate right	20	15
Extreme right	4	3
Total	134	100

Source: Interviews with Brazilian industrialists held in
1986–1988.

mented that leftist mobilization in the factories and trade
unions no longer concerned them, since the left had abandoned its revolutionary zeal. These industrialists stated that the
left had learned, after twenty-one years of repression, that radicalism was a self-destructive path. These industrialists also
mentioned that the international left's symbols of the 1960s
(such as the Cuban Revolution, Fidel Castro, and Che Gue-
vara) had been replaced by perestroika, glasnost, and Lech
Walesa—hardly symbols that would threaten business leaders.

Some industrialists also believed that workers were passive,
or that the labor movement was too weak to threaten business.
This view was probably influenced by the tepid support among
workers for the general strikes the leadership called during the
New Republic. For example, on 20 August 1987 the labor federations called a general strike to demand real wage increases,
agrarian reform, the inclusion of workers' rights in the constitution, and a debt moratorium. A poll conducted by the *Folha
de São Paulo* showed that although 87 percent of the population considered the workers' demands just, only 39 percent

would honor the strike. Indeed, rank-and-file support was low. Even in the "militant" industrial suburbs of São Paulo, participation only reached about 20 percent. FIESP reported that while the normal absentee rate for workers was 3 percent, it reached only 5 percent on the day of the strike.

Finally, several industrialists believed that the labor movement contributed to, rather than threatened, political stability. This opinion was undoubtedly formed after the participation of labor and various political parties on the left in the Constituent Assembly, during which they proposed changes in the national labor relations system that the most powerful trade unions had already achieved in collective bargaining. Some industrialists clearly viewed labor and the left as willing to work through democratic channels to attain moderate demands.

In sum, there was no consensus among industrialists that labor was a threat in the 1980s. First, owing to domestic experiences and changes in the international left, few members of the business elite viewed labor as radical. Second, during the democratic transition industrialists proved capable of controlling labor through individual and collective means, including collective bargaining and key legislative victories (for example, the defeat of the job security measure) in the Constituent Assembly. Thus authoritarianism was not necessary to protect business from labor. Indeed, since a number of industrialists insisted that an intransigent response to labor demands heightened rather than reduced labor demands, authoritarianism may actually have been viewed as more disruptive than democracy.

The Expropriation of Private Property

The central threat to private property during the New Republic was agrarian reform, and industrialists were ambivalent toward it. On one hand, many believed that agrarian reform might resolve the problems of urban migration and meager agricultural production. On the other hand, they feared legislation permitting the government to expropriate private land, since it might lead to the expropriation of industrial firms.[43]

Not surprisingly, attitudes of rural business leaders toward the agrarian reform were unambiguous: they actively organized to defeat it. They also engaged in individual strategies to oppose threats to their property. In particular, they sponsored violence against rural organizers and their supporters (such as in the church, the legal community, and trade unions).[44] These landholders' use of violence obviously threatens democracy, since it denies peasants their fundamental rights to political representation and organization, liberty—and, at times, life. Government authorities' failure to fully investigate and prosecute these rural crimes, thereby granting landholders virtual immunity, further weakened the principle of rule by law. Thus, when landholders felt threatened by agrarian reform, their reaction to those fears threatened democracy.

Agrarian Reform Faced with the pervasive problems of skewed land distribution, rising rural violence, and popular pressure for change,[45] the Sarney government made agrarian reform one of its top priorities. Despite initial intentions, however, the program failed. At the end of Sarney's term in 1989, only 10 percent of the land initially targeted was actually expropriated and only 6.3 percent of the settlement target was reached.[46]

Although one explanation for the failure of agrarian reform is structural and technical constraints,[47] the primary obstacle was opposition from landholders. Ironically, Sarney stated in May 1986, "The agrarian reform will go forward despite pressure from those who hope to slow it. . . . I will not lose my courage."[48] However, even before he made that statement, he had compromised the goals of the reform in response to pressure from landholders and their allies in the military and the government. This was true of substantive changes in agrarian reform policy (for instance, the focus on public over private land distribution and the increase in compensation to land-holders) as well as in the personnel in charge of the reform.[49] Nevertheless, landholders were not satisfied with limiting their political pressure to modifying or delaying Sarney's agrarian reform, or influencing the appointment of the reform's administrators. They also took direct action to defeat agrarian reform in the Constituent Assembly. Landholders' interests were represented in the Assembly by existing institutions, such as the CNA (National Confederation of Agriculture) and the state Federations of Agriculture designed by the corporatist state, and a traditional "parallel" association, the Brazilian Rural Society. However, many landholders felt that these associations were better equipped to handle backroom negotiations with government officials for private interests than participate in open and democratic debate on agrarian reform under way in the Constituent Assembly. Thus a new organization was formed in 1985 (and officially registered in 1986): the UDR (Union of Rural Democracy).[50]

The UDR succeeded in its principal aim: to defeat agrarian reform legislation. The 1988 constitution protects from expropriation any productive property, thereby leaving only infertile lands unsuitable for agricultural production available for expropriation.

In some respects, the UDR pursues its goals through the democratic process. It elects representatives and candidates to public office, lobbies the government, shapes public opinion against the agrarian reform, and informs its members on agrarian issues. The UDR also promotes a "pragmatic" agricultural policy that includes making technology available to farmers and agricultural production more profitable.

However, its tactics are widely criticized. The UDR promotes particular candidates, often by using smear campaigns against competitors.[51] Its aggressive lobbying strategy in the Constituent Assembly led the president of the Brazilian Bar Association to label it "dangerously *golpista*."[52] The UDR twice blockaded the streets of Brasília with trucks and tractors to protest the agrarian reform proposal. It also organized young supporters (widely referred to as the "agroboys") to demonstrate in the halls of the Constituent Assembly.[53] These demonstrations often led to violent clashes with representatives of rural workers.

Violence has not been limited to the legislative hall, however. During the Constituent Assembly's debate on the agrarian reform, the Brazilian Bar Association referred to the escalating number of assassinations in the countryside as "a virtual civil war." One UDR leader confirmed suspicions that the UDR bought and distributed the weapons used to assassinate rural organizers and their supporters attempting to implement the land reform.[54] However, despite this open admission and the fact that landholders associated with rural violence belong to UDR, official investigations have failed to implicate the organization or its members in these rural crimes.

There is little question that the UDR has been politically powerful, popular among landholders, and effective in its efforts. However, it is doubtful that the UDR can provide a democratic alternative to violence as a means of defending landholders' interests.

Rural Violence   Landholders are not solely responsible for the rising rural violence; the government itself must also be held accountable for its failure to protect against the violations of human and civil rights in the countryside. The Brazilian government accepts the claims made by Amnesty International, the Brazilian Bar Association, and the Ministry of Agrarian Reform and Development that a large number of killings over the past five years were commissioned by members of the politically powerful landed elite and that state authorities (that is, the police and the judiciary) often failed to act decisively and independently to investigate and prosecute those cases. Indeed, Amnesty International found only two cases in which hired gunmen were convicted and sentenced, and in none were the landholders ordering the murder arrested. The government characterized this failure as the result of administrative problems of poor pay, inadequate training, overwork, and weak local and state authority structures inherited from twenty-one years of centralized military rule. The Brazilian government also listed individual "shortcomings" to explain the failure of the police and judiciary to conduct prompt and impartial inquiries into violent crimes against rural workers, indigenous Brazilians, and their advocates. Prejudice against peasants led to police intimidation and human rights abuses, which eroded trust in local authorities and deterred other peasants from reporting violent crimes.[55] Police and judges also permitted their personal relationships with landholders and hired gunmen to color their investigation of crimes against peasants.[56] Indeed, Amnesty International found that the police rarely interviewed witnesses or interviewed, detained, or arrested suspects in these rural crimes. When they did detain suspects, they were often immediately released without charge, papers on the case were "mislaid," or the suspect escaped from jail. Instead of addressing these problems, the judiciary relied solely on the incomplete findings of the police investigation. It neither called for further investigation nor carried out an independent inquiry.

Although Brazil acknowledged that under international law it has a responsibility to protect human rights, it stated that out of deference to the constitution-based federal structure, and in order to build strong local institutions and thereby restore democracy, it would not intervene directly. Instead, it would endeavor to educate the public and investigate grievances brought to the government's human rights agency.

Amnesty International argues that the government has failed to intervene even in cases where the violations of human rights fell within the federal government's jurisdiction.[57] It also argues that under the constitution, the federal government is authorized to intervene when state authorities do not act or where there is danger to social or political order. In the case of rising rural violence, both justifications for intervention apply. By refusing to use its full powers to ensure that the rule of law is respected in all parts of the union, the Brazilian government has ignored the problem of rural violence and thereby weakened democracy.[58]

In addition to Amnesty International, several worldwide entities, including the United States government,[59] the International Commission of Jurists, the ICFTU (International Confederation of Free Trade Unions), and Americas Watch, have pressured the Brazilian government to intervene, investigate, and prosecute human rights violations.[60] However, this international pressure has only occasionally proved successful. The most prominent example of successful international pressures concerns the murder of Francisco Alves ("Chico") Mendes on 22 December 1988.

Mendes's murder prompted an outcry against the Brazilian government's complacent and complicitous attitude toward rural violence. Mendes was a rubber tapper in Acre, a national trade union and landless peasant leader, a militant in the Workers' party (PT), and an internationally renowned environmentalist. In his defense of the rainforest, he led rubber tappers in direct confrontations with ranchers who were burning the forest for pasture. He also convinced international banks to stop loaning money for ranching in the Amazon and to suspend financing to the Brazilian government until it began to protect the environment.[61] Soon after he was killed, the Brazilian ambassador to the United States received petitions with 4,104 signatures demanding a trial for the responsible landholders. The judge in the case also received voluminous correspondence from concerned foreign citizens.

Brazil responded to international pressure. The government abandoned its noninterventionist stance and used the National Intelligence Service (SNI) and the federal police to aid the Acre

TABLE 6.5   Rural Assassinations in Brazil
during the New Republic, 1985–1989

	No. of Victims	% Increase/ Decrease
1985	125	—
1986	105	–19
1987	109	4
1988	93	–15
1989	56	–40

Source: Comissão Pastoral de Terra in *Rural Violence in Brazil: An Americas Watch Report* (New York: Human Rights Watch, February 1991), 29.

police. In addition, the federal government and its Ministry of Foreign Affairs were kept abreast of all developments in the investigation. The police investigated the case and arrested two suspects, Darci Alves Pereira, who fired the fatal shots, and his father, Darly Alves da Silva, the rancher who ordered the assassination. These suspects were brought to trial, the first jury trial in twenty-two years in Xapuri, found guilty, and sentenced to nineteen years in prison each.

As table 6.5 illustrates, the number of rural murders fell dramatically after the Mendes case. There are two conflicting explanations for this salutary development. On one hand, international and domestic pressure—as in the Mendes murder—may generate more consistent investigations and prosecutions that could greatly deter violence in the Brazilian countryside. This interpretation lacks support, however, since Mendes's murderers subsequently escaped from jail and the government has not intervened in other cases. Alternatively, when landholders are guaranteed their right to private property—as in the 1988 constitution—they will reduce their violence against rural organizers.

In short, a significant group of landholders felt threatened by agrarian reform efforts. They offset those threats by using violence against peasants, environmentalists, rural workers, and supporters of all these groups. They also engaged in political efforts to defeat agrarian reform legislation. Their efforts were often successful. While they have not eliminated rural social movements, they have remained generally immune from prosecution for their violence against rural organizers and their supporters. Furthermore, they successfully defeated the agrarian reform legislation in the 1988 constitution. Thus, landholders are unlikely to deliberately undermine the democratic transition, since they have retained both influence and protection throughout the political process. However, their tolerance for democracy is sustained at an extremely high cost to that political system.

In analyzing the economic crisis, changes in labor relations, and threats to private property during the New Republic, I have shown that business leaders faced many of the same threats they encountered in the pre-1964 coup period. However, in contrast to their responses during that period, they protected themselves individually from the government's unfavorable policies and programs and collectively influenced governmental decisions. In other words, the democratic transition provided business with sufficient individual and collective political power to render overthrow of the system unnecessary.

Business Leaders' Political Power and Preferences

As in other countries, Brazilian business leaders enjoy a "privileged position" in government that guarantees them a disproportionate influence over political outcomes.[62] This position is derived in part from their significance to the economy. Capitalist governments often avoid policies that might lead business leaders to reduce the services (such as jobs and goods) and revenues (like taxes) they provide to the nation. For example, the New Republic government modified its economic policies in response to threats of massive business collapse, excessive rates of unemployment, and reduced national revenues, production, and services.

Business leaders also derive their privileged position and undue influence over policies from their extensive political resources: financial, organizational, and social. Their financial resources come from their personal wealth, firm profits, and business organization budgets. The staff, expertise, technology, and materials provided by business associations comprise their organizational resources. And they derive their social resources—contacts and connections with government officials—from traveling in the same social circles, attending the same schools, parties, or social clubs, and trading occupations—that is, business leaders often pursue political careers, and public officials often retire to jobs in the private sector. In Brazil, urban and rural business leaders have used their financial and organizational resources to elect sympathetic government officials, shape popular opinion, and lobby for their demands. Their social status gives them more influence than other social sectors over key appointments in the ministries of Finance and Agriculture and Development.

Despite these sources of influence, business leaders have not achieved all their demands. One key obstacle is diversity. Firms vary in size, location, vulnerability to economic fluctuations, and access to credit, subsidies, and incentives. As a result, policies do not affect all businesses in the same way, causing business leaders to view government policies differently. In addition, the different ages, personalities, backgrounds, experiences, and ideologies of business leaders create diverse interests and opinions within the business community. Without agreement on policies or issues, leaders cannot tap the collective financial, organizational, and social resources within the community. Thus, when business leaders disagreed on policies, or when individuals found the means to protect their firms from unfavorable policies on their own, the business community failed to win its demands (for example, on the unrestricted right to strike, reduced work hours, and shop floor committees). On the other hand, business leaders universally feared limitations on their ability to hire and fire at will by the job security measure, and landholders generally feared expropriation of land. Such unanimity allowed them to unite their resources to defeat those measures. In other words, business's use of collective action to influence policy outcomes is greatest when there is a universally perceived threat coupled with the absence of individual means for reducing that threat.

Due to the diversity within their community, business leaders are most effective at vetoing specific policies rather than constructing alternatives. While they may agree that a specific policy threatens them, diversity within the business community is likely to prevent them from agreeing on an alternative. Thus business leaders rely on other social sectors (such as politicians) to develop and implement those alternatives. For example, business proved capable of defeating the job security measure, but could not agree on any alternatives to it. A conservative block in the Constituent Assembly, the Centrão, defeated the job security measure by proposing an alternative program (indemnity). Business leaders probably would not have been able to endorse this alternative, since it had little support within the business community.

Business's political power is also limited by poor leadership. Although business associations could provide that leadership, their strength depends on their ability to defend the broad interests of the business community and bring tangible benefits to individual firms.[63] For example, the UDR accomplished its chief goal by defeating agrarian reform. It is unlikely that the UDR will permanently withdraw from politics even though it has achieved its goal. Instead, it will no doubt remain dormant until threats of agrarian reform resurface. If it does disappear, it will only do so along with the hope for agrarian reform.

FIESP has faced more serious internal dissension than UDR, which weakens its leadership potential. Its members criticize its acquiescence and accommodation, as well as its failure to adopt a modern and democratic strategy to defend industrialists' interests. For example, one of FIESP's members stated, "FIESP has extraordinary force, but doesn't know how to use it."[64] Another stated that "FIESP is completely tied to the state" and therefore incapable of adequately defending business interests.[65] While some attribute this strategy to deeply ingrained corporatist patterns of behavior, others accuse FIESP directors of acquiescing in order to win personal favors from the government and of ignoring their obligation to represent the interests of the business community.

FIESP's members have also criticized it for representing only certain types of firms, although critics disagree as to which ones. While some believe that FIESP represents only small conservative traditional firms,[66] others claim that it represents only large domestic or foreign industrial monopolies. My analysis of FIESP's directorate and base of support suggests that FIESP appeals most to conservative industrialists from large firms, regardless of nationality.[67]

Business leaders' frustration with FIESP's strategy and failure to provide tangible benefits led them to form competitive and specialized trade associations.[68] These associations eroded some of FIESP's power in the business community, without supplanting its monopoly of representation. Thus business associations grew more fragmented, rather than united, during the New Republic.

Business leaders' political power has a definite bearing on their political attitudes. First, given the diversity within the business community, one cannot describe business leaders as inherently democratic or authoritarian. I found three broad groups within the business community: a minority that strongly defends democratic rules and procedures; another small group that strongly endorses authoritarian rule; and the majority, which is indifferent to political systems.[69]

Second, business leaders are capable of mobilizing to limit social democracy. For example, by defeating the agrarian reform measure, landholders prevented the distribution of land and political resources to peasants. Similarly, by defeating the job security measure, business leaders retained the right to fire labor leaders who mobilized workers to defend their rights. As long as they are able to restrict democracy by acting collectively within the system, they will not see the transitional government as having gone too far, thus safeguarding the democratic transition.

This appears to confirm O'Donnell and Schmitter's assumption that business leaders will accept only a restricted democracy. However, even if business leaders fail to restrict democracy, the inherent limitations on their political power will usually prevent them from successfully toppling the democratic government, as O'Donnell and Schmitter predict. The consensus necessary for toppling a democratic government depends on four principal factors: (1) a crisis severe enough to threaten nearly all business leaders and a lack of individual and collective protection from that crisis; (2) strong leadership emerging from the business community to mobilize its members against the government; (3) the government's failure to protect the nation from business's threats to reduce employment, investment, and production; (4) other social actors joining business leaders in their "veto" of the democratic government and installation of an authoritarian alternative. (Business leaders on their own might agree to undermine the government, without agreeing on an alternative.) While all of these conditions explain the success of the 1964 coup,[70] they are unlikely to recur in light of the current domestic and international political climate.

In sum, Brazilian business leaders adapted to the New Republic government even though it often threatened their interests. They tolerated this unsatisfactory situation because they could circumvent the economic crisis, modify the government's economic policies, retain control over organized labor, and eliminate threats to private property. Their success in these endeavors depended on effective individual and collective action. It also depended on the government's responsiveness to business needs. The Sarney government listened to business leaders' demands because it both feared political reprisals from business and depended on their supply of goods, jobs, and revenues.

The Collor de Mello Government and Threats to Business Leaders

The Collor de Mello government elected in 1989 initially proved less responsive to business's needs than its predecessors. This surprised business leaders, since most had supported Collor in the elections. However, their initial distrust of business-state relations during this period never led them to mount an opposition to democracy. And, as Collor modified his positions over time, these tensions diminished. In this section, I will analyze the threats to business leaders from the economy, labor relations, and agrarian reform, as well as their political power, during the early years of the Collor administration.

The threats business faced during the New Republic did not dissipate with the Collor de Mello government. However, business used both the individual and collective means developed during the New Republic period to influence and offset negative government policies.

Economic Crisis

Industrialists believe that they lost influence during the Collor government. This was partially apparent in his appointment of Zélia Cardoso de Mello, a former member of the Communist party, to the Finance Ministry. Collor ignored both business leaders' alternative recommendations for, and protests against, the Cardoso appointment.

Another example of business leaders' lack of influence was the Collor Plan, an economic program designed without business input and announced shortly after Collor took office in March 1990. On one hand, the plan included provisions endorsed by industrialists: privatization of state enterprises, reduction of government expenditures, and control over inflation. However, it threatened businesses by freezing savings accounts over $1,000, partially closing the "overnight," cracking down on capital flight, reducing import barriers, freezing prices, and increasing taxes. Moreover, Collor announced—and imposed—prison sentences for individuals who violated the program. Collor further alienated business leaders by casting aspersions on them and blaming them for the economic crisis.[71]

At first, business leaders protested the government's plan, but they also appeared willing to give it time to succeed in reducing inflation and stabilizing the economy. By most accounts, it has failed. Collor reduced government expenditures by eliminating jobs but has not successfully privatized state enterprises or reduced inflation. Prices rose 1,795 percent in 1990, outpacing 1989's 1,765 percent increase. The plan stimulated rather than halted the ongoing recession in Brazil.

However, while the economy continued to deteriorate, business leaders retained some, albeit limited, influence and protections. For example, judgments against members of the business community under Collor's plan were overturned in courts of law. Businesses did lay off workers. In addition, when Collor dismissed his finance minister (after her romantic involvement with the married justice minister), he replaced her with Minister Marcílio Moreira, a conservative more in line with private-sector interests.

Capital-Labor Relations

Relations with labor did not threaten business leaders during the Collor administration for three reasons. First, economic decline continued to weaken the labor movement in Brazil. Second, Collor placed the Ministry of Labor in conservative hands. Collor first appointed A. Rogério Magri, the conservative trade union leader of the *sindicato de resultados* strain, to that position. Although Collor later dismissed Magri because of his involvement in a bribery scandal, he replaced him with another conservative minister. Third, the severity of the crisis led business and labor to unite in protest against the Collor Plan. Indeed, rather than increasing capital-labor tensions, the Collor government—albeit unintentionally—reduced them. While this kept business leaders from mounting an opposition to democracy, it also represents the continued failure of social and economic distribution programs in Brazil.

The Expropriation of Private Property

Collor campaigned on a platform for "constitutional reform," which included eliminating the ban on expropriating productive land, giving way to a viable agrarian reform. However, landholders had little to fear from Collor's pronouncements, since he appointed—and retained despite numerous ministerial shuffles—as minister of agriculture Antônio Cabrera Filho, a wealthy cattle farmer from São Paulo and active member of the UDR.[72]

Collor also twice reversed his positions regarding the environment. During his campaign, Collor was allied with Amazonino Mendes, governor of Amazonas, who once offered to distribute free chain saws to clear the rainforest. However, once elected he appointed José Lutzemberger, an internationally renowned environmentalist, to head a conservation agency called IBAMA (Brazilian Institute for the Environment and Natural Renewable Resources). In direct contrast to ranchers' and developers' interests, Lutzemberger has publicly opposed the construction of roads into the Amazon and clear-cutting of forests. Collor also ordered the destruction of landing strips in the Amazon used by ranchers and miners invading indigenous lands, and announced the demarcation of lands for exclusive use by indigenous groups. Despite these bold initial moves, Collor subsequently dismissed Lutzemberger because of his outspoken criticism of the Collor government, and indigenous lands have yet to be distributed.

Business Leaders' Political Power

On one hand, under Collor, business lost some of its influence. Initially Collor was unwilling to negotiate with business leaders, openly attacked them, appointed cabinet members whom they vehemently opposed, and adopted policies inimical to their interests. On the other hand, Collor modified both his initial attitudes toward business and his policies. Moreover, evidence suggests that business began to break out of the corporatist mold, strengthening organizations and increasing business autonomy from the government. Mario Amato's reelection to the FIESP presidency in 1989 was disputed by forces within FIESP that accused the organization of failing to allow democratic participation in decisions. Amato responded to these protests by announcing a reorganization within FIESP's board of directors. He claimed that the appointment of these directors would now be based on their business expertise, rather than personal loyalty and friendship. Although it is too early to judge the impact of this change on FIESP's political activities, it may lead to more effective leadership in the business community.

Conclusion

The evidence presented in this chapter supports a new interpretation of business-state relations in the emerging Latin American democracies. As in the earlier experiment with democratic rule, business leaders faced economic decline, labor mobilization, and expropriation of private property. However, in contrast to that earlier period, they are unlikely to endorse an authoritarian reversal. That is, as long as certain conditions present during the transition period prevail throughout the consolidation phase. The Brazilian case reveals two sets of conditions that have militated against business leaders' involvement in an authoritarian reversal.

First, authoritarianism no longer represents a model for resolving national problems in Brazil. It has been discredited both domestically and internationally. The military regime's mismanagement of the economy, reliance on arbitrary repression to guarantee social order, encroachment on the private sector by expanding state enterprises, and exclusion of business influence in government decisions, led leaders who had formerly endorsed—or at least passively accepted—the military regime to question the regime's capacity to govern effectively and defend business interests. In addition, foreign governments and international organizations attached moral stigmas and tangible costs to authoritarian rule, leading nations around the world to begin democratic transitions. The authoritarian model of government lost its appeal for business and allied sectors. In short, as long as business leaders and their allies perceive that the domestic and international costs of authoritarian rule exceed its benefits, they are unlikely to endorse it.

Second, business can adapt to, and even benefit from, emerging democratic rule. The Brazilian case suggests that liberalization can provide business leaders with more opportunities to influence government policies than they enjoyed under authoritarian rule. In addition, their experience under the emerging democracy may reduce their fears of economic decline, labor radicalization, and the expropriation of private property. Their perception of threats also changes with international trends, such as the end of the cold war. Moreover, their own success in their efforts—individual and collective—to mitigate potential threats reduces their fears. They are reassured to realize that democratic rule will not necessarily undermine business interests. In other words, when business leaders perceive that their intrinsic interests are protected and they have some influence over the policies that affect them, they are likely to accept the prevailing political system. Rather than mobilize to overthrow it, they attempt to restrict its policies. When united, business leaders have effectively limited redistribution programs and social protections for marginalized groups. If newly emerging democratic governments are to overcome the obstacles to social democracy from business, they must exploit the fragmentation within the business community by negotiating agreements with its progressive sectors, thereby undermining the formation of a united front. Without unity, business leaders will be less successful in their efforts to limit the rights and protections of marginalized social groups.

Notes

1. Larry Diamond and Juan J. Linz, "Introduction: Politics, Society, and Democracy in Latin America," in *Democracy in Developing Countries: Latin America*, ed. Diamond, Linz, and Seymour Martin Lipset (Boulder, Colo.: Lynne Rienner Publishers, 1989), 1–58.

2. Guillermo O'Donnell and Philippe Schmitter, *Transitions from Authoritarian Rule: Tentative Conclusions about Uncertain Democracies* (Baltimore: Johns Hopkins University Press, 1986), 27.

3. For a more detailed discussion, see Leigh A. Payne, *Brazilian Industrialists and Democratic Change* (Baltimore: Johns Hopkins University Press, 1994).

4. See discussion on the threats of political uncertainty and the left in ibid.

5. Aldo Lorenzetti quoted in "FIESP decide ampliar apoio a Sarney e intensificar 'lobby' no Congresso," *Folha de São Paulo*, 15 October 1987, 30.

6. For example, although the government promised not to freeze prices and wages before the Summer Plan, the plan as implemented included price and wage freezes.

7. Walter Sacca, director of the Economic Department of FIESP, quoted in "Empresarios acham que Cruzado II ja está demorando," *Estado de São Paulo/Jornal da Tarde*, 20 November 1986, 13.

8. "Indústria critica 'instabilidade' da política econômica," *Folha de São Paulo*, 30 December 1986, 25.

9. "Empresários pedem regras mais claras," *Folha de São Paulo*, 9 July 1987, 23.

10. Walter Sacca, quoted in "Empresarios acham que Cruzado II ja está demorando," 13.

11. Thomas E. Skidmore, *The Politics of Military Rule in Brazil, 1964–85* (New York: Oxford University Press, 1988), 305.

12. For example, while these economic policies often froze wages after they had been averaged over a previous period, prices were never averaged, but simply frozen at their current rate or, at times, allowed to increase before they were frozen. Leigh A. Payne, "Working-Class Strategies in the Transition to Democracy in Brazil," *Comparative Politics*, January 1991: 221–38.

13. Peter Flynn, "Brazil: The Politics of the Cruzado Plan," *Third World Quarterly* 8 (October 1986): 176–77.

14. William C. Smith, "Heterodox Shocks and the Political Economy of Democratic Transition in Argentina and Brazil," presented at the XIV International Congress of the Latin American Studies Association, New Orleans, 17–19 March 1988, 14. See also Skidmore, *Politics of Military Rule in Brazil*, 281.

15. These shortages were primarily in meat, dairy, and soybean products.

16. Sarney responded by calling businessmen "anarchists." See "Sarney acusa empresários de pegar anarquia," *Folha de São Paulo*, 10 January 1987, 17; and "Empresários ameaçam desobedecer governo," *Folha de São Paulo*, 22 August 1987, 17.

17. Matias Machline quoted in "Machline defende fortalecimento do mercado interno," *Folha de São Paulo*, 6 August 1987, 25.

18. Interview with a director of a medium-sized metalworking company, 8 October 1987.

19. The remaining 1 percent stated that they paid above the minimum wage but did not know exactly how much. In addition, 18 percent did not know how much they paid their employees.

20. "Empresários fazem acordo em vários estados," *Folha de São Paulo*, 14

August 1987, 26; and "Empresas ignoram o Plano Bresser e antecipam residuo," *Folha de São Paulo*, 4 October 1987, 46.

21. "FIESP sugere abono para assalariados," *Folha de São Paulo*, 18 June 1987, 25; and "FIESP preve uma redução no rendimento do assalariado," *Folha de São Paulo*, 19 June 1987, 19.

22. "Empresários admitem apoiar a paralisação," *Folha de São Paulo*, 28 July 1987, 21.

23. Feres Abujamra quoted in "FIESP decide ampliar apoio a Sarney e intensificar 'lobby' no Congresso."

24. Industrialists from foreign firms were less fearful than those from Brazilian firms. While 52 percent of those from Brazilian firms felt threatened by the New Republic, only 25 percent of the industrialists from U.S. firms and 39 percent from other multinational companies felt threatened. In addition, only 40 percent of those from firms with some export production were threatened compared to 60 percent without it.

25. Clovis Rossi, "98% dos empresários não confiam no governo Sarney," *Folha de São Paulo*, 9 February 1988, 5.

26. Of industrialists I interviewed, 76 percent of those from traditional firms (in wood, paper, leather, furs, textile, clothing, food, beverage, glass, and ceramic manufacturing) favored centralized negotiations through business associations, compared to 56 percent from nontraditional firms. In addition, 67 percent of those with memberships in prominent business associations—particularly FIESP—favored such negotiations, compared to 52 percent of those with memberships in less important ones. Last, 75 percent of the industrialists from firms founded before 1930 supported centralized negotiations, compared to 55 percent of those founded after 1930.

27. Interview with a director of a very large multinational corporation, 27 July 1987.

28. Interview with an executive of a very large metalworking company, 11 October 1987.

29. Interview with a director of a medium-sized Brazilian company, 1 October 1987.

30. Interview with a director of a medium-sized company, 24 September 1987.

31. Comment made in a meeting I attended of owners of small businesses on 12 May 1988.

32. Interview with a director of a large multinational metalworking company, 15 July 1987.

33. Interview with a director of a small company, 16 May 1988.

34. Albano Franco, head of the CNI, stated that the forty-four-hour week might cause difficulties, but "in truth, firms are not going to close because of these changes" ("Empresarios pressionarão PMDB para fixar indenização para demitidos," *Folha de São Paulo*, 4 November 1987, 8). In addition, the most "progressive" members of the business community announced that they could accept the forty-four-hour week, but not the job security measures.

35. Indemnity was already part of Brazilian law and had not provided any protection for workers, although its supporters suggested that by increasing the amount four times, the new indemnity would do so (Skidmore, *Politics of Military Rule in Brazil*, 291–92).

36. These industrialists all shared the following characteristics: (1) they were Brazilians, (2) were born in a capital city, (3) had a college education, (4) claimed religious affiliation, (5) had some experience abroad, (6) had became industrialists after the 1964 coup, and (7) defined themselves as right wing (although not extreme right). Although they feared the New Republic and viewed labor as extreme left, they did not fear labor during the New Republic.

37. "Luis Eulálio critica os partidos," *Jornal do Brasil*, 26 January 1985, 18.

38. Interview with a director of a very large Brazilian metalworking firm, 20 November 1987.

39. In addition, 23 percent placed the more conservative labor federation, CGT, on the extreme left. Nationality of the firm was a significant variable in my analysis of industrialists' views of these labor federations and PT; industrialists from Brazilian firms were more likely to place the labor federations and PT on the extreme left (Payne, *Brazilian Industrialists*, 94–102).

40. Interview with a director of a small metalworking company, 29 September 1987. This view was also expressed in an interview with a president of a very large multinational corporation, 16 November 1987.

41. Some executives distrusted Medeiros' intentions. They felt that he had not rejected his past membership to the Brazilian Communist party (PCB), would use a pragmatic appeal to win power, and then radicalize the labor movement.

42. Of the industrialists who considered Medeiros to be on the extreme left, none were from the metalworking sector (Medeiros's sector). A large percentage were from U.S. firms: 38 percent compared with 4 percent from Brazilian and 2 percent from other multinational firms considered Medeiros to be on the extreme left.

43. See Luis Eulálio Bueno Vidigal Filho, "Contribuição para a futura constituição brasileira," pamphlet, 1985, 33–34; and Confederação Nacional da Indústria, "Proposições iniciais do empresariado industrial à Assembléia Constituinte," pamphlet, March 1987, 60.

44. *Brazil: Authorized Violence in Rural Areas* (London: Amnesty International Publications, September 1988).

45. These demands primarily came from: the National Conference of Brazilian Bishops (CNBB), the Pastoral Land Commission (CPT), the Movimento de Trabalhadores Rurais Sem Terra (Movement of Landless Rural Workers), the rural labor federation, CONTAG, national labor organizations, and individual rural trade unions.

46. The targets and accomplishments reported by government and nongovernment sources are often conflicting. The figures I have provided here are those that are most consistently reported. However, I regard them with much skepticism and use them only as indicators rather than facts.

47. The government lacked the time and the resources to overcome the problems of: (1) measuring the productivity of different tracts of land to determine whether they could be legally expropriated; (2) evaluating the land's worth; (3) supplying services to new landowners (such as credit, transportation, technology, and storage facilities); and (4) developing a government budget for agrarian reform. Moreover, the government faced the problem of establishing land rights in a country where plots of land have overlapping, conflicting, and multiple titles. Another problem the Sarney government faced was a high turnover rate in the Ministry of Agrarian Reform and Development. In four years, Sarney had four different ministers of agrarian reform and development: Nelson Ribeiro, Dante de Oliveira, Marcos de Barros Freire, and Jader Barbalho.

48. "O recuo no campo," *Veja*, 28 May 1986, 20.

49. The first director of INCRA, José Gomes da Silva, resigned in opposition to the emasculation of the reform. He was replaced by Pedro Dantas, who was allegedly supported by the National Security Council. Dantas, in an effort to appease landholders, increased the level of compensation for land expropriated from private landholders from 2 billion to 8–14 billion cruzados. See "O recuo no campo." At about the same time, Sarney fired minister of agriculture and development Nelson Ribeiro, due to pressure from landholders, the military, and the conservative members of Sarney's cabinet, who viewed Ribeiro as too closely allied with the progressive church and rural trade unions. Sarney's third minister, Marcos de Barros Freire, was killed in an airplane crash along with INCRA president José Eduardo Raduan in September 1987. Allegations of sabotage were never confirmed.

50. For more information on the UDR, see Leigh A. Payne, "The Traditional Right in New Democracies: The Landed Elite in Brazil," presented at the XVI International Congress of the Latin American Studies Association, Washington, D.C., 4–6 April 1991.

51. "UDR discute estratégia nacional para eleger prefeitos e vereadores em 88," *Folha de São Paulo*, 24 November 1987, 6.

52. Marcio Thomaz Bastos in "OAB denuncia 'golpismo a direita,'" *Folha de São Paulo*, 11 November 1987, 9.

53. These youths are typically young landowners or teenage children of landowners. On one occasion they followed Sandra Cavalcanti, a conservative member of the Constituent Assembly, calling after her "Communist, Communist," because she had voted in favor of the agrarian reform.

54. Salvador Farina, leader of the UDR in Goiás, quoted in Susanna Hecht and Alexander Cockburn, *The Fate of the Forest* (London: Verso, 1989), 161.

55. Police officers told Amnesty International investigators that one could not believe anything peasants said and that the police should not have to investigate peasants' complaints of harassment and death threats. Amnesty International also found evidence that peasants were illegally detained, beaten, and threatened with execution by the police.

56. Amnesty International reported that hired gunmen and police jointly carried

out raids on peasants, hired gunmen were often seen in police uniforms and frequented police headquarters, and police were reported to have delivered death threats from landholders.

57. Amnesty International cites two examples: the murders of miners on the Tocantins bridge and violent conflicts on indigenous lands.

58. Under the Brazilian civil code, landholders have a right to defend their land by force but only if the right of possession is under immediate attack. On occasion, landowners have also been the victims of rural violence. However, Amnesty International found that between January 1985 and June 1987, 23 landowners and 90 of their employees died (40 percent due to conflicts between the landowners and their employees), compared to 485 peasants, rural workers, indigenous Brazilians, and their supporters. (Note that Amnesty International's figures are somewhat higher than those cited by the Comissão Pastoral de Terra; see table 3.5.)

59. United States Government, *Country Reports on Human Rights Practices for 1986.*

60. Human Rights Watch, *Rural Violence in Brazil: An Americas Watch Report* (New York: Human Rights Watch, February 1991).

61. The UDR was accused of murdering Chico Mendes because it was threatened by the rubber tappers' successful organizing efforts. Indeed, just before Mendes's murder, Sarney signed two agreements granting the land reserves for which rubber tappers had mobilized. However, the UDR has denied the accusations. Although the murderers are members of the UDR, the organization's regional president, João Branco, denounced them. Nonetheless, former national UDR president Ronaldo Caiado has railed against the "imperialist" pressures from correspondents of the BBC and the British *Guardian* in their coverage of the Chico Mendes murder.

62. For a discussion of these resources, see: Fred Block, "The Ruling Class Does Not Rule: Notes on the Marxist Theory of the State," in *The Political Economy: Readings in the Politics and Economics of American Public Policy,* ed. Thomas Ferguson and Joel Rogers (Armonk, N.Y.: M.E. Sharpe, 1984), 36–37; Charles E. Lindblom, *Politics and Markets: The World's Political-Economic Systems* (New York: Basic Books, 1977), 171–78; Ralph Miliband, *The State in Capitalist Society* (New York: Basic Books, 1969), 146; Theda Skocpol, "Political Responses to Capitalist Crisis: Neo-Marxist Theories of the State and the Case of the New Deal," *Politics and Society* 10, 2 (1980): 160; and David Vogel, "The Power of Business in America: A Re-Appraisal," *British Journal of Political Science* 13 (1983): 29–42.

63. Víctor Pérez Días, "Governability and the Scale of Governance: Mesogovernments in Spain," Instituto Juan March de Estudios e Investigaciones, Centro de Estudios Avanzados en Ciencias Sociales, Working Paper 1990/6 (June 1990).

64. Interview with a president of a very large metalworking company, 12 November 1987.

65. Interview with a director of a small Brazilian company, 10 September 1987.

66. Interview with a director of a very large Brazilian company, 23 November 1987. One industrialist accused the owners of these firms of behaving as though it were 1910. Interview with a president of a very large Brazilian firm, 23 September 1987.

67. Of the sixty-seven directors in the 1986–1989 FIESP directorate: 18 percent were from small businesses (under 500 employees), 28 percent were from medium firms (500–1,999 employees), and 33 percent were from large firms (over 2,000 employees). As far as I could discern, not one of the directors came from a firm with under ten employees. However, since I could not trace the size of the firms of 20 percent of these directors, my finding that FIESP primarily represented large firms may be incorrect. Moreover, the industrialists who considered FIESP an important instrument for defending their interests tended to identify with the right wing in the country and possessed some foreign capital (Payne, *Brazilian Industrialists*, 114–19).

68. An organization that attempted to compete with FIESP was the National Grassroots Business Association (Pensamento Nacional de Bases Empresariais— PNBE) which primarily represented small- and medium-sized industries in São Paulo but also included owners of industries of all sizes and from different areas of São Paulo, Rio Grande do Sul, and Rio de Janeiro. Small business associations and trade associations also increased their autonomous activities during this period.

69. Payne, *Brazilian Industrialists*, 84–122.

70. Ibid., 16–38.

71. At one point he called business leaders who raised prices the "exploiters of chaos" (Jorge Caldeira, "Fascínio e susto," *Istoé-Senhor*, 21 February 1990, 24–27).

72. Collor first appointed Marcelo Paiva Abreu, who quit reportedly due to disagreements with the minister of finance. Collor replaced him with Joaquim Roriz, who resigned two weeks after being sworn in, allegedly to run for governor of Brasília. Political analysts suggest that he resigned when farmers objected to Collor's economic package, which included an end to farm subsidies and taxes on agricultural incomes. Cabrera was the third appointment and, at twenty-nine, is probably the youngest minister in the republic's history.

Leigh A. Payne and Ernest Bartell, c.s.c.

7. Bringing Business Back In

Business-State Relations and Democratic Stability in Latin America

In theoretical discussions, Latin American business leaders are stereotyped as a monolithic group of weak political and economic actors who depend on an authoritarian state to protect their rent-seeking ventures. These old stereotypes do not reflect the significant political and economic changes that have occurred over the last two decades in Latin America. Business leaders today play an increasingly significant and autonomous role in national politics and in the development of economic policy. Moreover, they generally advocate less state intervention in the economy rather than state-led economic policies.

While Latin America's business elite no longer merits its characterization as weak, authoritarian, and protectionist, neither has it been transformed into a hegemonic group capable of shaping the economic policies of the new democratic governments to satisfy their own interests. Instead, business leaders have become strong enough to adapt to certain economic and political changes and constrain others, while still remaining vulnerable to government controls. Given these changes, it is imperative to develop a fresh approach to contemporary business-state relations in Latin America and to analyze their implications for democratic stability in the region.

The Weak Business–Strong State Paradigm

Business leaders are described in much of the theoretical literature as politically and economically powerless, and therefore dependent upon a strong, usually authoritarian, state to defend their interests. Their weakness is attributed to two main factors: inferior social status and the problematic position of Latin American economies within the global economy.

Albert Hirschman suggests various reasons why Latin American entrepreneurs have failed to achieve the same political and economic power as their counterparts in the advanced industrial world. He argues that they often come from immigrant or minority backgrounds; they fail to innovate or experiment and instead tend to copy foreign products and import ideas, processes, and technology; they have limited international prestige and contacts and do not produce enough for the export market. As a result, Hirschman concludes, Latin American industrialists have not achieved the kind of social status needed for political and economic influence in government.[1]

According to the theory of the bureaucratic-authoritarian state,[2] which is built largely on assumptions in *dependencia* approaches to economic and political development,[3] the timing of development in Latin America, and the resulting subordinate position of Latin American economies in the world market, created a weak bourgeoisie. In Argentina, Brazil, and Chile in the 1960s and 1970s, for example, entrepreneurs faced economic bottlenecks and rising popular unrest. In the eyes of business, the populist governments in those countries were unwilling and unable to protect the private sector from the dual threat of economic decline and popular mobilization.

Moreover, business leaders lacked the power to effectively defend their interests within the competitive democracies of the time. Thus, they allied themselves with the military and with technocrats to undermine democratic governments and implant authoritarian regimes. These regimes effectively and violently suppressed popular dissent and attempted (with varying degrees of success) to ameliorate economic conditions. The weak business–strong state paradigm is most obvious in the historical context of the 1960s. Even where business did not support authoritarian rule and a bureaucratic-authoritarian state failed to evolve, it was nonetheless too weak and too dependent on the state to oppose and defeat authoritarian rule, and instead acquiesced to those regimes (for example, in Bolivia and Mexico).

However historically accurate this characterization may be, recent changes in Latin America suggest that the weak business–strong state paradigm is outmoded. Its assumptions about entrepreneurs' political and economic weakness, and their reliance on an authoritarian state, do not hold up in the current international context of economic and political liberalization. Nonetheless, the concept continues to influence contemporary approaches to business-state relations in Latin America. In one of the few efforts to discuss business leaders and the transition to democracy, O'Donnell and Schmitter argue that entrepreneurs will support such a change as long as the transition forces do not go "too far" in their demands. If they do, business will again call for an authoritarian solution.[4] Implicit in this view is the assumption that business will again be unable to defend its interests in a competitive democracy and therefore will rely on a strong authoritarian state for protection. The evidence provided in this volume offers an alternative interpretation.

From Historical Conjuncture to Active Adaptation: A New Approach to Latin American Business-State Relations

As the case studies in this volume attest, the economic and political power of Latin American entrepreneurs has increased. In direct contrast to the old stereotype, business has played an increasingly assertive role in pressuring the government for economic policies rather than acquiescing to those dictated by the state. In addition, the fact that these leaders have often been at the forefront in demanding less state intervention in the economy challenges their portrayal as dependent on a strong state. Moreover, business has been increasingly willing to adapt to democratic change instead of advocating authoritarian rule. Indeed, in some cases (again, Mexico and Bolivia are examples), business leaders played a significant role in opposing authoritarism. The transformation from acquiescence and dependence to increasing autonomy from the state and economic and political power reflects changes that have occurred over the past two decades.

Emerging Economic Power

In the 1990s the Latin American private sector has increasingly become the primary engine of economic growth. This new role for business results from a convergence of four historical trends in Latin America, as elsewhere, over the past two decades: (1) the failure of state-led strategies; (2) the relative success of free-market strategies; (3) the lack of alternate models for state-led growth; and (4) international pressure for change, especially from economically advanced capital-exporting nations.

First, Latin American governments began to find the pattern of state-led growth that had characterized most of the major economies of the region from the end of World War II until the 1970s unsatisfactory. The statist orientation of these economies adhered in varying degrees to the protectionist, import-substitution models of industrialization (ISI) recommended by the Economic Commission for Latin America in the postwar years. Although during the banner years of ISI in the 1960s and 1970s Latin American economies showed some of the highest growth rates in the world, this success soon came to an end. Once the "easy" phases of import substitution had been completed (such as in the domestic production of consumer nondurable goods and noncapital-intensive, technologically uncomplicated intermediate goods), the quality of results under ISI regimes began to deteriorate and to vary widely among countries. Inflationary development finance, negative real interest rates, the disincentives of controlled relative prices (such as in agricultural sectors and through complex combinations of tariffs), import controls, and differential exchange rates generally failed to resolve and sometimes exacerbated the externally generated crises of the 1970s and 1980s—for instance, the oil crises and especially the external debt crises.

The heterodox policies of Argentina and Brazil in the mid-eighties attempted to achieve economic stabilization by "concertation," that is, by involving the private sector (both business and organized labor) in a process of implicit consensus building to eliminate inertial inflation through voluntary agreements to freeze prices and wages and to eliminate indexing. In effect, these policies sought to maintain a dominant role for the government in the economy while at the same time acknowledging the importance of the private sector. Yet these policies also failed, leaving variations on the neoliberal economic system as winners by default.

In short, the statist economic regimes of both the ideological right and left performed poorly in the years preceding the democratic transitions. This was caused by the exhaustion of growth policies based on import substitution, the growing inefficiency of government economic bureaucracies, unanticipated external shocks, or some combination of these deterrents. Given the failure of prior policies, the new democratic governments searched for viable alternative growth strategies.

Second, many countries that adopted neoliberal policies—for example, the export-led Asian "tigers"—were more successful in achieving growth targets than state-led economies. Chile was able to achieve both economic growth and moderate inflation because of its radical and sustained policies of economic liberalization. The relative prosperity of export-oriented, market-driven, open economies challenged the sluggish performance of protectionist state-led national economies and helped to generate pressure from domestic business for market liberalization.

Third, the worldwide collapse of socialist economic systems left Latin American governments without viable statist alternatives to their own interventionist economic models. The premier models of state-led systems in Eastern Europe and the former Soviet Union had failed to survive in the contemporary era, and the leaders who replaced the old communist order adopted free-market strategies.

Fourth, Latin American governments were pressured to adopt free-market policies to help service their foreign debt. Three of the countries analyzed in this volume—Argentina, Brazil, and Chile—have the largest amount of aggregate or per-capita foreign debt in the hemisphere. Foreign banks pressured Latin American governments to increase their ability to service their debts by improving balance-of-payments performance, liberalizing markets, and privatizating state-owned enterprises, thus emphasizing private-sector activity for efficient domestic resource allocation and for expansion of export earnings.

The Bolivian case study specifically reveals the importance of this international pressure. Catherine Conaghan argues that business leaders in that country succeeded in promoting democracy and free enterprise only when backed by international pressure for such change, especially from the Reagan administration. In Mexico, international financial institutions pressed for greater economic liberalization and created an ideological tide against state intervention and favoring market solutions consistent with the demands of many domestic business leaders.

With the adoption of market-oriented policies by the new democracies because of the failure of alternative models, examples of successful economic liberalization, and international pressure, the private sector has assumed an increasingly significant role throughout Latin America. This shift away from state intervention is especially evident in the responsibility of the private sector for mobilizing national savings and investment necessary to achieve growth targets, as well as creating jobs and generating foreign exchange through improved trade balances and attracting foreign capital. With this shift comes a reordering of economic values and objectives. A new emphasis on competitive efficiency and aggregate growth replaces the focus on economic and social distribution (that is, state-dictated wages policy, profit sharing, and property and income redistribution). Because the new values are applied to government as well as private-sector performance, more attention is paid to the direct costs of government social policies and their efficient administration than to distributional and nonmarket economic objectives. This normative shift is especially apparent in arguments for privatizing public services and enterprises—even those, like Chile's national copper mining firm or Brazil's petroleum corporation, that yield a surplus on operations that is used to finance social programs.

The success of neoliberal policies depends on an appropriate response from the private sector. Without private investment and efforts to increase domestic output, these policies will fail. Yet, as the case studies in this volume indicate, business leaders' acceptance of these policies, and their success under them, vary. For example, Chilean business leaders—at least those who survived the economic crises of the 1970s and early

1980s—have emerged as quintessential "Chicago Boys"—endorsers of neoliberal development strategies. For most business leaders in Chile, and to a considerable extent in Argentina and Peru, state-owned enterprises are at best relics of an inefficient past and at worst potential threats to the future of private enterprise. Bolivian business leaders also demanded an end to state-centered solutions and advocated a new liberal economic strategy for development. Brazilian business leaders, on the other hand, appear to be much less intimidated by sharing markets with state-owned enterprises, even those that dominate their respective markets. Moreover, Argentine and Brazilian business leaders have pursued contradictory policies: some favor neoliberal strategies, others seek protection, and others demand neoliberal strategies in certain policy areas while seeking protection in others.[5] Peruvian business leaders also continued to seek protectionist policies, despite the trend toward market orientation. The case studies in this volume suggest why there are such different views about neoliberal policies: varied experience under statist regimes and growing competitiveness in liberalized domestic and international markets.

Latin American business leaders had different experiences under statist regimes. Not all were negative. Thus, despite the shift in policy direction and public discourse, statist-oriented policies of the ISI era continue to have appeal in many Latin American countries, including some of the most heavily industrialized, such as Brazil and Mexico. In those cases, ISI policies stimulated the creation and expansion of protected and powerful domestic firms engaged in consumer durables and heavy capital goods. At the same time, promotion of exports in those countries can be attributed as much to the evolution of state promotion of trade and industrial production as to the current trend toward liberalization.[6] Thus, since many sectors depend (and may continue to depend) on state incentives and subsidies, they endorse these policies in addition to neoliberal strategies that create profitable opportunities.

Where state-led development has been very disappointing, business leaders were less likely to endorse state-led policies. Chile under the Allende regime is a case in point. Fear of expropriation and suffocating regulation of prices of inputs and outputs raised strong opposition to any form of state intervention. In addition, business leaders who survived economic crises without state protection and who perceived themselves as capable of functioning in a neoliberal international economy were more likely to become adamant defenders of a free economy. Despite the economic crises that all Latin American authoritarian regimes faced after the halcyon days of ISI development, some sectors of their economies grew and became powerful economic actors. As these sectors developed, they became more autonomous from the state and more capable of defending their interests without state help. Consequently, they became stronger advocates of market-oriented economic strategies. For example, Chilean agricultural exporters who survived the orthodox economic experiment of the Pinochet regime proved that they could succeed in such an environment, further explaining their adamant defense of neoliberal policies. Survivors of economic restructuring in Bolivia also adapted to the neoliberal international economy and became advocates of market-oriented policies. The uneven response among Argentine and Brazilian business leaders reflects their varying successes and failures in the international economy.

The case studies in this volume suggest that it is simplistic to assume that Latin America's business leaders have a rigid or monolithic attitude. At the same time, businesses in all these countries shared two overarching concerns regarding government policy making: respecting economic competence and protecting private property rights. One complaint voiced by leaders in virtually all the countries studied, one leveled at both statist regimes and some of the new democratic regimes, concerns inconsistencies and unpredictable fluctuations in government policies that interfere with the economic decision making that is necessary for survival in competitive markets. Such complaints are especially evident in reactions to price controls, whether imposed as part of Allende's program for social redistribution in Chile or by the democratically devised concertation programs for economic stabilization under the Austral Plan in Argentina and the Cruzado Plan in Brazil. The private sector's growing importance to the success of economic policy in the new democracies has severely curtailed the freedom of the new regimes to use direct intervention in market pricing as a tool for economic redistribution and forming social policy.

One reflection of business leaders' concern over government competence is their refusal to support authoritarian regimes. It is no coincidence that entrepreneurs in Argentina, Brazil, and Mexico all began to withdraw their support from the authoritarian regimes during periods of economic crisis. However, these case studies suggest that business leaders are less concerned with national growth than with the competence, consistency, and stability of the state's economic decisions. The Mexican case suggests, for example, that business leaders mobilized against the state while the economy was growing but economic policy was becoming increasingly uncertain, unpredictable, and incoherent. In a similar vein, business leaders in Chile and Brazil who shifted their support to a democratic regime did so during a period of relative economic growth. These studies thus suggest a much greater concern by business leaders for upholding stable rules of the game—and protection against losses—than for macroeconomic growth and overall gains.

A second broad consensus among business leaders in these countries is their demand for the preservation of property rights. Without the guarantee of this fundamental rule of the capitalist game, risk-taking and incentives to make long-term investments are curtailed. Indeed, for business leaders a threat to property rights is a threat to their very survival.

In short, business leaders have varying degrees of economic power in Latin America. Nonetheless, they share a growing tendency to adamantly demand, or passively accept, a reduced economic role for the state, thereby undermining one of the main pillars of the old business-state paradigm. Moreover, business's demands on the state appear to have changed. While the state is still expected to protect the rules of the capitalist order, specifically private property rights, business leaders are less concerned with overall economic growth than with competent and predictable management of the economy.

Emerging Political Power

There is little doubt that business leaders have enhanced their political power and organization during the political opening in Latin America. New business associations have formed to represent, defend, and inform the business community. Businesses have lobbied legislatures and the executive. Representatives of business have promoted candidates to public office and run for office themselves. Both collectively and as individuals they have begun to ally themselves with politically active community groups. Where political parties are historically strong (as in Chile, Mexico, and Peru), business leaders have formed or joined political parties to pressure for change.[7] Business leaders and associations have also engaged in antigovernment demonstrations, or have threatened to do so.

The enhanced political power of business is in part a result of the economic changes discussed above. As it becomes more important in the economy, business has acquired more financial, organizational, and social resources with which to influence political and economic outcomes. Moreover, economic liberalization has given business a larger role in determining economic policy than ever before.

Political liberalization has also meant more power for business. Latin America's entrepreneurs, no doubt, viewed liberalization as inevitable. After all, during the 1980s, most countries in the region were undergoing some sort of political opening, due to domestic pressures, direct and indirect influences from foreign governments and international nongovernmental organizations, the collapse of authoritarian rule, and the absence of alternate solutions. Thus, rather than reject an inevitable process, business adapted to it.

In their adaptation, business leaders did not merely "tolerate" the political opening; they seized and exploited new political opportunitites to defend their interests. Indeed, in some cases business leaders were motivated to actively support the political opening due to their experiences under authoritarian rule. O'Donnell and Schmitter suggest that business leaders will tolerate a political opening when they view the authoritarian regime as "dispensable."[8] However, the reactions of business in the case studies presented here suggest that other factors, in addition to the regimes' success or failure at achieving their original goals, prompted an endorsement of or adaptation to political opening. In particular, the case studies suggest that business leaders were motivated by the authoritarian regimes' incompetence and lack of legitimacy, their exclusion of business influence, and their inability to guarantee adherence to the rules of the capitalist game.

First, as mentioned, business began to withdraw support from the authoritarian regimes when those regimes proved unable to manage the economy effectively. Yet, regime competence also had a political component. The regimes' flagrant abuses of human rights to control civil opposition, and international and domestic attention to those abuses and pressure for change, led business leaders to question the government's legitimacy in Argentina, Bolivia, Brazil, and Chile. In Argentina, the Malvinas War debacle led business to challenge the authoritarian regime's competence to govern. In Mexico, business is attuned to the domestic and international condemnation of the PRI-controlled regime's repression, exclusion, fraud, and corruption, which challenges its legitimacy. Business's concern is based on a demand for stability and predictability. Incompetent and illegitimate regimes cannot offer the equilibrium needed for making long-term investment and production decisions.

The exclusionary nature of authoritarian regimes eventually affected business leaders, who withdrew their support from or mobilized against authoritarian governments when they perceived that they had lost influence over their policies. In Brazil, for example, business leaders began to clamor against the regime after it eliminated both the formal and informal channels of influence upon which business had traditionally relied. The Brazilian and Mexican cases (in addition to the Peruvian case under democratic rule) suggest that business began to view clientelistic and corporatist arrangements as constraining its influence, prompting it to demand autonomous forms of political expression.

In some cases business also felt threatened by the authoritarian regime's disregard for the rules of capitalism. In the case of Mexico and Bolivia (in addition to Peru under democratic rule), the regimes nationalized private enterprises, prompting business leaders to unite against those authoritarian regimes. In their eyes, nationalizations are tantamount to an ideological war against the private sector, against which they must mobilize in self-defense. While objective observers would not accuse Brazilian's regime of being anticapitalist, business leaders opposed what they considered to be "socialistic" tendencies in the state-capitalist policies of the regime. The authoritarian regime did not expropriate private firms, but rather preempted private domestic investment through the proliferation of state-owned enterprises and subsidies for multinational corporations.

These examples of expropriating or squeezing out private enterprise are the most dramatic assaults. However, in some cases, specifically Chile and Mexico, business proved highly sensitive to antibusiness rhetoric. In Chile, acquiescence to the democratic transition was tempered by fears of antibusiness bias in Chilean culture and political institutions. In Mexico, business leaders felt vulnerable to the widespread perception that they had little role to play in the economic and political health of the country. In these cases, business leaders mobilized against this attitude, organizing public relations campaigns and emphasizing the common interests shared by both business and broad national groups.

In short, business leaders not only adapted to the political opening, they exploited it. They used it to capture new political opportunities with which to defend their interests independently from the state. In addition, they were motivated not only by the inevitability of the democratic transition but also by their frustrations under authoritarian rule. They perceived the authoritarian regimes as incompetent, exclusionary (with regard to business influence), and unreliable (in guaranteeing the observance of capitalist rules). Thus accepting the democratic transition was an attempt to protect their interests by reversing the preexisting pattern of acquiescence or collaboration with the state. Whether business sustains this support for democracy will depend in part on the new democratic governments' competence, inclusion of business influence, and ability to guarantee adherence to the rules of the capitalist game.

It is too early to fully evaluate the new governments' success on these three points. There are some positive trends in Argentina and Chile. Business leaders in both countries are increasingly reassured that the Menem and Aylwin governments have the capacity to govern, will not threaten property rights, and will promote free enterprise. Indeed, the move toward privatization and away from nationalization has reassured most business leaders in Latin America that free enterprise is no longer in jeopardy. This perception has been heightened by the collapse of the communist regimes in Eastern Europe and the disorganization of the left throughout the world. Furthermore, the representative nature of the political regimes, coupled with business's significant resources, give these leaders significant political influence within the new democracies. They have founded more combative business associations, formed alliances with middle-class organizations, and joined or established political parties. And these organizations have successfully defended many business interests.

On the negative side, incompetent governments in Bolivia, Brazil, and Peru have increased business leaders' concern about economic and political stability in these countries. In addition, while the new governments have generally protected capitalist rules, business is wary of the political power shown by popular social groups who demand a redistribution of wealth and income. They continue to mobilize against these efforts, thus increasing domestic class conflict and undermining the government's efforts toward increasing economic and political equality.

Implications for Democratic Stability

Both democracy and capitalism are likely to prevail in Latin America in the foreseeable future. Alternate models of political and economic development are not currently viable because of the failure of statist development models, the collapse of authoritarian regimes, the decline of international socialism, and international pressures favoring both democratic and capitalist systems and supported by business, organized labor, political parties, and other key social actors.

One might assume that the coexistence of capitalism and democracy will lead to greater political and economic stability in Latin America. After all, private investors should provide the investments, production of goods, and employment opportunities that encourage growth and economic and political stability. In addition, as business leaders participate more in economic decisions, they should demand more market reforms, thereby strengthening the development of capitalism in Latin America.

Yet these systems are not intrinsically linked. There is no guarantee either that democracy will strengthen the private sector and reliance on market mechanisms, or that a strong private sector and market economy will lead to a more stable democracy. Instead, democratic stability remains vulnerable to the political and economic behavior of the private sector. It is unlikely that business leaders would deliberately destabilize a democratic government. After all, their interests are not inimical to democracy, and their harsh experiences over a disastrous decade make it unlikely that they would prefer authoritarianism over democratic rule. Nonetheless, the priorities of business leaders are primarily economic, and they have the economic and political means to hamper both democratization and liberalization: they could refuse to save and make productive investments, send capital abroad, cut production, lay off workers, refuse to comply with legal regulations, and disrupt the economy in other ways. Moreover, the impulse to resort to these strategies and undermine a democratic opening could arise from a position of either weakness or strength.

Threats from a Weak Private Sector

Although business leaders have become increasingly powerful in Latin America, certain weaknesses continue to prevent them from achieving their political demands, and this threatens their support for democracy. These limitations result from: (1) fragmentation within the business community; (2) problems of leadership and representation; (3) a sense of social inferiority; and (4) deficient entrepreneurship. If business leaders feel they cannot defend their interests within a competitive democracy and cannot survive within a neoliberal international economy, they may look to an authoritarian system for protection.

Fragmentation of the Business Class Government policies have different impacts on business because of diversity of size, sector, production techniques, geographic location, marketing possibilities, and the nationality of foreign firms. In addition, industrialists have different ideologies, which prevents them from working in unison. Thus, collective action and effective political power is often checked by the inherent diversity of business leaders' needs and views.

Leadership and Representation Problems Business leaders' collective power has also been limited by the business associations themselves, whose leaders are often co-opted by the government or who represent only one sector of the economy. As a result, associations have often failed to defend the broader interests of business leaders. Instead, they have been accused of corruption, particularly of accepting government bribes or favors in exchange for their acquiescence. The failure of an association to defend business interests can create the impression that only the interests of a few powerful firms are represented in government. This, in turn, can make entrepreneurs feel that they have been excluded from government policies, thus undermining business support for the regime.

Social Inferiority Business leaders will be more likely to support a democratic government that represents all social sectors if they feel that they are themselves accepted as legitimate by other social sectors. If their values seem to vary from the dominant norms of society, they may be less inclined to support representative democratic processes that potentially threaten their interests, and more likely to resort to individualistic, self-interested behavior.

Chile provides an example. Despite its modernization and openness to the world, Chilean society can be described as in the Hispanic tradition, valuing intellectual effort, political endeavor, and public-sector administration over business administration, and assigning a higher ethical value to labor than to management.[9] Consequently, despite the success of businesses that survived the competitive opening of the economy and reaped a disproportionate share of the gains from economic growth, Chilean business leaders feared for their position under the new democratic regime. They believed that despite their economic power, they lacked sufficient political clout to maintain the support of a government that might yield to popular pressure for economic intervention and could stifle a growing market economy. Thus they continue to feel insecure and defensive about the legitimacy of their values, especially the pursuit of profit, in Chilean society and culture.

Insufficient Entrepreneurship Advocates of liberalizing Latin America's national economies acknowledge that only a "modest" number of small and medium-sized firms in Latin America have successfully met the challenges of international competition.[10] Those challenges imply risk, and the classic stereotype of Latin American business leaders is that they are averse to taking risks, having become used to corporatist dependence on patronage and state protection against the competitive challenges of the free market.

While the survivors of Chile's economic restructuring see themselves as risk takers (although they have yet to face some of the hazards of becoming integrated into the international economy through a complete business cycle), many business leaders in Latin America are still risk averters in the marketplace, especially in the financial markets. Many Brazilian firms are content to share domestic markets protected from international competition—even at the cost of bureaucratic government regulation, domination of some markets by state enterprises, and inefficiencies that make them less competitive in export markets. Likewise, investors in Argentina and Mexico who are now bringing their "flight capital" back home often tend to invest that capital in more liquid portfolio assets and short-term monetary instruments that can easily be converted back into flight capital, rather than in riskier long-term investment in physical assets or facilities for domestic production of goods and services.

There is some truth to the claim that Latin American business leaders' traditional fear of risk is simply a rational response to the instability inherent in economies that have long been vulnerable to intervention by governments whose tenure depends on achieving their own goals, whether they are goals of equity or of growth. Excessive inflation, inconsistent policies on wages, prices, and interest rates, and ineffective tax codes and tax enforcement all help explain why businesses will commit themselves to the domestic economy only for short-run economic gain, while sending long-term capital commitments abroad. In addition to these anxieties, low savings and capital flight contribute to the economic weakness of Latin American business.

If Latin American business leaders do lack entrepreneurial skills, the market-driven economic growth promised by the neoliberal model is unlikely to develop. Thus Latin American governments cannot rely on the private sector to strengthen capitalist democracy. A weak private sector will not create jobs, expand incomes, improve the quality of goods and services, or compete effectively in international markets. Nor will it generate enough income to reduce poverty and invest in education and productive human capital, or create enough public revenues to develop essential infrastructure and provide social services.

In sum, these four typical weaknesses of business leaders just outlined have the potential to destabilize democracy in the region. Even if democratic governments are able to produce competent economic policies and protect capitalist rules, they may become vulnerable to opposition if business lacks enough influence over the regime. If business leaders feel alienated from the political process because of their social inferiority, fed in part by their lack of entrepreneurship or even their own weak collective action, they may attempt to restore their political influence and gain attention from the government in ways that have in the past destabilized governments and political systems. So political marginalization of business could lead to a repetition of the kinds of events that toppled Latin American democracies in the 1960s and 1970s.

Threats from a Strong Private Sector

While democratic stability is clearly vulnerable to opposition from a weak private sector, a business class that becomes too powerful may also threaten democracy. Businesses can become powerful by effective collective action, increased social status, and successful entrepreneurial activity.

Collective Action Government policies may have the unintended effect of uniting a fragmented business elite. For example, although Peru's and Mexico's business communities lacked sufficient cohesion to mount strong political force, they overcame this obstacle when their governments threatened to nationalize the banks. Brazilian landholders united and mobilized in the face of government attempts to expropriate and redistribute land. Chilean businesses appeared ready to unite to oppose any form of expropriation of private property. A generalized fear of events that cannot be controlled through individual political action may well galvanize business leaders against the government. This mobilization, however, is most likely to be defensive—motivated by perceived threats and the desire to overcome them rather than a desire to promote policy initiatives based on consensus.[11]

Strong business associations can overcome business's weak social leadership. The tradition of co-opted and corrupt business leaders and associations is not inevitable. The Peruvian case demonstrates that effective leadership can evolve within business associations. Leaders can build strong institutions by finding strategies to unite disparate forces within the business community. In other words, as other analyses of collective action demonstrate, when business leaders perceive that associations can deliver tangible benefits, they are more likely to join them.[12] So, when CONFIEP in Peru forced the government to limit tax increases and back down on its efforts to nationalize the banks, business leaders and the government both began to view CONFIEP as a serious force to contend with. Its membership swelled after it proved that it could achieve specific important goals.

While overcoming fragmentation and weak representation will reduce business leaders' political isolation, it will also increase their ability to influence democratic policy. This power can have negative consequences for democracy. As demonstrated in the Brazilian case, business leaders can effectively veto social redistribution policies, thus undermining the government's attempts to extend economic and political rights to more people.

Heightened Social Status Where business leaders either retain or raise their social status, they are much more capable of becoming an autonomous political force and therefore more willing to work within the system than to disrupt it. However, improved social status depends on a widespread perception that business leaders can make a positive contribution to society. This perception is not necessarily related to economic success. Business leaders in Brazil and Chile illustrate this point. While generally confident of their own ability to compete in the international neoliberal system, Chilean business leaders have viewed themselves as socially inferior. Paradoxically, except for leaders in export-oriented sectors, Brazilian business people doubt their ability to compete in open markets and support protectionist policies, but consistently manifest social and political self-confidence. They identify their own materialist values with the dominant cultural values of Brazilian society. Thus, Brazilian business leaders enjoy sufficient social status to achieve high positions in public office and to lobby effectively in the legislature.

Heightened social status for business leaders, while it enables them to become integrated into the political system, also has negative implications for democracy. By accumulating political power, business leaders can effectively hold the democratic government hostage to private-sector demands.

Entrepreneurship Political power is often derived from economic success. In turn, economic success in Latin America today is defined by firms' capacity to adapt to free and flexible prices, competitive markets, and open economies. Business competence defined by these conditions varies with the nature and extent of competition and length of experience with competitive challenges. Chilean business leaders have earned a reputation for competence that is due in large part to their increasing familiarity with the technical know-how for competitive efficiency and survival in the international marketplace. As the Bolivian and Peruvian case studies indicate, attempts at similar competitive restructuring have not always worked politically in fragile democracies. Chile was able to use its comparative advantage in climate and access to nonproprietary agricultural technology to develop nontraditional exports in fruit and wood products which, by generating foreign exchange to pay for imports, acted as replacements for the relatively inefficient import substitutes that were driven out of the market by Chile's rapid opening to foreign producers.

Brazil has one of the world's ten largest industrial economies. However, in an open economy its industries must compete with firms from countries that are capital-rich and endowed with advanced patented technology. While Brazilian firms in some sectors of the economy (such as production of auto parts) meet export market tests for competence, other sectors are characterized by high costs and outdated technology (for example, the much criticized computer industry). It is not surprising that business leaders in Brazil have shown less than unanimous support for liberalization of the Brazilian economy.

In sum, Latin American business leaders have become increasingly strong through increased collective action, improved social status, and economic competence. While they have not achieved political hegemony, business leaders may still be able to hamper liberalization. Increased business power could constrain the advancement of social democracy in Latin America. In some cases business leaders have rejected distribution programs that might equalize power among social groups. They have opposed land reforms and tax reforms designed to foster redistribution, price controls, employment security, and public expenditures for social welfare programs. Their resistance to reallocative measures, especially when coupled with their own weak entrepreneurship, has led to growing poverty, worsening employment opportunities, less equitable income distribution, and declining access to social services.

Even when the private sector is economically strong, self-interested behavior by business can result in inequities that jeopardize the prospects for capitalist democracy. Moreover, collusion among firms and exploitation of emerging market opportunities by the strongest firms and groups can result in oligopolistic and monopolistic rents, and thus inefficient allocation of national economic resources. Traditional patterns of bribery, collusion by powerful economic interests with government policy makers and administrators, along with other corrupt practices typical of Latin America, may persist and undermine constructive links between democracy and capitalism.

Finally, business leaders may be able to limit political agendas, political expression, and broad participation. This is particularly true regarding organized labor and the left. Even when they are not threatened by these groups, business leaders have attempted to constrain their power by collective bargaining and lobbying in the legislature. Given the superior social, organizational, and financial resources available to business in relation to labor and the left, they have often succeeded.

Artful Negotiation: Strategies to Build Democratic and Economic Stability

Thus democratic stability can be threatened, paradoxically, by business leaders who are either too weak or too strong politically. Business support for democratic institutions and its constructive participation in democratic processes are important to regimes whose economic policies and programs for growth, employment, and fair allocation of resources depend on substantial economic liberalization. Yet the goals of business, however conditioned by local cultures, do not automatically coincide with those of a democratic society. Hence the private sector must be supported in its role as an engine of economic growth, but not to the extent that political participation becomes manipulation or domination and threatens destabilization.

The experiences detailed in this volume suggest a series of measures that could help ensure constructive relationships between Latin American democratic regimes committed to economic liberalization and to developing private sectors capable of encouraging the success of liberal economic policies and programs. One overriding concern that surfaces explicitly or implicitly in these studies is the plea for consistency and durability in the economic rules of the game.

One characteristic of Latin American business leaders, through a long history of frequent and drastic changes in economic regimes, is adaptability—a feature easily overlooked in a macroeconomic analyses of costs and benefits of specific policies and programs. Brazilian business has adapted to various kinds of bureaucratic intervention in the marketplace, albeit with inevitable costs. Chilean business adapted successfully not only to the state interventionism of the 1960s, but also to the radical liberalization of the 1970s, with its two waves of bankruptcies. Peruvian business rapidly adjusted to nationalist, populist, and neoliberal economic regimes in rapid succession. And Argentine business leaders, noted for their proclivities for sending capital abroad, were quick to bring back that capital, even if on a speculative basis, when warranted by economic opportunities.

Nevertheless, there are certain limits to business's power of adaptation, beyond which the macroeconomic costs and sociopolitical effects are likely to lead to nonproductive business behavior and economic destabilization. Enforcement of private property rights is almost universally offered by business leaders as a necessary condition for both their productive behavior and their support for democratic institutions. Chilean business leaders who supported the "revolution in liberty" of the Christian Democratic party during the 1960s, in a country that had not experienced a serious disruption of democracy in living memory, supported a military coup after only three years of a democratically elected socialist regime that initiated a major nationalization program. Business peak associations came into their own in Peru only after the nationalization of banks threatened property rights. Brazilian landholders also organized an effective political movement when threatened with even a mild land reform.

Without denying that Latin American business leaders have a cultural history of rent-seeking behavior, one can still argue that uncertainties about the stability of the rules that ultimately determine economic values make risk-averting short-run maximizing behavior seem rational. A shared desire for observing consistent and enduring rules of the game helps to explain the apparent differences in business attitudes toward price regulation in Latin America. In Chile, memories of coping with a ballooning, bureaucratic system of comprehensive and inconsistent price controls under the socialist regime were still vivid as business leaders considered their prospects under a possible transition to democracy. Not surprisingly, they had little tolerance for economic programs based on price intervention.

On the other hand, Brazilian business found it easier to adapt to an evolving system of price interventions as well as to the inflationary effects of fiscal and monetary policy in a predictable, bureaucratic apparatus of a familiar corporatist society, especially when measured against the benefits of relatively protected market shares. (Complaints by foreign business executives suggest that this was a weightier burden for them.) When the rules of the game are consistent and enduring, adaptation is less costly and business is thereby freed to pursue its own objectives. In this respect, consistency of the rules may be as important as their substance in gaining the support of business for a specific regime. And it is consistency and durability, as well as the content of economic policies and incentives, that help define business's perceptions that a government is "probusiness."

Of course, the content of economic policies is also significant. In virtually all the countries analyzed here, a favorable economic climate was identified with macroeconomic policies of monetary and fiscal stability. Moreover, economic incentives are important. Simply "getting the prices right," for example, allowing price consistency across markets for inputs and outputs, maintaining positive real interest rates at competitive levels in relation to productivity, and so on, can generate incentives through the market mechanism that will elicit business support, as indicated in the case studies of Bolivia and Chile.

However, economic incentives also imply specific kinds of intervention by the state to stimulate growth, employment, savings, and investment through private-sector responses. Although the rhetoric of laissez-faire is widespread in the Latin American private sector, those who support market-oriented economic policies and regimes still acknowledge and even expect government direction in economic life. Consequently, within the framework of a market economy, business can be expected to respond to incentives created by government industrial policy, including economic targets and other kinds of planning. Business people expect economic policy to favor the private sector, such as incentives for private savings and investment through special bank credits and favorable interest rates, and they explicitly press for technically qualified public servants, not only as ministers but also as managers of government agencies that administer those policies.

The strength of democratic governments depends in part on regular communication and their accessibility to various interest groups. Individually, Latin American business leaders have forged channels of communication and access, both legal and extralegal, and under a variety of political regimes. If the private sector is to contribute to democratic stability, however, it must represent its interests fairly and equitably, according to social norms. This means that business must enjoy regular access to policy determination and administration without contending with the weight of antibusiness sentiments in government; by the same token, business interests must refrain from cultivating irregular, preferential, and corrupt relations with government.

For governments, this virtuous middle way implies the need for both fairness and shrewdness in negotiating with business to maintain a playing field considered "level" by business but also to avoid vulnerability to pressures that the combined resources of business can construct. These can range from mobilizing political opposition within the business sector and among the population at large to the various forms of economic boycott that are available to business in a free-market economy—for example, failure to save and invest, capital flight, and noncompetitive and nonproductive rent-seeking behavior. The liberal paradigm, unlike the corporatist model, includes political as well as economic incentives for government to strengthen competition in the domestic economy. Fostering competition plays on the inherent weakness of associations of business firms, whose interests may overlap but are seldom identical.

Strategies to divide and conquer are not limited to dealings with business, but can be applied to other sectors as well. As the case studies on Argentina and Bolivia indicate, liberalizing governments have pursued policies that have weakened and divided once powerful labor movements and trade-union associations. Again, the objectives of increased economic efficiency and growth through competitive markets are used to justify policies that also curb the political strength of organized labor.

Nevertheless, the political prospects for Latin American democracy need not be limited by the strength of business relative to labor and other sectors, nor by the ability of business leaders to veto distributional policies. While capable of defensive collective action, business leaders, as indicated throughout this volume, lack the cohesion to formulate and implement policy, and they are susceptible to artful political strategy and negotiation by government officials.

The strategy of divide and conquer, of course, does have its limits, and its effectiveness will be conditioned by an adroit mix of sticks and carrots among economic incentives and regulatory controls which, in the ideal neoliberal world, will stimulate individual maximizing behavior that is consistent with national economic goals, such as growth and new jobs. For example, the Menem government's efforts in Argentina combined with unpopular economic reform measures to win public approval from business associations, despite specific complaints and lukewarm support from individual business people.

The Mexican case also provides evidence of clever negotiation. The Lopez Portillo government was able to divide and conquer business opposition by providing a rescue plan, expanding the nonbanking financial sector, and introducing market-oriented reforms. It also held both formal and informal meetings with the major businesses in the country, while marginalizing the middle-sized companies who were the most active in the opposition movement. This demonstrated the government's resolve to allow for some business influence, as well as its capacity to implement economic reforms. The Mexican case suggests that when business-government relations are good, business unity is low because the business sectors adopt a compliant and cooperative relationship with the government.

In the neoliberal economic framework, the competition introduced by policies of openness to the international economy contributes to the divide-and-conquer strategy without necessarily fostering the unholy alliances of domestic and foreign capital that were predicted by the dependency literature on open economies. The efficiency of competition, however, rests on assumptions that domestic markets are sufficiently well developed along competitive lines to preclude the degree of control and collusion that would bring market domination and unearned rents. At the same time, the more highly developed a competitive domestic market is, the less likely that comprehensive business associations will be effective. It is thus not surprising that business groups are less important political actors in contemporary Chile, Mexico, and Argentina than in the more rudimentary market economies of Bolivia and Peru. Nor is it surprising that business associations have not always been politically effective in Brazil, with its mixed bag of markets—some competitive and some still characterized by protection and market sharing.

If democracy and neoliberal economic models are not necessarily harmonious, the links between them will depend not only on economic policies that set fair rules, but also on the effectiveness of social and political institutions that govern their relations with one another. Democratic society is characterized by institutional checks and balances that prevent one social sector from dominating all others. Constitutionally independent branches of government, especially a sovereign judiciary, are obvious examples. It is interesting that in Chile sectors as diverse as business and human rights groups support the need for an independent judiciary. Judicial reform, where needed, would thus appear to be one strategy of democratic government that could win the support of business in union with other social sectors. An autonomous central bank that can act as a monetary check on the fiscal excesses of governments with short time horizons also elicits wide business support. Business associations, labor unions, the media, consumer advocates, and other economic interest groups all can serve as checks and balances in a democratic society, and democratic governments have an opportunity, at least to some extent, to orchestrate that process to strengthen support and reduce opposition within various social sectors, including business. The wide appreciation of the consultative efforts of the new democratic government in Chile and the alleged isolation of the first economic team of the Collor government in Brazil suggest that there is not yet a uniform appreciation of this source of stability in the new democracies of Latin America.

Business's demand for competent government hardly threatens democracy. Indeed, some discussions of the breakdown of democracy in Latin America emphasize that concerns about political leadership and government competence, rather than international capital and leftist subversion, were key factors that undermined the old democratic experiments.[13] The disturbing trend toward political mavericks and outsiders in Latin American politics raises questions about the future of competent government. Half of the countries included in this volume faced government leaders—Menem, Collor, and Fujimori—

who lacked the political expertise, support from a strong political party, or the majority support that could have helped to offset their weaknesses. Nonetheless, business has demonstrated considerable adaptability to varying levels of government competence. For example, when the Mexican government recovered from the Echeverría period and again showed that it could respond to crises, many business leaders retreated from their support for political change and resumed the status quo ante: acquiescence to the PRI government. In a similar vein, Argentine entrepreneurs were skeptical of democracy and feared the possible rebirth of Peronism, state centrism, and labor strength. However, they have kept an open mind and have begun to view democracy as a less risky venture than authoritarian rule.

It appears that business leaders' fears of democracy have been largely assuaged in Latin America. Relatively conservative leaders have seized the helm of each of the new democracies studied in this volume. The left in most cases has lacked sufficient coherence to challenge the conservative trend, and organized labor during the recent economic crisis has been generally weak.

Fears of democracy by Chilean business leaders, like those of their counterparts in Argentina, have been relieved during these first few years. Chile is the one case where the business leaders who survived the orthodox economic policies of Pinochet fared well under authoritarian rule. In light of their experience with the previous democratically elected socialist regime, it is not surprising that business leaders feared that a transition to democracy might erode their gains, produce more state-centered economic policies, and generate ideological warfare between the left and the right and conflict within the left. However, the Aylwin government quickly established communication with the private sector and did not reverse the process of economic liberalization, thereby avoiding ideological antagonism. In their adaptation, these business leaders sought ways to restrict some aspects of the liberalization while benefiting from others.

The Argentine case suggests that government can win support from business leaders by providing channels of influence within government. While business leaders were skeptical of the democratic governments, and particularly a Peronist nemesis, Menem has so far overcome this bias against him by promoting policies that reassure rather than challenge business leaders. This would suggest that business can be open to specific policies rather than judging them by ideological labels. Menem has cultivated this assurance by appointing business leaders to ministries and consulting with them on government strategies.

But these positive impressions cannot be generalized to other cases. In Peru, democracy brought increasing social and political upheaval, particularly because of the Shining Path guerrillas and the military's efforts to combat them. Business leaders in Peru and Brazil also recognized that democracy does not guarantee government competence. While the Aylwin and Menem administrations assuaged many anxieties on that score, the Alan García government in Peru and the José Sarney and Fernando Collor governments in Brazil heightened business fears.

Moreover, economic crises continue to challenge the abilities of the new democratic leaders. Hopes for Brazil's rapid economic improvement under democracy have gone unfulfilled. The numerous and dramatic economic plans proposed by both Sarney and Collor failed miserably. Brazilian business leaders have nowhere to turn: both democracy and authoritarianism have failed to produce the conditions necessary for long-term business confidence.

At least in the short term, Latin American business is unlikely to deliberately sabotage democratic stability. However, attitudes may shift as a result of changes in international attitudes toward democracy, serious threats to business owing to the policies or antibusiness rhetoric of democratic governments, collective amnesia about the disasters of authoritarian rule, or the discovery of viable political alternatives. Moreover, business leaders may inadvertently undermine democratic stability as they pursue their own interests. Therefore, only a vigilant and competent government, capable of astute strategy and artful negotiation with business leaders and their adversaries, will be able to assure democratic equilibrium.

Notes

1. Albert O. Hirschman, "The Political Economy of Import-Substituting Industrialization in Latin America," in *A Bias for Hope: Essays on Development in Latin America*, ed. Hirschman (New Haven: Yale University Press, 1971), 96–98.

2. Guillermo O'Donnell, *Modernization and Bureaucratic-Authoritarianism* (Berkeley: University of California, 1973).

3. Fernando Henrique Cardoso and Enzo Faletto, *Dependency and Development in Latin America* (Berkeley: University of California Press, 1979); and Peter Evans, *Dependent Development: The Alliance of Multinational, State, and Local Capital in Brazil* (Princeton: Princeton University Press, 1979).

4. Guillermo O'Donnell and Philippe C. Schmitter, *Transitions from Authoritarian Rule: Tentative Conclusions about Uncertain Democracies* (Baltimore: Johns Hopkins University Press, 1986), 27.

5. William R. Nylen, "Liberalismo para Todo Mundo, Menos Eu: Brazil and the Neoliberal Solution," in *The Right and Democracy in Latin America*, ed. Douglas A. Chalmers, Maria do Carmo Campello de Souza, and Atilio A. Boron (New York: Praeger, 1992), 259–76.

6. See Jaime Ros, "Mexico's Trade and Industrialization Experience since 1960: A Reconsideration of Past Policies and Assessment of Current Reforms," Working Paper no. 186 (Notre Dame: Kellogg Institute, January 1993); and Jeffrey Cason, "Development Strategy in Brazil: The Political Economy of Industrial Export Promotion, 1964–1989," Ph.D. diss., University of Wisconsin, Madison, 1993.

7. Business leaders did not use political parties in Argentina, where there is little ideological distinction between parties; nor in Bolivia, where parties and politicians shift according to political winds; nor in Brazil, where party loyalties and parties themselves are highly ephemeral.

8. O'Donnell and Schmitter, *Transitions from Authoritarian Rule*, 27.

9. See Guillermo Campero, "Los empresarios ante la alternativa democrática: El caso de Chile," in *Empresarios y Estado en America Latina*, ed. Celso Garrido N. (Mexico City: CLACSO, 1988), 262.

10. Gunther H. Muller, general manager of the Inter-American Investment Corporation, cited in *The IDB*, May 1992, 12.

11. By contrast, for example, the Business Council for Sustainable Development, made up of fifty executives of major firms in the OECD countries, is ahead of most national governments in pressing for long-term environmental reforms.

12. Mancur Olson, *The Logic of Collective Action* (Cambridge, Mass.: Harvard University Press, 1965).

13. Alfred Stepan, "Political Leadership and Regime Breakdown: Brazil," in *The Breakdown of Democratic Regimes: Latin America*, ed. Juan J. Linz and Alfred Stepan (Baltimore: Johns Hopkins University Press, 1978); and Juan J. Linz, "Crisis, Breakdown, and Reequilibration," in *The Breakdown of Democratic Regimes: Latin America*, ed. Juan J. Linz and Alfred Stepan (Baltimore: Johns Hopkins University Press, 1978).

Notes on Contributors

CARLOS H. ACUÑA is a Researcher at the Centro de Estudio de Estado y Sociedad (CEDES) in Buenos Aires, Argentina, and Professor of History at the University of Buenos Aires (UBA). He is coauthor, with William Smith, of "The Political Economy of Structural Adjustment" in his coedited volume, *Latin American Political Economy in the Age of Neoliberal Reform* (1994). In addition, he is the author of "Politics and Economics in the Argentina of the 1990s" in his coedited volume, *Democracy, Markets, and Structural Reform in Latin America* (1994). Both volumes are coedited with William Smith and Eduardo Gamarra.

REV. ERNEST BARTELL, C.S.C., is Executive Director of the Helen Kellogg Institute for International Studies and Professor of Economics at the University of Notre Dame. Among his publications are "John Paul II and International Development," in *The Making of an Economic Vision*, ed. O. Williams and J. Houck (1991), and "Private Goods, Public Goods, and the Common Good: Another Look at Economics and Ethics in Catholic Social Teaching," in *The Challenge of the Common Good to U.S. Capitalism*, ed. J. Houck and O. Williams (1986). He is currently conducting research on the private sector and democracy in Chile and Brazil.

CATHERINE M. CONAGHAN is a Queen's National Scholar and Associate Professor of Political Studies at Queen's University in Kingston, Ontario. She is the author of *Restruc-*

turing Domination: Industrialists and the State in Ecuador (1988) and coauthor, with James Malloy, of *Unsettling Statecraft: Democracy and Neoliberalism in the Central Andes* (1994).

FRANCISCO DURAND teaches political science at the University of Texas at San Antonio. He is the author of *La década frustrada: Los industriales y el poder, 1970–1980* and "La nueva derecha peruana: Origenes y dilemas" (*Estudios sociológicos de El Colegio de México*, May–August 1990), as well as other monographs and articles on the Peruvian business sector. His latest book is *Business and Politics in Peru* (1994).

BLANCA HEREDIA is Assistant Professor in the Department of International Studies at the Instituto Technológico Autónomo de México (ITAM). She is the author of "Politics, Profits and Size: The Political Transformation of Mexican Business," in *The Right and Democracy in Latin America*, ed. Douglas Chalmers, Atilio Borón, and Maria Campello de Souza (1992); "Estructura política y reforma económica: El case de México," *Política y gobierno* (1994); and other articles on business and economic policy making in Mexico.

LEIGH A. PAYNE is an Assistant Professor of Political Science at the University of Wisconsin, Madison. She is the author of "Working-Class Strategies in the Transition to Democracy in Brazil," *Comparative Politics* (1991) and *Brazilian Industrialists and Democratic Change* (1994). She has begun a new research project on authoritarian movements and democratic consolidation in three Latin American countries.